Personal Finance on Your Computer: Starter Kit

By Phillip Robinson

MIS:
PRESS

A Subsidiary of
Henry Holt and Co., Inc.

First Edition—1995

Printed in the United States of America.

Library of Congress Cataloging-in-Publication Data

Robinson, Phillip R.
    Personal finance on your computer : starter kit / by Phillip Robinson.
  —1st ed.
        p.   cm.
    ISBN 1-55828-420-6
    1. Finance, Personal—Data processing. I. Title.
HG179.R5478   1995
332.024'00285'416—dc20   95-18260
                                                                              CIP

10 9 8 7 6 5 4 3 2 1

MIS:Press books are available at special discounts for bulk purchases for sales promotions, premiums, fund-raising, or educational use. Special editions or book excerpts can also be created to specification.

For details contact: Special Sales Director
                        MIS:Press
                        a subsidiary of Henry Holt and Company, Inc.
                        115 West 18th Street
                        New York, New York 10011

Associate Publisher: Paul Farrell
Managing Editor: Cary Sullivan
Development Editor: Judy Brief
Copy Edit Manager: Shari Chappell

Production Editor: Anne Alessi
Layout: Patricia Wallenburg
Technical Editor: Rich Jaroslovsky
Copy Editor: Gwynne Jackson

Acknowledgments

A special thanks to Intuit, for their trial software,
and to everyone at all the companies mentioned in the book.
Your cooperation is much appreciated.

Table of Contents

CHAPTER 2   35

CHAPTER 3   65

CHAPTER 4   93

CHAPTER 5   111

CHAPTER 6 121

CHAPTER 8   201

CHAPTER 9   **223**

CHAPTER 10   241

Introduction

A year ago I wrote *Welcome to... Personal Finance on Your Computer*. That book listed and described personal computer programs that help you save, invest, budget, calculate taxes on, and even spend your money. In the back was a floppy disk with a single program—Windows on Wallstreet—for planning investments.

Now I'm back with this more complete book on using computers for personal finance. You'll find three big improvements over that *Welcome to...* book:

ⓒ More and the latest information on the full range of personal finance software

ⓒ Many personal finance programs on a CD-ROM, not just one program on a floppy disk

ⓒ Tutorial examples—step-by-step explanations of putting key programs to work

The programs on the CD-ROM in the back of this book pack in a bunch of personal finance programs, for everything from planning budgets to reconciling your checkbook to preparing tax returns and even trading stocks and bonds on-line. These programs are *demo* or *trial* versions of popular commercial software: that is, they'll help you with basics, they'll show you how it's done, but if you want complete power and control, you'll need to go out and buy the complete programs.

The chapters of this book still list your personal finance program choices, both for PC-compatible and Apple Macintosh computers.

But the book does more than that. It shows how to use one or two example programs from each category. I'll lead you through setting up those programs, entering typical data, producing results, and guessing what those results mean. Start at the beginning, read through to the end, follow the examples along the way, and your finances should soon be better organized and better planned.

Chapter 1, "Setup," tells you how to get equipped to run those programs, from the computer (if you don't already own one), to the *peripherals* (hardware extras such as printers, modems, and the like to fully exercise the programs), to *general-purpose software* that any computer should have (such as word processors), to the *on-line services* (for research and stock trading).

Chapter 2, "Plan," covers personal financial planning programs. Before digging into details of your finances, before investing a penny, you need goals. These programs help you get those hopes and dreams and fears out of your head and down on computer disk. Do you have kids to put through college? A comfortable retirement in mind? Or even just a dream vacation or home to buy? These programs help you quantify what you want and what it will take to get there.

Chapter 3, "Record," describes personal accounting programs (more commonly known as *checkbook register* or *personal finance* programs). Once you know where you want to go, you need to know where you are. These programs help you keep track of what you have, what you own, and what you're spending.

Chapter 4, "Pay," is the place you pay your current bills. Using the same basic programs as Chapter 3, you can record checks you write by hand, automatically record checks the computer prints, or even pay bills electronically through the phone.

Chapter 5, "Budget," takes the information you've recorded and the bills you've paid, and creates your actual budget from them. This shows in numbers or charts how much you spend each month and on what. After you recover from the immediate shock, you can create a planned budget and see where you need a financial diet to reach it.

Chapter 6, "Tax," shows you how the right program can simplify income-tax-return preparation and minimize your income tax payments. The programs will eliminate mathematical mistakes, search for missed deductions, and avoid the

IRS' favorite audit alarms. Use a modem with one of these programs and you can even get your refund back faster.

Chapter 7, "Invest," shows how your computer can help you choose, buy, and sell stocks, bonds, and other securities. You'll have more control, understand more about what you've got and where it's going, and even save money on trades.

Chapter 8, "Protect," has programs for creating wills and other estate-preservation documents. Here's the place to keep your money or pass it on to the people you most care about.

Chapter 9, "Learn," may seem a little late. But don't worry—you've been learning all along. This chapter just tells you how and where to learn more, from magazines and books to on-line sites you reach through your modem and phone to research numbers and discuss investments.

Chapter 10, "Sources," lists the manufacturers and suppliers of the products I mention in this book. Not only can they tell you the latest on the products—prices, specifications, abilities—but they're the most likely sources for new products in personal finance.

Remember: take computer advice with a grain—or even a pound—of salt. While computers are great at calculating, comparing, and remembering, they don't know context. In other words, they can be full of data but downright dumb. The advice you find is really human advice, but given by someone who doesn't know you or your situation. Sometimes it is top-notch. Sometimes it stinks. And often it is just debatable. Pay attention to the numbers and to your own common sense. If you're thinking of making any big move, pass it by your favorite human advisor.

Enough of this! Go ahead, get started. You may soon find yourself addicted to knowing more about your money.

CHAPTER 1

Setup

Before you can use any personal finance program, potent or puny, you need a personal computer system. I say *system* because you need more than just the main computer. You need:

- 💰 the computer, naturally
- 💰 a printer, to print checks, reports, and other documents
- 💰 a modem, to get on-line information through the phone line
- 💰 general-purpose software, for writing, calculating, and so on
- 💰 an on-line service, an information source for the modem to call

This chapter gives some tips for choosing these things.

The Hardware

You need a computer to run personal finance programs. Some computers are large *desktop* models; some are lightweight portable models known as *laptops* or *notebooks*. You can buy them from a computer store, from a warehouse or department store, or even through mail-order.

T I P

If you already have a computer, skip to the section on printers. If you don't have a computer, personal finance alone may be reason enough to get one. After a couple of years you could save or earn enough to justify the cost. Think about all the other possible uses, too—from bringing work home, to learning, to fun. But if your finances are very simple—a single job, a single savings account, the 1040EZ form for your taxes—then perhaps you should stick to paper-and-pencil financial organization and maybe a Nintendo or Sega system for fun and games.

PC or Mac?

There are two basic types of personal computers: PCs and Macs, or to be more verbose, *PC-compatibles* and *Apple Macintoshes*. Each has its own programs. PCs cannot run Mac programs. The latest Macs can run some PC programs, but they have trouble with programs that contain lots of sophisticated sounds and video clips. These problems may be ironed out soon, maybe even by the time you read this book.

T I P

Some of the most advanced investment analysis programs run only on PCs, not on Macs. If that's a key interest and you're a Mac owner, you may need to either switch to a PC or buy one of the latest Macs, a *PowerMac*, which can run PC software.

PCs follow the basic design IBM invented in the 1980s. You can buy *peripherals* (extra hardware you plug into the computer, such as printers) and programs that will run on any computer advertised as "PC-compatible" (see Figure 1.1). Hundreds of companies make PCs. About 80% of the world's personal computers are PC-compatibles, so there are more programs and peripherals for them than for any other kind of computer.

Figure 1.1 Typical PC.

The Apple Macintosh comes only from Apple Computer Inc. (In early 1995, a few other companies started announcing Mac-compatibles, and more of these may appear by the time you get this book.) About 10% of the world's personal computers are Macs. There are peripherals and programs created specifically for Macs, which PCs can't use. Although there aren't as many programs or peripherals for Macs as there are for PCs, there are still plenty for most tasks. And some PC peripherals can be used on Macs with small changes, such as a different cable or installation program. However, some PC peripherals won't work on Macs at all.

During 1994 Apple introduced a new line of Macintosh computers that can run basic PC programs. These *PowerMacs* won't run all PC programs; they have a hard time with the latest audio and video elements in some programs. But they'll run nearly all personal finance programs—outside of those problems. This flexibility makes Macs more attractive as financial systems.

During 1995 the first Macintosh-compatible computers appeared. There were only a few examples out while I wrote this book, but the competition should mean lower prices and better performance in Macs. A typical Mac is shown in Figure 1.2.

Figure 1.2 Typical Macintosh.

PCs are traditionally less expensive and harder to use than Macs. They were cheaper because many companies made them. The competition pushed prices down. PCs were more difficult to use because their fundamental software, called DOS, is difficult to use (see Figure 1.3). You had to learn a different way to operate every DOS program.

```
DOS          <DIR>      01-04-80   8:30a
NECUTILS     <DIR>      01-04-80   8:30a
WINDOWS      <DIR>      01-04-80   8:31a
CSERVE       <DIR>      01-04-80   8:34a
WINWORKS     <DIR>      01-04-80   8:35a
DEMO         <DIR>      01-04-80   8:36a
KIDPIX       <DIR>      05-06-94   3:08p
GT!          <DIR>      05-11-94   7:05a
DFPICS       <DIR>      06-14-94  10:09a
DFLITE       <DIR>      06-14-94  12:35p
DF           <DIR>      06-14-94   7:14p
PP30         <DIR>      06-15-94   2:12p
TYPEP30      <DIR>      06-15-94   2:23p
DRAWP10      <DIR>      06-15-94   2:25p
MYBRO        <DIR>      06-15-94   2:28p
BROCHURE     <DIR>      06-15-94   2:35p
COMMAND  COM    52925   03-10-93   6:00a
WINA20   386     9349   03-10-93   6:00a
VERSION           109   01-04-80   8:34a
CONFIG   SYS      433   06-09-94   4:16p
AUTOEXEC BAT      408   06-01-94   4:30a
       21 file(s)     63224 bytes
                   81788928 bytes free

C:\>dir c:\*.exe _
```

Figure 1.3 DOS display.

Macs have newer fundamental software than PCs. This software, called the *Mac OS*, uses *icons*—small graphic images on the screen—and standard *menus*—lists of commands (see Figure 1.4). You control these, choosing among the icons and menus, by moving a *mouse* (see Figure 1.5).

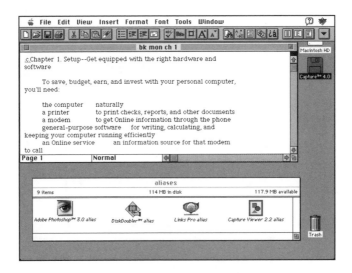

Figure 1.4 Macintosh display.

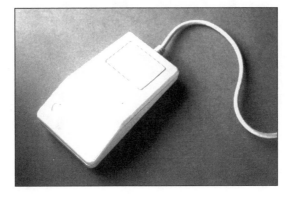

Figure 1.5 Mouse.

But PCs are getting easier to use because of new easier foundation software called *Windows* (see Figure 1.6) and OS/2 (see Figure 1.7). These programs add icons, menus, and the mouse to the DOS foundation. They don't yet have the underlying structure that makes connecting new peripherals or installing new programs as easy as on the Macintosh. Newer versions, such as Windows 95, may come closer, but it will still probably be simpler to add things to a Mac.

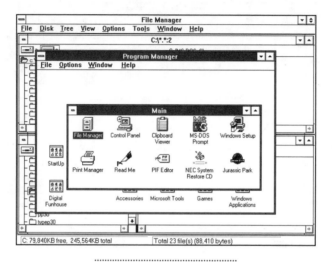

Figure 1.6 Windows display.

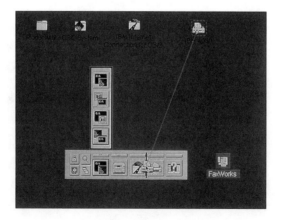

Figure 1.7 OS/2 screen.

There are more finance programs for PCs than for Macs, especially for investment analysis. This is probably because there are so many more PCs—a larger market to sell programs to—and especially more PCs in business, where finance software is more valued. Still, there are enough Mac programs in each category that you can get along even with an older Mac. The PC-versus-Mac decision boils down to the following considerations:

🐷 PC—more program choices, the cheapest, the most difficult to set up and use

🐷 Mac—fewer program choices, more expensive than PCs, the easiest to set up and use

🐷 PowerMac—the most program choices, the most expensive (but not by much), very easy to set up and use

If you're about to buy a computer, you have to choose between a Mac and a PC. Ask yourself these questions:

🐷 Will you be heavily into investment analysis? A PC (or PowerMac) is best.

🐷 Otherwise, are you already experienced with a PC or Mac? Stick with it.

🐷 Do friends, colleagues, or customers use PCs or Macs? Stick with them.

🐷 Can you afford to pay a little more and gain easier setup? Mac has an edge.

🐷 Do you have small children who will use the computer? Mac has a big edge.

Whatever you choose, don't buy any model that is totally new. It could have *bugs* (flaws that can cause mistakes, halt programs, and even lose information).

One last bit of advice on choosing between Mac and PC. I've met a number of people who switched from a PC to a Mac and stayed. I've met few who have switched from Mac to PC and were glad, except computer journalists and corporate systems specialists who are glad to be more in the mainstream. The journalists were thrilled with the larger number of programs and peripherals appearing for PCs and Windows, giving them more to write about. The systems specialists were more comfortable with the variety of sources of PCs and the greater number of tools available to connect them to large networks of computers. If you're going to compute your cash at home and you don't have PC work to bring home from the office, I suggest you try a Mac first.

There are both PC and Macintosh programs on the CD-ROM included with this book.

What to Look for in a PC

PC-compatibles are built of standard components by hundreds of companies. You need to determine the levels you need of the following:

- 💰 **performance:** how fast the computer calculates, prints, and so on
- 💰 **reliability:** whether it breaks down or has trouble using programs
- 💰 **support:** how easily and quickly it gets fixed

Spend more, and you generally get more in each category. Spend smarter, and you can get more of each without spending too many dollars.

I suggest you look for the following:

- 💰 a processor, at least a 66-MHz 486 chip, but a Pentium is better
- 💰 4 MB of memory (a real minimum), 8 MB is better
- 💰 a hard disk drive, at least 250 MB, but 500 MB is better
- 💰 a floppy drive, one 3.5-inch drive is plenty
- 💰 a 14-inch SVGA monitor (the display screen), 15 or 17 inches is better
- 💰 a mouse and keyboard, whatever feels good to your fingers
- 💰 a 9600-bps data/fax Hayes-compatible modem, but 14.4 Kbps is better
- 💰 a double-speed CD-ROM drive, not strictly necessary but highly recommended
- 💰 DOS version 6 or later and either Windows 3.1 or later or OS/2 2 or later
- 💰 a one-year or longer on-site service warranty
- 💰 a toll-free technical support help phone number

Companies I've heard good things about, although naturally they are all also the targets of some complaints, include IBM, Compaq, Packard-Bell, Dell, Gateway, NEC, AST, and Hewlett-Packard.

A PC will cost $1500 to $2500. A portable PC (see Figure 1.8) with the same abilities will cost $2000 to $3500. That's a lot more to pay unless you truly need the ability to move the computer from room to room or from office to home to remote site.

Figure 1.8 Portable PC.

What to Look for in a Mac

Macs are built only by Apple, although a few other companies have announced they'll get into the game soon. As with PCs, you'll choose a particular Mac model based on the following criteria:

🐷 **performance:** how fast the model calculates, prints, and so on

🐷 **reliability:** whether it breaks down or has trouble using programs

🐷 **support:** how easily and quickly it gets fixed

Spend more, and you'll get more performance. Reliability and support are pretty equal among models because one company is behind them all.

Macs come in "families." I suggest the *Performa* family for personal finance and general school and home use on a tight budget (see Figure 1.9). The *PowerMac* family is best for personal finance and business or multimedia use. The *PowerBook* family is portable. The particular model numbers within the familiesare constantly changing. Each family has lower-priced models with slower processors, midrange models with faster processors, and top-range models with the fastest processors. Moving toward the top of the range will also buy more memory and disk capacity, although you can add these to the slower-processor machines. Get at least 8 MB of memory and a 250-MB disk. Also, make sure it has a 9600-bps Hayes-compatible data/fax modem, although 14.4 Kbps is better. Get a CD-ROM drive if you can afford the extra $200 to $300.

Figure 1.9 Mac Performa.

All of the PowerMacs and (confusingly) some of the latest Performas (such as the 6118CD), use the *Power*PC processor chip (see above). This lets them run PC programs, if they have enough memory and the added SoftPC or SoftWindows software (see Figure 1.10). If you like Mac and you can afford a PowerPC-based Mac, go for it. You'll buy the most flexibility of any computer.

Figure 1.10 PowerMac running SoftWindows.

A Mac should cost about $1500 for the lowest Performa, $3500 for the highest PowerMac, or $3000 for a solid PowerBook (see Figure 1.11). Make sure the price you're quoted on a Performa or PowerMac includes a display screen (also known as a *monitor*). That may add $500 to the price. Again, the PowerBook's extra cost is high, unless you truly need the ability to move the computer from room to room or from office to home to remote site.

Figure 1.11 Mac PowerBook.

Printers

A computer without a printer; can be a lot of fun, but it isn't practical, especially for financial work. You'll want to print the following:

- checks to pay bills
- reports on your financial status
- charts on your financial status
- lists of your possessions or assets and liabilities for your own records or for a bank or insurance firm

There are three kinds of printers to consider: impact, inkjet, and laser. Whichever you buy, make sure you get the cables, interface, and software *drivers* (utility programs that help the computer and printer understand one another) for the computer you use. Windows users, for example, need a good Windows driver and PC cables and connectors. Mac owners need different cables, connectors, and software. Some printers can be moved from PC to Mac or back by changing these options. Some printers cannot move back and forth because they have built-in circuits and programs that will work with only one or the other type of computer.

Impact printers (see Figure 1.12) hammer tiny pins against an inked ribbon, pressing it against the paper. They are the noisiest, slowest, and lowest-quality printers; they are also the cheapest. But the only reason to buy one is if you're printing on multiple-carbon-copy forms. Other printers don't press against the page and so can't handle carbon copies. If you want more than one copy with any other printer, you must print the page again.

Figure 1.12 Impact printer.

Inkjet printers (see Figure 1.13) shoot tiny droplets of ink at the paper. They're almost as quiet as laser printers but only half as fast. Their output looks a lot better than dot-matrix results. The graphics are smoother and the text more professional. Many inkjet models also print in color. It can be wonderful if you have kids who will use the computer or if you'll be creating presentations on it. Even financial charts look better in color. Hewlett-Packard and Canon are good names in inkjet printers for both PCs and Macs.

Figure 1.13 Inkjet printer.

Laser printers (see Figure 1.14) work in pretty much the same way as copy machines. They shine a laser on the surface of a special drum, creating a pattern of static charges there. Those charges attract ink powder called *toner*. The drum then rolls against the paper, leaving the toner image on the paper. Heat then melts the toner so that it sticks to the paper. Laser printers create the highest-quality prints and are the fastest and quietest. But they don't print through layers or in color. Traditionally they have been the most expensive, once costing more than an entire computer. But recently they have dropped down to the $500 to $1500 range.

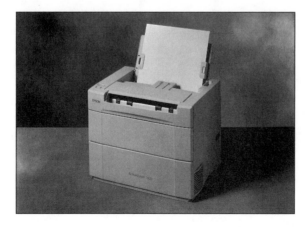

Figure 1.14 Laser printer.

If you have a PC, make sure the laser printer you get has HP LaserJet compatibility. This is also known as having PCL-4 or PCL-5 (a printer control language from HP) built in. The HP LaserJet is by far the most popular laser printer. It set the standard in printers for PCs, much as the IBM PC set the standard in personal computers. Most programs expect and know how to work with an HP LaserJet.

If you have a Mac, make sure the laser printer you get has PostScript compatibility. There are some good and inexpensive printers that don't, but PostScript adds as little as $100 to the printer's price, and it assures you that any text or charts you print will be as sharp as if they were from an expensive corporate printer.

If you're hoping to pay bills with your computer, look for a laser printer with an *envelope feeder*, a mechanical part that holds envelopes and feeds them one at a time to the drum. HP, TI, NEC, Canon, Apple, and Brother are trustworthy companies producing laser printers.

Printer Summary

💰 If you must print carbon-copy forms, buy an impact printer.

💰 If you're sharing the computer with kids, get a color inkjet printer.

💰 If you must print hundreds or thousands of pages, such as because you're printing work projects and other tasks in addition to your personal finance stuff, get a laser printer.

Otherwise, it's a toss-up between faster, monochrome laser printers and slower, color-capable inkjet printers. Note that printers can be difficult to set up. Your best bet is finding a dealer or friend who will handle that chore for you.

Modems

A modem connects a computer to your telephone line. The name *modem* is short for MOdulator/DEModulator because it *modulates* (translates) computer information into telephone tones and back again. You need a modem to send and receive computer information through the phone lines.

What kind of information can you send and receive? There are millions of computers out there connected by modems to phone lines. With a modem, your computer can talk to any of them. Some of those other computers are full of information ranging from the latest stock and bond prices to company reports, government projections, airline schedules, and discussion bulletin boards full of advice, both good and bad.

There are two places a modem can attach to your computer: inside or out. *Internal modems* (see Figure 1.15) cost less than external because they don't have a case and power supply. They plug into and occupy one of the limited number of slots inside a typical desktop computer. *External modems* (see Figure 1.16) connect to a *port* (an electronic socket) outside the computer. Typically it is a serial port.

Figure 1.15 Internal modem.

Figure 1.16 External modem.

The Hayes company dominated the modem market for years. It set the standards for modems, much as IBM did for PCs and HP for laser printers. Most programs that operate modems therefore assume you have a modem that comes from Hayes or will work like a Hayes modem. Most modem makers design their product to act like Hayes modems. Just be sure you ask for a *Hayes-compatible modem*.

Modem speed measures how fast the modem can move information through the phone line. This is measured in bits per second, or bps. Sometimes you'll see the term *baud*, which is used interchangeably with bps. Modems that transfer data at 300 bps and 1200 bps are too slow. Get at least a 9600-bps modem. You may have trouble finding one; the newer, faster 14.4-Kbps modems have crowded them out of the market at a very small increase in price. Make sure the modem you get meets the standards of V.32 (pronounced vee-dot-thirty-two) for 9600 bps or V.32bis for 14.4 Kbps.

You should also ask for a modem that has some fax ability (most do). Although it isn't necessary, it shouldn't cost any extra, and it may come in handy for sending or receiving faxes. (Make sure it does both.) Your computer documents that display on screen can be sent to other computers with fax modems or to standard fax machines. Fax machines, in turn, can send documents to your computer. Ask for a modem that follows the Group 3 standard, the latest for faxing.

CD-ROM Drive

A CD-ROM is a *disc* (spelled with a *c*) that can hold more than 500 MB of information. Traditional floppy *disks* (spelled with a *k*) hold only 1 MB. The capacity of CD-ROMs is necessary for more and more computer pursuits. Large collections of data, such as historic stock prices, will only fit on CD-ROMs. (They'll also fit on the large computers you can reach through a modem, and that information can be kept more up-to-date than a CD-ROM. But you don't have immediate access and ownership of modem-accessed information. Often, you also pay a lot more for it.) In addition, the latest versions of some personal finance programs add *multimedia* tutorials and help. The sound, video, and animation of multimedia take up a lot of space on CD-ROMs.

A CD-ROM drive adds about $200 to the price of a computer but is definitely worth the cost. You can add a CD-ROM drive to a computer that doesn't have one, but it isn't easy; you have to plug in interface boards, install drivers, and set configurations. Have a dealer or expert friend do it for you.

However you get the CD-ROM drive, be sure to ask for at least *double-speed*. That measures the cruising speed at which the drive delivers information to the computer. Single-speed won't play video well. Quad-speed is worthwhile if you're also going to play games and educational discs.

Ask for 300-ms (milliseconds) or faster *access time*. Access time measures how quickly the drive can look up one particular piece of information; the shorter the time the better. An access time of 200 ms is great, and 150 ms is the absolute best. Finally, if you're adding a CD-ROM drive to your PC, ask for a SCSI interface. That's the easiest and most flexible way to connect a CD-ROM drive.

If you want to play multimedia finance titles, which include more help information and video and sound clips explaining details, or other multimedia titles (for fun), you'll also need to add speakers and a *sound card* (a circuit board capable of producing better sounds than the simple circuits already in the PC) to the typical PC. Macs have the sound circuits built in, but they may need added speakers for multimedia. Some computers have a CD-ROM drive built in (see Figure 1.17); some need to have one added (see Figure 1.18).

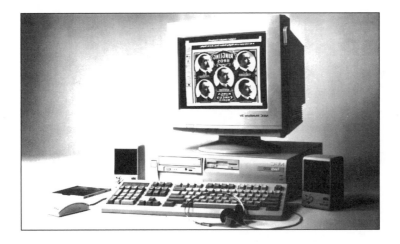

Figure 1.17 Computer with built-in CD-ROM drive.

Figure 1.18 CD-ROM drive to add to a computer.

General-Purpose Software

Financial programs are your goal, but there are other programs you'll want, just to get your computer running, tuned, and ready for typical tasks. These general-purpose programs range from *operating systems*—the fundamental software a computer needs to turn on—to the word processor you'll want for writing letters or financial reports.

Operating Systems

For operating systems, a Mac needs at least System 6, but the newer System 7.0 or 7.5 is better. A PC needs at least DOS 5, but one of the newer versions of DOS 6 (called 6.0, 6.1, and so on) is better. A PC is easier to use if it has Microsoft Windows or IBM OS/2 software, which add to DOS, making it easier to use. Get Windows 3.1 or the newer Windows 95 when it is available, or get OS/2 3.0 Warp. Windows is better for beginners, OS/2 for advanced users. To use Windows or OS/2 your PC will need at least a 486 processor and 4 MB of memory.

Remember that the PowerMac models of Macintosh, when equipped with enough memory and the SoftPC program, can run DOS and Windows programs. That may be the most flexible approach, although it is still rather new and not completely effective yet.

Spreadsheets

A *spreadsheet* program organizes numbers and word labels into rows and columns, with formulas that can relate the numbers (see Figure 1.19). That is, it's a grid on the screen where you can type some numbers, and then some formulas, and then have those formulas generate more numbers as results. Accountants, scientists, and managers love them, but spreadsheets don't have any ready-to-use formulas. If you wanted to analyze a loan payment, for example, you would have to enter the equations yourself. Sometimes you can buy *templates* for spreadsheets that have the equations, but finding and using these is not for beginners. Microsoft Excel, Lotus 1-2-3, and Novell Quattro Pro are some of the best spreadsheet programs.

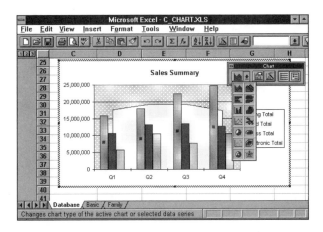

Figure 1.19 Typical spreadsheet display.

Word Processors

You've probably heard of and used word processors (see Figure 1.20). These are programs for typing, moving information around on the screen, and printing words. They'll help you produce anything from a letter to a book. No computer is complete without some word processing capability. Microsoft Word, WordPerfect, and Lotus Ami Pro are three of the most popular word processors.

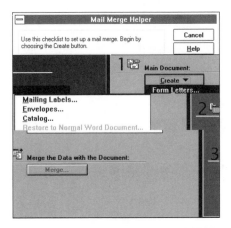

Figure 1.20 Typical word processor display.

Suites and Works

Many people buy a spreadsheet, a word processor, and a *database* program (that stores lists and tables of information) for their computers. Each program alone may cost $100 to $300. Software companies have started selling these programs bundled together in *suites* for a total cost of only $300 to $700. You pay less per program when buying a suite, but you may get programs that you don't really need, such as a *presentation* program (for making visual aids for speeches or charts for meetings) or an *E-mail* program (for sending electronic messages through a network of computers). The programs within a suite work together better than programs chosen randomly, such as a spreadsheet from one company and a word processor from another. Microsoft Office, Lotus SmartSuite, and Novell PerfectOffice are the best known suites.

Works programs cost less than suites. These aren't marketing deals, packing full professional programs into one big box. Instead they are single programs with the most used features of each major function—word processing, spreadsheeting, databasing. They cost $150 to $250. Microsoft Works and Claris Works are two of the best-known packages.

Utility Programs

Utility programs perform little labors. They organize the programs and documents on your disks, speed printing, and make sure no viruses are attacking your information (computer *viruses* are nasty little programs that duplicate themselves and overrun your other programs). Utilities are not as vital as they were a few years ago because operating systems now come with many of these abilities. Still, there are many utilities that can add to the safety and efficiency of your computing; Symantec's Norton Utilities and Central Point's PC Tools are the best-known.

Software Summary

An operating system will come with your computer; try to get System 7 or later for a Mac and Windows 3.1 or later or OS/2 3 or later for a PC. Get a Works package or a suite if you're in business and have a bigger budget. Use the utilities that come with your operating system, and you're ready to go with general-purpose software.

How to Buy Software and Hardware the Smart Way

There are many ways and places in which to buy *software* (programs) and *hardware* (computers, printers, and modems) these days.

Computer stores are small retail shops. They offer local expert help in buying and setting up systems. But computer stores may have higher prices than some other sources.

Computer superstores are supermarkets of computer stuff. These have lower prices than small retail stores and a larger selection, but they cannot provide the same personal help. Warehouse stores have small computer sections tucked in with clothing, appliances, and just about everything else under the sun. These can have very low prices, but they carry only the simplest hardware and software and provide very few choices.

Mail-order companies often have the lowest prices. They can also be the hardest to contact when you need help, although some try hard, with toll-free numbers and around-the-clock experts, and you may prefer their service to that of local stores. Many mail-order hardware companies even provide *on-site service*— technicians that will come to your place to fix a problematic computer.

Choose the source that you're most comfortable with. Storefronts and mail-order companies are no good if they don't want to help. You need to check their reputations with friends, business bureaus, and computer magazines. Incidentally, if the store or mail-order company that sells you hardware or software can't help with problems, most computers and programs come with the manufacturer's phone number. Call; the quality of these tech support lines is an important facet of any computer purchase.

List Prices Versus Street Prices

One upon a time, software and hardware companies created and packaged their software, then shipped it off to retail stores with a wholesale price (which the store paid) and a suggested list price (SLP) or suggested retail price (SRP) (which customers were expected to pay). The store would keep the difference between the list and wholesale prices. This was generally a substantial amount, even if the store discounted the retail price by 10 to 20%.

Then along came mail-order outfits that took hardware and software orders over toll-free phone lines and delivered the goods via Federal Express or some other shipping service. The customer calls and gives a credit-card number, and the company ships the program. The program is exactly the same as the one you can buy in a store—the same disks and manuals in the same box. Some stores add service to the equation by helping you install and set up the program or system, but so do some mail-order firms. Mail-order firms only provide over-the-phone advice. If you have trouble with the program, you'll call the same technical support people at the software company, whether you buy retail or mail-order.

Because mail-order firms don't have storefronts to keep up and because they often work in low-wage areas, they sell at a substantial discount from the list price. You can get software for 30 to 40% off the list price.

Retail stores fought back, with deeper discounts. Soon no one paid list price or anything close to it. The 30 to 40% discount off list price, available either at discount computer stores or through mail-order, came to be known as the *street price*. This is not official, although it can be standard from one outlet to another. Even the software makers acknowledge it; they now set their list prices to evoke the desired street price. Some hardware makers don't even have an official price because they hate seeing it compared negatively to the mail-order price when they know that no one buys at list price.

Some programs are free. These *public-domain programs* are yours for the asking from computer clubs or computer bulletin board systems. (A BBS is a computer set up with lots of information on its hard drive and a modem attached to a phone so other computers can call it and trade messages, grab software, and look up information.) You're not free to sell public-domain programs, only to use them. Some are excellent, others aren't. Finding the best means trying several and reading computer magazines regularly. What you get for paying for a commercial program is a much higher quality percentage and the probability of a large company ready to fix problems you have with software and to introduce new versions with new features that will let you do more without having to learn a whole new program.

Then there are *shareware* programs. These are free for you to try, but if you keep them you're supposed to send in a registration payment of $25 to $75 (depending on the program). There's no enforcement of this beyond moral suasion. As with public-domain software, some shareware is great, and some is bad. You need to test and read reviews to find the good stuff. If you're considering software that's expensive in the commercial world, say, a $500 program, and you have computer knowledge and time, you can save a lot of money by digging through shareware. If the commercial program costs only $50 or so or if you don't have computer expertise, then shareware is not for you. Look instead for special deals on commercial software, such as bundling, competitive upgrades, and introductory prices.

Bundling is the practice of adding a program for free to computer hardware or another program. For example, you might get Microsoft Money (a personal finance program) with Microsoft Works, or you might get Quicken with a new PC. *Competitive upgrades* are attempts to win you over from some other program. These upgrades let you trade in (some companies ask for proof, others don't) your current spreadsheet or finance program for the latest version of this company's program, at a discount price.

Introductory prices range from $10 for a program that's normally $100 (frequently called "free with shipping and handling") to $100 for a $250 program. It costs a software company a lot of marketing money to make a first-time customer of you. If you like the software, you're likely to buy new versions each year with relatively little effort from the software company's advertising and sales departments. So software companies are always eager to gain new first-time customers. Also, most categories of software tend to develop dominant companies. New companies to the category have a hard time persuading customers to buy from them rather than from the tried-and-true companies. To gain new customers and to tempt people away from dominant players, software companies sometimes offer very low "introductory" prices. These can be as little as $5 to $10, really just enough to cover the price of the software materials and shipping and handling, not enough to pay for development of future versions or even for technical support on the phone. Although these deals are often set to end on specific dates, they typically continue longer than that. People don't like paying $69 for something today that was nearly free yesterday.

Summary on Buying Software

Buy software where you get the best price unless you have some local outlet that may charge a little more but will help you when you have trouble. All questions go back to the software maker anyway, no matter where you buy the package, so you may as well search for introductory prices, competitive upgrades, mail-order catalogs, or other routes to the lowest price. When choosing programs, just remember to ask about the publisher's technical support policy:

- How long does it last?
- Is the call toll-free?
- Is there fax and on-line support?
- What hours is it open?
- How long will you wait on hold?
- How useful are the answers?

The programs on the CD with this book are *trial versions*. That doesn't mean the same for each program. Some lack major features such as printing. Others are older versions, lacking the latest improvements in the commercial program. Some are just demos—they show you what the program does but don't actually let you do it.

Upgrades are software companies' offers for owners of older program versions to move up to the latest program version at a discount price. Some of the programs on this book's CD offer upgrades at special discounts.

On-Line Services

You may have heard of the *information superhighway*. That's just the latest catch phrase attached to the way information can be sent through phone lines (and later through cable TV lines and satellites). This information can be words, numbers, pictures, even sound and video clips.

The key to this information exchange is a personal computer. With a modem and a typical phone line, plus some telecommunications software, your computer can talk to other computers all over the world. Some of these computers are other people's personal computers. Others are large mini- or mainframe computers.

Some of those larger computers are attached to many telephone lines at once and connected to huge disk drives with databases chock-full of news, photos, books, and financial statistics. Access to these computers is sold as an *on-line service*. Typically you pay a start-up fee and a monthly subscription fee. That buys you the phone number for your computer modem to dial, a voice number to call with problems, a manual explaining which commands to use to get what information, and a password that will tell the service to accept your computer's call.

Most services also have *surcharge* information, special databases they're attached to and that they charge more for, perhaps on a per-minute basis (which is often more during business hours and less after). Most services also offer E-*mail*—the ability to send and receive written messages, sometimes with attached computer documents—to anyone else on the service. More and more on-line services have interconnections to one another. That lets you move E-mail from one machine to another. Many now also offer a partial or complete interconnection to the *Internet*. That's the name given to the many educational, governmental, and research computers in the world that are interconnected as a large web permitting the exchange of messages and computer documents, which can be words, numbers, video, sound, and so on from any connected computer to any other.

A few years ago, you would have used a telecommunications program (that came with your modem in a works program or suite or that was sold independently to work with standard modems) to dial an on-line service. When you connected you would see a list of text describing available commands and information. You would respond with typed, abbreviated commands.

You can still operate some on-line services that way, but many are now offering *front-end* or interface programs. These are known as GUI (graphic user interface) software, which makes choosing commands and information easier. These programs run on your PC or Mac and present menus, icons, and other elements that simplify finding what you need. They work the way the Mac operating system or Windows does (as explained earlier in this chapter), with most commands available by simply clicking the mouse on a picture icon on the screen. Prodigy and America Online typify this trend; they are described later in this chapter. Some of the older services, such as CompuServe, now offer interface programs you can choose instead of the original (still available) abbreviated, typed commands.

You don't need an on-line service subscription to balance your checkbook and compute your taxes. But if you want to, you can do the following with an on-line service:

💰 pay bills electronically instead of printing checks

💰 have 24-hour instant access to your accounts instead of going to an ATM

💰 monitor investments automatically instead of looking through newspapers

💰 buy and sell investments 24 hours a day instead of calling a broker

You should get a modem and a subscription to an on-line service. You'll also gain E-mail, airline and hotel reservation services, discussion groups on computer and noncomputer topics, and much more.

Here are brief descriptions of the major commercial on-line services. There are many other places a modem can call, such as large and small bulletin board systems. These can offer some of this same information, as well as E-mail, discussion groups, and programs you can *download* (pull in) through the modem and run on your own computer. When you choose an on-line service, consider the following:

💰 software compatibility—the front-end interface must run on your computer

💰 startup price—should be 0 because many are given away for free

💰 monthly price minimum—as low as possible, typically $10 or less

💰 surcharges—as low as possible for information you'll regularly use

💰 local-call prices—the service should provide a local or toll-free number for access

💰 financial compatibility—should work with the personal finance programs you choose

💰 software options—a service with optional programs for easier use

💰 great extras—such as games, shopping, and more

Here are the big competitors in the on-line service game:

💰 Dow Jones News Retrieval

💰 CompuServe

💰 Prodigy

💰 America Online

💰 Reuters Money Network

💰 GEnie

💰 Internet access providers such as Netcom

If you plan to analyze and trade stocks and bonds through your modem, read Chapter 7 before choosing an on-line service.

The Internet

In the past year a number of direct Internet access services have become affordable: Netcom (see Figure 1.21), Slipnet, Pipeline, and Cerfnet are four of the big names. Using their software—which includes E-mail, file transfer (called FTP), discussion groups (called Usenet or Newsgroups), and search utilities (such as Gopher)—you can find and exchange information on finances. Most also offer a web browser program for searching through World Wide Web (WWW) computer sites on the Internet. You won't find the instant stock quotes, mutual fund analyses, and other such services as easily on the Internet, but they are there, and you will run into nearly endless libraries and discussion groups on all subjects, including finance.

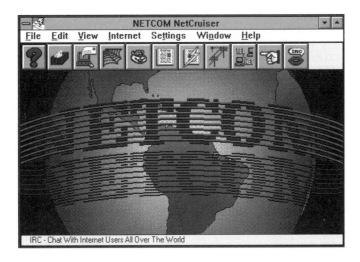

Figure 1.21 Netcom direct access to the Internet.

CompuServe Information Service

CompuServe is the second largest on-line service, with nearly 2 million subscribers, including hundreds of thousands in Japan. It has E-mail, news (including AP and Reuters feeds), sports, weather, references, shopping, financial information, stocks and investment tracking, games and entertainment, and travel services.

Although lighter on entertainment or family-oriented services than Prodigy or America Online, CompuServe does have forums for discussing every topic in the world, and it is probably the best service for businesses. It has more information, from historical stock data to agribusiness weather reports to Dialog databases. It also has screening programs for investigating investments. It is certainly the most popular place for computer software and hardware companies to set up their on-line support facilities.

Figure 1.22 shows a CompuServe menu without a graphics interface. You can access a variety of financial and nonfinancial information without graphics, on any computer, just by pressing numbers from a menu such as this. Figure 1.23 shows the CompuServe Information Manager, or CIM, interface software that makes the service easier to use.

```
 5 Travel
 6 The Electronic MALL/Shopping
 7 Money Matters/Markets
 8 Entertainment/Games
 9 Hobbies/Lifestyles/Education
10 Reference
11 Computers/Technology
12 Business/Other Interests
[25H[JEnter choice !7
[H[JFinance[;75HMONEY

[7HBASIC PRODUCTS
 1 Basic Quotes
 2 FundWatch Online By Money Magazine
 3 Basic Company Snapshot
 4 Issue/Symbol Lookup
 5 Loan Analyzer
EXTENDED PRODUCTS
 6 Market Quotes/Highlights
 7 Company Information
 8 Brokerage Services
 9 Earnings/Economic Projections
10 Micro Software Interfaces
[25H[JEnter choice or <CR> for more !
```

Figure 1.22 CompuServe without graphics interface.

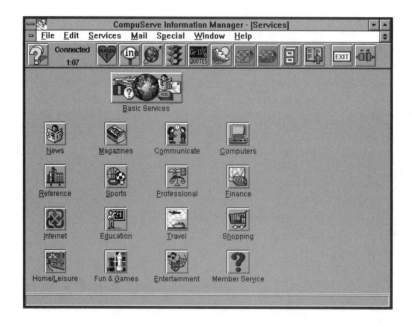

Figure 1.23 CompuServe graphics interface.

Dow Jones News Retrieval

This service, called DJN/R for short, has lots of financial information, which, because of the name, should come as no surprise (see Figure 1.24). Many people get it with the MCI Mail E-mail service. The information comes from the Wall Street Journal and the Dow Jones News Service wire information. The Dow Jones Text Library is a database of all Dow Jones publications and 1400 other general and trade publications, including major newspapers and magazines. This may be the most complete source of financial information, including Standard & Poors and Dun & Bradstreet reports, but it is also the most expensive.

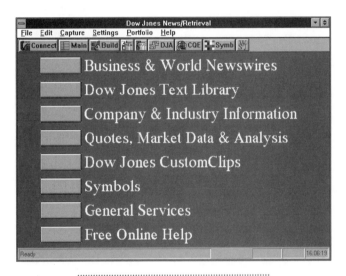

Figure 1.24 Dow Jones News Retrieval.

Prodigy

IBM and Sears got together to make Prodigy. It is the largest service, if you count all of the members of the signed-up families, which Prodigy does. It comes a close second to CompuServe for finance information. There aren't as many discussion areas, investment tools, or financial databases, but Prodigy can be cheaper and easier to use (see Figure 1.25). It is also a better choice for anyone wanting entertainment and nontechnical information. It has news, on-line encyclopedias, travel, shopping, and E-mail features. Prodigy does have more financial information than America Online, including an extra-cost feature called The Strategic Investor, a collection of investment analysis tools and databases. Closing stock quotes are free with the basic subscription, as are two hours per month in the financial bulletin boards and Dow Jones news section. Prodigy recently added surprisingly complete Internet features, permitting access to that huge but disorganized world of on-line information.

Figure 1.25 Prodigy.

Prodigy can be used only with its own front-end graphics software, which unfortunately is sometimes slow to display changes on screen. And outside the basic screens, you'll run into advertisements on screen, which bother some people.

GEnie

General Electric's GEnie service has about 350,000 subscribers. It gives them access to important databases such as Dialog, Businesswire, and TRW and to numerous discussion forums (many of which are devoted to computers). It includes E-mail, a chat area for typed conversations, entertainment forums on films and literature, and some computer company support areas. A graphics interface is available for Windows—called Aladdin—and there's one for the Mac too. Gateways from GEnie let you get at yet more information, such as the Dow Jones databases. You can also use GEnie without the special software. There is an on-line program for analyzing stocks. However, a big negative for GEnie is the high price you pay to use it during business hours (see Figure 1.26).

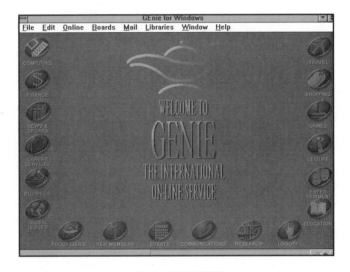

Figure 1.26 GEnie.

Delphi Internet

The Delphi service has databases of its own, as well as multiplayer games, software, business and finance data, news, weather, and sports. But Delphi is mainly known for its complete connections to the Internet. Most on-line services that talk of Internet access have only E-mail, not all the other database access that makes the Internet what it is. But the others are working hard to catch up to Delphi (see Figure 1.27).

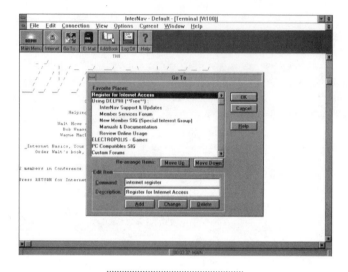

Figure 1.27 Delphi Internet.

Reuters Money Network

Devoted solely to financial data, the Reuters Money Network from Reality Technologies offers stock quotes, securities reports, and company news (see Figure 1.28). Soon it will add on-line trading of stocks and bonds. If numbers are what you want, not the financial discussion groups or all the other features of an on-line service, consider Reuters. You might even use it with a more general on-line service.

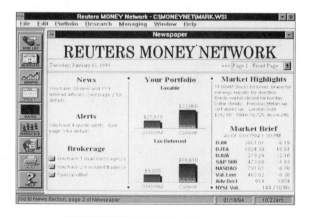

Figure 1.28 Reuters Money Network.

America Online

America Online is the newest major on-line service and the fastest growing; it claims nearly 2 million subscribers. The graphics front-end software for it is free, packaged with many computer magazines and products. AOL historically had less investment information than some of its competitors, but it is so much easier to use that it is popular with some investors. The interface makes the E-mail and bulletin boards easy too. This could make it suitable for a family that wants to learn about on-line information. It has news, shopping, some important databases, newspapers and magazines in full text, and special events, as well as some computer company support areas (see Figure 1.29).

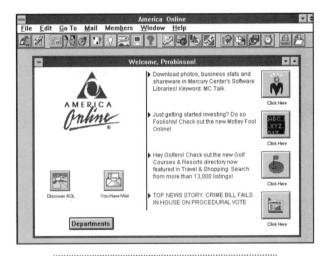

Figure 1.29 The personal finance area in AOL.

Mutual fund analysis takes you through several windows, telling which ratings you want. You see results, such as in the rankings of the top 25 funds over a 10-year period. And you can choose a specific stock ticker symbol and see the latest quote information. For less numeric advice, you can use the unique Motley Fool area on AOL, where all sorts of people interested in personal finance swap stories and suggestions (see Figure 1.30). In Chapter 10 I'll use America Online as the example for learning more on-line, so you'll see more figure examples there.

```
┌──────────────────────────────────────────────────────────┐
│ ▤▤▤▤▤▤  Top 25 of All Funds (Ranked by 1 ▤▤▤▤▤▤        ▤ │
│ Top 25 of All Funds (Ranked by 10 Yr Annualized Return)  ▲ │
│                                                     ▸      │
│ AS OF 07/31/94                                             │
│                                                            │
│                         3 Mth  1 YR   3 YR   5 YR    10    │
│ YR                                                         │
│                    Mstar Total  Total  Annlzd Annlzd      │
│ Annlzd                                                     │
│ Fund name          Obj  Rtg  Return Return Return Return  │
│ Return                                                     │
│ ================================ === ===== ====== ====== ====== ====== │
│ ======                                                     │
│ 20th Century Giftrust Invest  SC ***** -1.92  11.74  24.31  18.43 │
│ 24.20                                                      │
│ CGM Capital Development    G  ***** -6.12   5.92  19.83  21.22 │
│ 22.44                                                      │
│ Merrill Lynch Pacific A    WP ****   3.55  14.32  10.90  10.10 │
│ 21.83                                                      │
│ Fidelity Adv Inst Eqty Grth  G ***** -2.76   5.58  12.61  18.85 │
│ 21.06                                                      │
│ Fidelity Sel Health Care   SH ****   6.05  20.72   3.26  16.41 │
│ 20.74                                                    ▼ │
└──────────────────────────────────────────────────────────┘
```

Figure 1.30 AOL's Motley Fool investment discussion area.

Summary of On-Line Services

As the commercial on-line services add Internet access and retain their well-organized financial data, you're probably in the best shape with a good service and a knowledge of Internet techniques. CompuServe is the best for pure finance; Prodigy does well for finance plus family use; America Online falls somewhere in between. By the end of '95 you may also be able to check the quality of a new Microsoft Network.

Chapter Summary

You'll need a computer (PC or Mac) with peripherals (a printer, probably a modem, and a CD-ROM drive), some general-purpose software (works or suite), and an on-line service subscription. You may want to put off getting a subscription until you've read through more of this book in case you fall in love with a program that prefers a particular service, but America Online, CompuServe, and Prodigy are easy ways to start.

Now on to the first step for computerizing your finances: planning what you want.

CHAPTER 2

Plan

When you travel, the first step is deciding where you want to go. When you tackle your personal finances, the first step is deciding what you want to afford.

- $ Do you want to buy a home, a better home, or pay off the one you have?
- $ Do you want children?
- $ Do you want to save for college, for your kids or yourself?
- $ Do you want a vacation? What kind—sitting in a hammock or cruising to Mexico?
- $ Are there major goodies you'd like to present yourself or someone else with, material goods such as cards, boats, jewelry?
- $ Would you like to retire someday, and what kind of retirement are you hoping for?
- $ Do you want to give or leave money to family, friends, or worthy causes?

These are all common aspirations and they all take uncommon money. For most of these goals, you'll need a certain amount of money, the kind of money that won't appear in one fell swoop but must be saved and earned over time.

So the first step is to consider these things: house, education , children, vacations, possessions, retirement, gifts, insurance.

Seriously consider what you'd like and the minimum you'll be comfortable with. Dream, think, write it down. The computer won't help much with this, except perhaps if you have a word processor you'd like to put to work saving your thoughts.

Get ready with that list, with those visions. Now you need to calculate what they will cost. Put some numbers beside the items. Do you want a $200,000 house or a $1,000,000 house? (Think in today's dollars. Let the computer worry about inflation adjustments later.) How much do you think the childrens' education will set you back? (Remember that even as college costs climb, so do the percentage of those costs paid by scholarships, so just think in today's dollars and typical costs.) Keep assigning prices to those visions. Some of the planning programs will help you hone these numbers, but you're better off starting with what you already know.

Now you're ready for the programs. They'll put firmer prices on what you're thinking, and will use their calculating strengths to figure:

    💰   How much it will cost in the future

    💰   How much you'll have to save to have that future (including interest and taxes along the way)

Only then will you be ready to tackle the *how* questions:

    💰   How much should I save each month?

    💰   How should I use retirement plans at work?

    💰   How much will I get from social security?

And so on.

Software can't help you much with the dreams, but it can help enormously with the *how much* and *how* questions. Such software ranges from bare-bones calculators to almost personal advisors and explainers.

This chapter describes the programs that can help, and shows you some examples of using them step-by-step.

Planning Features within Checkbook and Investment Programs

Your first stop should be a personal finance program such as Quicken or Managing Your Money. Although these are largely thought of as checkbook registers, bill payers, and so on, most also have some planning features for everything from retirement to home buying to taxes. They may be as simple as a calculator that will tell you how much of a mortgage you'll qualify for, and a retirement advisor that will show how much you need to save month-by-month from now until that important age. Since you're going to get one of these anyway for tracking your expenses, budgeting, and paying bills, you may as well see what sort of planning abilities are thrown in.

Microsoft/Novell Money

What started as Microsoft Money may now become Novell Money. After a couple of years selling this Windows program and moving it up to version 3.0, Microsoft offered to buy Intuit and its Quicken program. Because Quicken and Money were direct and significant competitors, the US government's Justice Department inspected the deal for antitrust implications. Microsoft sought to diminish those by selling Money to Novell, one of its chief competitors in the software business. (Novell is one of the world's largest software companies based on its dominance of the network software market—connecting computers together. It has since used that success to buy the WordPerfect company and its line of programs, such as the WordPerfect word processor.) This unsure status definitely hurts Money. You can't know who will be supporting it. And any improvements or new versions are on hold.

Money, by either name, has some elementary planning built in: calculators to show you how money or needs for the money will grow. There's a Savings calculator, a Retirement Planner, and an Interest Estimator. Each is a calculator aided by a *Wizard* (see Figure 2.1), a piece of programming that leads you through entering amounts in the right places.

The Savings calculator asks you to set a goal amount, estimate how many years you have to reach it, and what you're starting with. Then it can calculate the amount you'll have to contribute at any given return rate.

The Retirement planner does similar work in estimating what regular contribution you'll have to make to reach your hoped-for retirement income. You can use it to run *what if* calculations on different interest, inflation, and return rates.

The Interest estimator asks for the interest rate and time period, then calculates the interest.

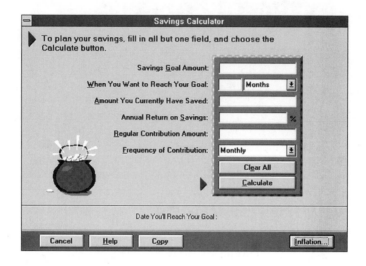

Figure 2.1 Microsoft/Novell Money has Wizards to help with planning.

Simply Money

Computer Associates is one of the world's largest software companies. Many of its programs are for accounting on large, corporate computer systems. Its personal computer program subsidiary is called 4Home Productions. Most have the brand name *Simply*, as in Simply Money and Simply Tax. They come in both DOS and Windows versions.

Simply Money is a checkbook register/budgeting/bill-paying program, a direct competitor to Quicken. But it too has some planning abilities. Some of these are calculators for loans, investments, interest, dividends, refinancing, life insurance, ARMs (Adjustable Rate Mortgages), and college. These are all outside the main program, as independent programs of their own.

The Life Insurance calculator, for example, not only calculates among all the relevant factors (Social Security, mortgage payoff, investments) it also adds advice (see Figure 2.2). There's a help window explaining insurance factors. And there's a bottom line *you should have this much* figure.

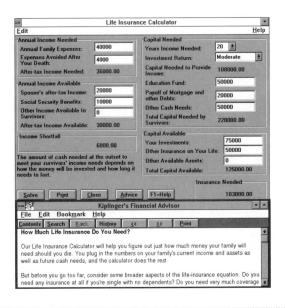

Figure 2.2 Simply Money's Life Insurance calculator comes with advice.

The College Planning calculator, for another example, also comes with an advice and explanation window. The calculations here are much simpler. You just say when your child will enroll and how much you have, and the calculator shows how much you'll need. This is almost too simple, in some ways, if you're interested in what annual increases in price the calculator assumes.

Money Counts

An inexpensive checkbook register/bill-paying program from Parsons Technology, Money Counts doesn't offer much in the way of planning. You will find one unique element here, though: the InterestVision calculator. This is probably the most precise and flexible calculator for interest—either on savings or on debts—of any I've seen.

Parsons does also offer separate planning programs for Retirement and Education, which are actually the Price Waterhouse programs mentioned later in this chapter. And they sell Home Buyer and Car Buyer Companion programs which lead you through the ups and downs of different approaches and help you calculate such niceties as car options and home closing costs.

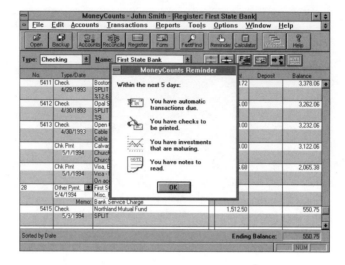

Figure 2.3 Money Counts.

Quicken

Quicken for Windows has only a little planning ability, mainly as calculators for loans, savings, college, retirement, and refinancing (see Figures 2.4 and 2.5). The latest CD-ROM version for Windows comes with the Wall Street Personal Finance Library a collection of articles described later in this chapter.

But if that seems skimpy for the most popular checkbook-register/bill-paying program, you can supplement it with the new Quicken Financial Planner program for retirement planning, described later in this chapter.

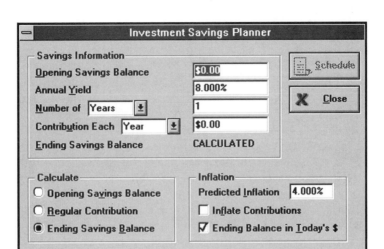

Figure 2.4 Quicken has a built-in planning calculator for investment savings.

Figure 2.5 Quicken helps you plan for home refinancing.

WealthBuilder

In this program you'll find some portfolio management, some personal finance organization, plenty of planning, a solid amount of asset allocation, and some security analysis. That's why it crops up in most chapters of this book. WealthBuilder starts with retirement planning, asking you questions in an interview style to get a line on what you want (see Figures 2.6 and 2.7). Then it suggests how you can divvy your investments and how much you'll need to get there. Figure 2.8 shows an example of WealthBuilder's advice. WealthBuilder will even let you know how close you are to your financial goals, as seen in Figure 2.9. The program comes in DOS, Macintosh, and Windows (new) versions from Reality Technologies. It also comes with a copy of Reuters Money Network for on-line analysis and investing. The Windows version comes with a free copy of the Jonathan Pond planner, described later in this chapter.

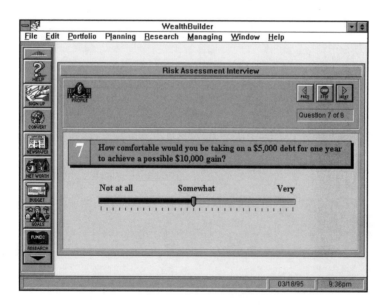

Figure 2.6 WealthBuilder planning starts by questioning you about risk—how much you want to live with.

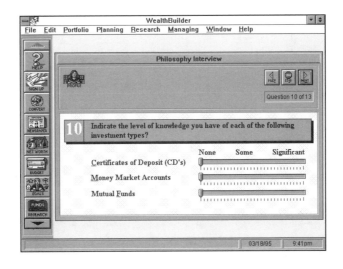

Figure 2.7 WealthBuilder's second planning step is to learn about your savings, income, and knowledge of investments.

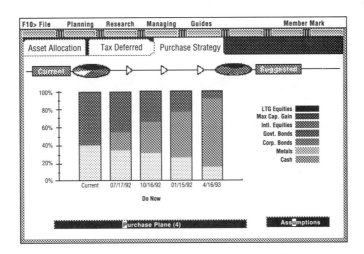

Figure 2.8 WealthBuilder then suggests asset allocation (see Chapter 7, "Invest" for details on this).

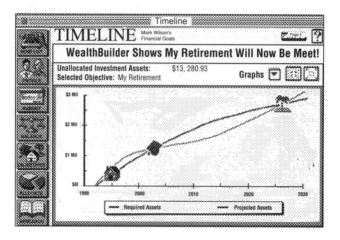

Figure 2.9 WealthBuilder planning concludes by graphing your progress toward goals.

Managing Your Money

This software from Block Financial Software (formerly MECA Software) is a checkbook register/budgeting/bill-paying/investment tracking program for DOS, Windows, and Mac. Within are planning modules for retirement, college, home buying, and other such goals. Managing Your Money has more planning built in than do most competing personal finance programs. It even has a menu just for planning, as seen in Figure 2.10.

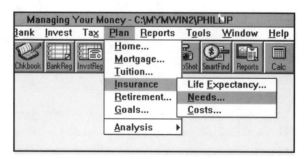

Figure 2.10 Managing Your Money has a full menu of planning help.

Managing Your Money calculates and analyzes mortgage refinance, college, insurance and retirement needs. IRAs, Keoghs, 401(K) plans, deferred annuities of company-sponsored retirement plans are all part of its understanding. And it is smart about those things, knowing, for example, about tax-free growth and lower tax rates at withdrawal.Figures 2.11 and 2.12 show samples of the help Managing Your Money provides. All along it adds advice, both on-screen and in the manual, that is clear and funny (coming from best-selling author Andrew Tobias).

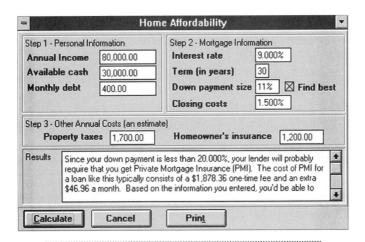

Figure 2.11 Managing Your Money has planning modules that not only calculate numbers, but tell you what they mean.

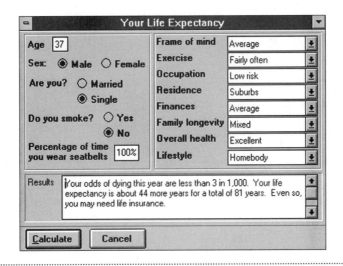

Figure 2.12 Managing Your Money even helps you calculate how long you'll have to keep up this computerized finance (and the life insurance to go with it).

Planning Information Programs

These programs package lots of words and pictures about planning with some calculators for specific planning problems. They help you calculate how much you should save, insure, and invest. All three packages described here are full of financial smarts and advice. Most come in CD-ROM versionswith additional information and video-interview clips that can help explain difficult concepts. (Unfortunately, all three are for PCs, not Macs.) Most of us could use one of these alongside whatever other planner we get. But don't leap to buy one until you get your other planning software. Some of the latest planning programs on CD-ROM come with free copies of one of these.

Jonathan Pond's Personal Financial Planner

Jonathan Pond is the author of nine books on personal financial planning including *The Personal Financial Planning Handbook*, *Safe Money in Tough Times*, and 1001 *Ways to Cut Your Expenses*. He is a CPA with a Harvard Business School education. Pond also writes for magazines and claims to appear in nearly 1000 radio, TV, and newspapers interviews each year.

This program organizes his advice onto floppy disks or a single CD-ROM. It starts with a "wealth test" that asks about your current financial records, savings, investment, and retirement plans. Then it quizzes you to see how much you know about personal finance. Next, using that information, the program suggests how you should build your own plans. Inside it you'll find:

💲 **Getting organized**—insurance, minimize spending and borrowing

💲 **Accumulating wealth**—in your home, in your investments, minimizing taxes on the way

💲 **Planning**—for retirement, for your estate

I especially like the list of "Ten simple things to do:"

1. Be happy with what you've got (live beneath your means).
2. Stop believing that because your income and assets may be limited, you can't do any financial planning.

3. Close all gaps in your insurance coverage.

4. Save at least 10% of your income.

5. Maintain a balanced investment portfolio appropriate to your financial situation.

6. Develop a reasonable investment strategy and stick with it.

7. Take advantage of tax breaks.

8. Recognize that it will cost a fortune to retire comfortably and begin preparing now.

9. Prepare and keep up-to-date necessary estate planning documents.

10. Take control of your personal finances.

Along the way you'll find examples, illustrations, exhibits, advice, suggestions, and on the CD-ROM version, even video clips of Pond pontificating, as seen in Figure 2.13.

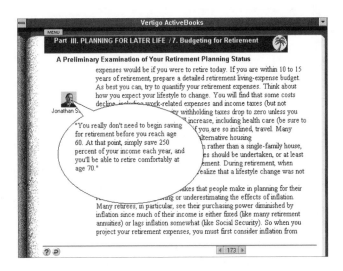

Figure 2.13 Jonathan Pond Personal Financial Planner is a full book on disc, computerized with cross-references and calculators.

This is not just a book on disc. It is an *ActiveBook*, in the company's words, where pages of explanations and illustrations also contain little worksheets. You type your numbers into these and the worksheets calculate results. It's like having a spreadsheet or calculator and a book rolled together (see Figure 2.14). And the book is much easier to move around in than a printed text because the many cross-references and icons let you instantly leap to look up any term, find related information, and so on. You can even backtrack to the pages where you've already been with the help of a **History** button. It also contains 20 minutes of video clips you can watch and listen to.

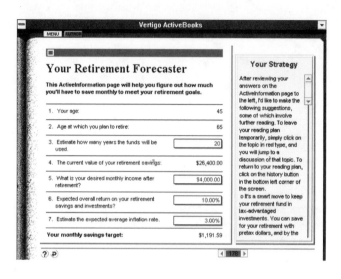

Figure 2.14 Pond's planner's built-in calculators make it an Active Book, which can both explain and figure.

The final result is a *Smart Planner Report*, a document you can print and take away. Plus you can always come back and work through the book again when your circumstances change. From Vertigo Development, it comes in both floppy and CD-ROM versions for Windows.

Wall Street Journal Personal Finance Library

From the same company that makes the Jonathan Pond Personal Financial Planner comes this collection of articles from the famous business newspaper's Your Money Matters column. Built into those columns in this computer version are interactive worksheets and calculators that let you immediately and directly figure what the advice means to you (see Figure 2.15). Topics include the best way to buy a new home, how to pay for college and retirement, the most effective way to establish credit, what lifetime savings can mean, and the most effective way to pay back student loans. Other interesting matters include debt reduction and investment strategies, with worksheets throughout so you can experiment with different approaches and see what the calculations turn out to be. You can buy this library alone on CD-ROM for Windows or you can get a discount by picking it up at the same time you buy the Pond disc.

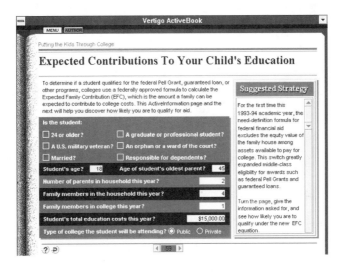

Figure 2.15 Wall Street Journal Personal Finance Library has articles with built-in calculators.

Your Best Money Moves Now

Another source of information on financial planning, also from Vertigo, is Your Best Money Moves Now. This collects 200 pages of information from *Money* magazine on stocks, insurance, health care, college education, and more. See Figure 2.16 for an example of the information provided by this program. It lists more than 3000 mutual funds and 1000 colleges that Money has ranked and lets you search through them to find your best fit. There's both expert text and interactive worksheets. You read, fill in forms, and then see suggestions and strategies from the experts. These cover investments, tax reduction, new Social Security laws, even health-care reform. And because it's on floppy, you don't need a CD-ROM drive.

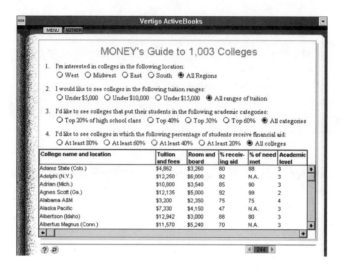

Figure 2.16 Your Best Money Moves Now has articles from Money Magazine on mutual funds and colleges.

Charles J. Givens Money Guide

Like Jonathan Pond Personal Financial Planner, Givens' guide is full of explanations, advice, and interaction (see Figure 2.17). Givens is the author of best-selling financial books such as *Wealth Without Risk*.

The program has three main sections to help you define your financial goals, organize your records, and teach you the basic principles of money management. The first section, called *Wealth Management*, gives you a ten-step process for getting organized. The second section, *Ten Biggest Money Management Mistakes and How to Correct Them*, is an interactive tutorial showing how to manage key financial issues such as insurance and savings. It focuses on saving for the future. The final section contains common questions and *Givens'* answers. All told there are 800 answers, 70 financial applications—such as built-in calculators and worksheets—and on the CD-ROM version, there are 131 video clips of explanations. From Friendly Software, it comes on either floppy disk or CD-ROM disc.

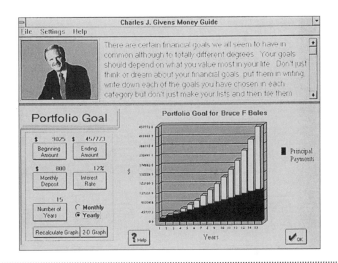

Figure 2.17 Charles J. Given's Money Guide can help you define your financial goals.

Home-Purchase Planning Programs

Buying a home is the largest purchase for most of us—if you figure that retirement costs more but is spread over some years. How expensive a home can you afford? How should you pay for it? Are you losing by renting? When should you refinance? Should you get an adjustable-rate mortgage or a fixed mortgage? There are so many questions.

And make no mistake that buying is generally a good idea. The government's mortgage interest tax deduction is the single largest loophole most of us will ever slip through. It wants you to buy, and makes it very enticing.

Naturally, the computer can help. There are basic home-buying planners built into the personal finance programs and the general planners described earlier. But there are some programs dedicated solely to homes. Let's take a look.

The Homebuyer's Guide for Windows

Here's a real specialist. Instead of general planning, you get homes and mortgages to the hilt. In this program, you'll find step-by-step information on mortgage comparisons, renting versus buying, debt-to-income ratios, prepayment schedules, refinance options, amortization tables, and more. You find all this through six menus: Preparation, Home Hunt, Financing, Offer, and Closing, which makes sense when getting a new home.

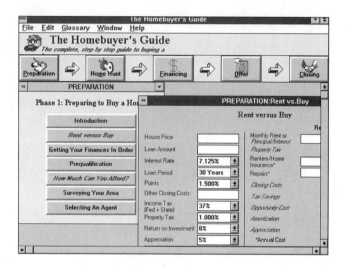

Figure 2.18 Homebuyer's Guide for Windows focuses on calculations and advice for financing options.

In The Homebuyer's Guide for Windows from *Tetra Solutions*, you can compare renting and buying, get advice on selecting an agent, get help with comparing the features of homes you see, be provided with financing options, calculate what you can afford, offer and negotiate, and handle escrow and closing along with inspections and disclosures (see Figure 2.18). The glossary of definitions should help explain the more technical terms. There's even a standard Fannie Mae (FNMA) loan application in the program (FNMA stands for Federal National Mortgage Association, a pseudo-governmental body helping to provide low-cost mortgages), one that many lenders will accept. The Guide is for PCs with Windows.

Education and Parenthood Planning Programs

Saving for the kids' college can be intimidating. It's coming sooner than retirement, most of us hope, and the costs seem to skyrocket every year. $20,000 a year seemed outrageous, but will soon feel old-hat as the top schools hit $25K headed for $30K. Add the Master's degree, Ph.D., or other professional school so many want for their children, and you're talking hundreds of thousands of dollars.

And in an economy asking more training of all of us, you may also be saving for some more college for yourself or your partner.

As you've seen in this chapter, simple calculators for education and college costs turn up in many personal finance programs. But there are now a few programs devoted specifically to this topic. They dig into more detail about how many years of what kind of school, and how you plan to save.

Price Waterhouse Education Funding System

This program comes in two versions, both for Windows. The inexpensive, "lite" version asks you what sort of education you're saving for, when it will come, and how much you already have put away. Then it guides you through balancing rates of return, possible annual contributions, and so on, to find out how and when to save. It contains helpful information and charts to show account progress. The advanced version also handles variable savings and investment return rates, gifts, part-time work, financial aid and variable education costs (see Figure 2.19).

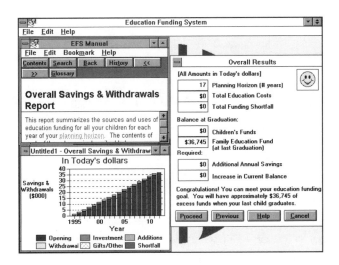

Figure 2.19 Price Waterhouse Educational Funding System helps you calculate and project college savings.

Quicken Parents' Guide to Money

A new planning program for Windows in 1995, this software guides parents through the various expenses of raising children, including education. Within you'll find tutorials, calculators, and advice. It comes on both floppy disk and CD-ROM. Of course, college-tuition planning is a central concern here. Figure 2.20 shows Quicken's main display.

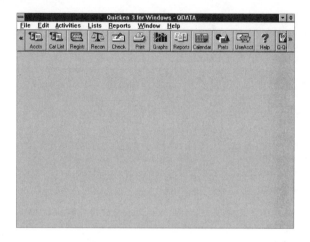

Figure 2.20 Quicken's main display.

Retirement Planning Programs

Retirement may be the single largest expense in your life. After all, a car costs $10,000 to $25,000. A college education $25,000 to $100,000. A home $100,000 to $500,000. (Of course you can spend more on any of those.) Retirement, if you're determined to live a long time, can mean 25 years times $30,000 to $70,000 per year, or an average of $1.25 million. That's for one person! Retirement is a bigger problem than it used to be because we live so much longer after work.

It could be even worse. Suppose you hope to retire early? That'll cut into savings and boost outflow. Where will you get that kind of money? Several places:

🐷   Savings over a lifetime of work is the theory

- ⑤ Interest over a lifetime of saving; the sooner you start the better
- ⑤ Pension from a lifetime of work, though these are harder to trust in an age of downsizing and multiple jobs in a lifetime
- ⑤ Social Security, which can add up to a lot, but because it is political it is hard to feel secure about (it's subject to governmental changes in times of tight federal budgets)
- ⑤ Your home, which is another form of savings, one the government encourages through the mortgage interest deduction on taxes
- ⑤ Your children, though whether they'll cost more when you're old or pay back more is also always an open question

You need to know how much to have, where it will come from, what to save now, and where to put those savings.

Some of the general-purpose planners—even the personal finance programs mentioned earlier—include retirement planning modules. But if you want to see more clearly and in more detail, you'll want a specialized retirement planner program such as one of these.

Rich & Retired is a Windows program from DataTech Software that helps you plan what assets to get and when. It handles assets you'll buy in the future, how to calculate how taxes will affect inherited property, and how to factor the percentage of assets to sell during retirement. You can print reports on yearly shortfall, yearly cash flow, yearly overview, lifetime overview, and more.

Destiny from Comtrad Industries has a portfolio manager and a retirement planning workbook. It guides you through understanding and calculating your own tax-deferred savings, investment diversification, inflation-adjusted savings, risk management, and asset allocation.

The Retirement Planning Kit from T. Rowe Price is for the PC and comes with a tutorial. T. Rowe Price is a famous mutual fund company, which naturally would like to convince you to save money, and save it in mutual funds. Still, this is a useful and inexpensive tool, not just an advertisement. What you'll need to save isn't stated as dollar amounts but as a percentage of what you make, which can help you feel better, but it isn't as clear a look to future circumstances.

Dow Jones' Plan Ahead for Your Financial Future is another PC program from a well-known financial name. It offers calculators and advice on retirement savings.

Prosper is a PC program that focuses on savings, investments, and inheritance for retirement and other similar financial goals. It builds a plan and advice, and has a database of mutual funds you might use for following that plan.

Price Waterhouse Retirement Planning System

Price Waterhouse is one of the biggest accounting firms. After accounting for corporations, it started helping the top execs with their accounting. Soon it was developing financial planning software for all levels of employees. Available for both DOS and Windows, this retirement planner is an easy way to draw those charts and tables showing what you'll need for the retirement you covet. It starts by asking your age, savings, pension expectations, and retirement goals (how nicely do you want to live?). It will estimate your Social Security take. Then it gives you the bottom line: what sort of retirement is coming if you follow your current path. The on-disk help information appears again to show you the ten steps to better retirement planning. Finally, you see a display ready for changes. As you fiddle with the numbers—how much you want in retirement, at what age you retire, how much you save annually now—the graphs change to indicate the future effects. Within this and the menu options you'll find easy revision of the plan, advice on investment choices, spousal benefits, and even estate planning. Figures 2.21 and 2.22 show examples of what you can do with this software. (The "lite" version is also available from Parsons Technology.) The company even offers an entire paperback book, 300 pages of it, devoted to retirement planning. (There's another book for tax planning.)

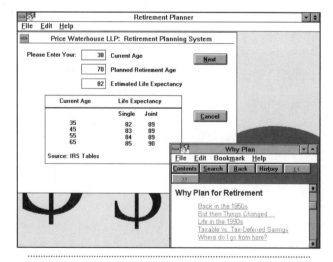

Figure 2.21 Price Waterhouse's Retirement Planning System starts by quizzing you about who you are and what you want.

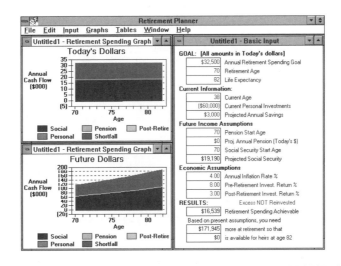

Figure 2.22 Price Waterhouse retirement planning lets you change your savings rates and goals, calculates the effects, and shows them instantly in graphs

Quicken Financial Planner

A new program for 1995 (along with the Quicken Parents' Guide to Money), this Windows software leads you from defining your current situation to a plan for reaching your goal. It asks you about your age and savings, your plans and investments. Then it helps you estimate what you'll need and how long you'll need it. There's a CD-ROM version with financial writer Jane Bryant Quinn appearing in video clips on screen.

Tutorial Example: Planning for Retirement with Quicken Financial Planner

Quicken Financial Planner, or QFP for short, provides easy and complete retirement planning. After you install it you'll soon see that you can work through it without even touching the menus. The work, from entering your own personal information to printing a plan, appears step-by-step on screen. You just read and answer the questions on each display, then click your mouse on the **Next** button to proceed or click on one of the notebook-style tabs on the far right to leap to another area of planning.

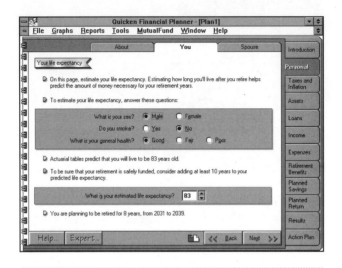

Figure 2.23 Quicken Financial Planner offers just a few buttons and notebook-style tabs for control, making it easy even for beginners.

As you work in QFP, you can click on the **Help** button, bottom left, for helpful instructions on answering the questions intelligently. Or you can click on the neighboring **Expert** button for Jane Bryant Quinn's suggestions and advice. See Figure 2.24 for a sample of a QFP screen. The Help or Expert information that appears will relate to the questions currently on screen. When you're done with the Help, press **Esc** to get rid of it.

Answering questions, you'll move through Personal Information, Taxes & Inflation, Assets, Loans, Income, Expenses, Retirement Benefits, Planned Savings, and Planned Return. You may notice that your answers to early questions affect which later questions appear. When you're asked what inflation rate you want to figure in, you won't be left alone. QFP displays historic inflation rates and suggests a reasonable, middle-of-the-road number. Throughout you can do all right with just the suggested values from the program (see Figure 2.25). But the flexibility to change them means you can work through QFP more than once, as times change and you change. You can even create different scenarios to see what changes in the economy or your plans affect what you'll need to save.

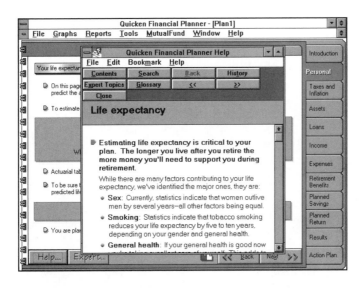

Figure 2.24 QFP offers both Help and Expert advice on answering the important questions.

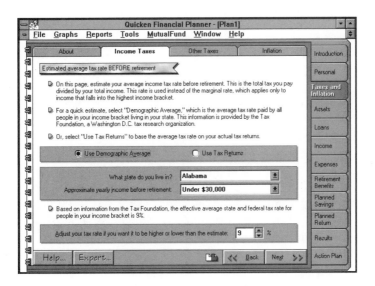

Figure 2.25 QFP lets you choose the numbers that will affect your future, but also shows you the range of choices and suggests a reasonable value.

QFP can grab a list of your assets from Quicken itself, saving you the trouble of typing all the values in again (see Figure 2.26). Next you'll get a chance to import. These links, like links you'll use later between your checkbook-register/bill-paying program and your tax preparation program, avoid math mistakes and save time.

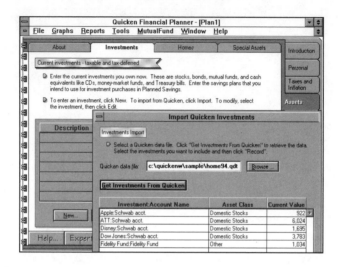

Figure 2.26 QFP can import asset and liability data from Quicken.

QFP will estimate your Social Security benefits and ask about your pension plan. Then it will want the details on your IRAs, Keoghs, 401(K) plans, and SEPs. Don't know what those are yet? You will soon, for any retirement planning. And descriptions are part of the QFP Help and Expert advice.

The next step is *asset allocation*. Where should you put your investments to gain that retirement you have in mind? QFP will ask you what sort of risk you're comfortable with, and then show you charts and tables with suggested divisions among safe and high-return investments, such as the one in Figure 2.27. The allocation will probably change after retirement, when most people want more security and are willing to tolerate less risk. QFP can chart that allocation too.

Results are the price of life here, and QFP shows those results in many different ways. You can see a graph of your cash flow, from today to and through retirement (see Figure 2.28). And that comes with a summary about trouble spots. There's advice available at the click of a button, and you can adjust all to today's dollars just by clicking a checkmark into the little box above the graph.

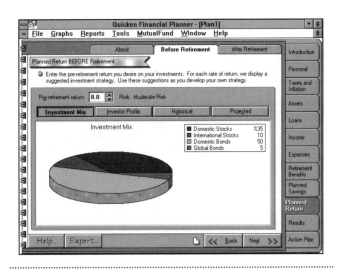

Figure 2.27 QFP suggests asset allocation for your investments. You choose the risk; QFP tells you where to put your money (in general terms).

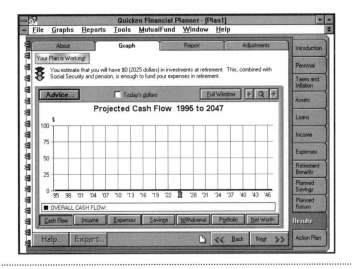

Figure 2.28 QFP shows results in charts of cash flow, income, and so on.

You can see similar graphs on expenses, income, savings, and your net worth. If you're more comfortable with numbers, you can view the results as tables, as seen in Figure 2.29. And within these you can use the QuickZoom feature. Double-click on any value to leap to the original details behind the final table.

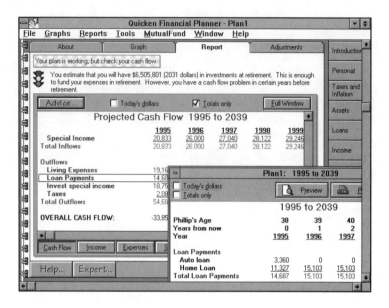

Figure 2.29 QFP can also show results in tables, with QuickZoom for double-click focusing in on the information behind any element of the results.

The Adjustments portion of results suggests what you can do to change any shortfalls. And as you make changes, such as promising to save a certain amount more per year for a certain number of years, QFP instantly calculates the effects.

Finally, you see your Action Plan. QFP shows how much you have planned to save and invest, month by month. To aid your investments, it has the Morningstar Mutual Fund data on many securities built in. Figure 2.30 illustrates such a task. You choose the investment factors important to you—which means knowing something about funds, though there is some built-in help—and the Search feature finds those matching your requests.

In the final display, shown in Figure 2.31, QFP suggests how soon you should revisit your plans. This planning maintenance schedule depends on changes in your life, naturally, and on the investments you choose. The last steps you should take at this point are:

1. Save your plan (from the File menu).
2. Print your plan (go back to the results or use the Reports menu).
3. Keep your dreams and plans handy for the next chapters.

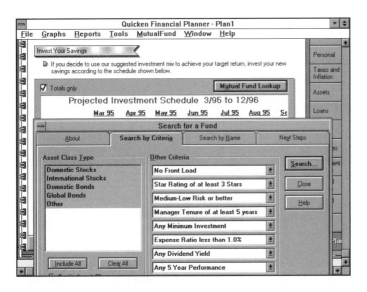

Figure 2.30 QFP will list what you plan to save and invest, and help you use Morningstar's data on securities to pick the right mutual fund for the investments.

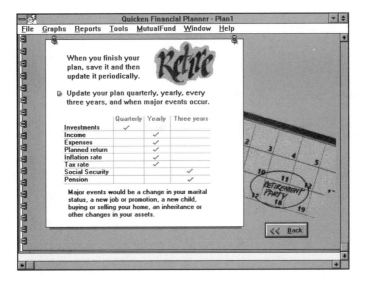

Figure 2.31 QFP's last act is to suggest a planning maintenance schedule.

Tips for Planning

Watch for these aspects of planning software:

💲 A multitude of *what if* scenarios—you should be able to challenge or change the program's assumptions. Remember, only you know your own life.

💲 Over-optimism—some programs suggest you'll earn 14% or more over the long term. That's quite unlikely. You'll have a hard time beating 10%, or even 5% when adjusting for inflation.

💲 Forgetting inflation—some programs will show you fantastic appreciation without noting that inflation will reduce the value of future dollars. Put a long-term inflation rate of 4 to 4.5% into your equations.

💲 Principal consumption—you don't have to leave lots of money behind for heirs. You can conservatively estimate your life span and then factor in some consumption of principal retirement.

💲 Tax considerations—make sure you're figuring either immediate or deferred taxes into your results.

💲 Social Security—it isn't gone, you know. See that its contributions or lack thereof are part of your plans.

💲 Doom projections—you may find that you'll need to save more every month, from now until eternity. Don't let that spook you. Just starting to do better is all that's necessary.

Summary—Dream, Plan, Then You're Ready to Budget

That about says it all. You need to start with wishes and desires. Put them down on paper, and be clear about them. Next, you use the software described here, from personal financial planners to specific tools. If you're on a tight budget, stick to the planning built into your central program. My favorite for this is Managing Your Money, though WealthBuilder comes very close. If you can afford more, get an informational resource such as Pond's CD-ROM, and then dig into the detailed planners: Homebuyer's Guide for you guess what, Price Waterhouse for education or retirement, or the Quicken Financial Planner for retirement.

Now you're ready to get the dollars those dreams demand. The first step: know what you have.

CHAPTER 3

Record

Now that you've looked to the future (Chapter 2), you're ready to look at today. This chapter is devoted to programs that let you record your finances to keep track of what you're getting and giving. The following chapters explain how the same programs automate bill-paying and then simplify budgeting.

Checkbook-Register Programs Start with Checks

The programs in this chapter are the heart of any computerized personal finance. In fact, they're often just referred to as *personal finance programs* although they don't cover the full gamut from on-line research through investing, protecting, and shopping.

What these programs do is record. They keep precise and organized records of what you've spent and what you've earned. Or rather, they let you keep those records, because the one key to using these programs is that you must enter the information. You must sit down with your computer and your receipts and your memories to put it all on disk. The computer cannot yet automatically monitor your movements and expenditures (though I'm not sure many of us actually want that development).

Originally, in fact, they were known as *checkbook register* programs (see Figure 3.1). They were replacements for the paper register, where you record the check numbers and amounts you've written, and occasionally try to balance the results. The computer's math abilities simplified the balancing.

Date	Num	Payee		Payment		Cl	Deposit	Balance	
		Memo	Category						
3/ 7/95		Cafe' Barrone		18 50				5,178 78	
		Lunch	Dining						
3/12/95		Juniper Landscape		56 78				5,122 00	
		monthly landscape	Landscape						
3/13/95		Mustard's		76 00				5,046 00	
		Dinner	Dining						
3/13/95		Starbuck's Coffee		17 85				5,028 15	
		breakfast	Dining						
3/18/95		ATM		40 00				4,988 15	
		need cash	Cash						
3/20/95	Sched	Dancer's Loft		35 00				4,953 15	
		membership fee	Fitness						
3/26/95	Num	Payee		Payment			Deposit		
		Memo	Category						

Figure 3.1 Personal finance programs make the on-screen account registers look as much like a familiar check register as possible.

Checks Alone aren't Enough— Adding Accounts

Keeping and balancing a checkbook are certainly fine goals for a computer program. But they aren't enough. Why write the checks and then type the results into the computer? Why not just type what you want and then have the computer both register it and print the checks? So that ability appeared in these programs. And as corporations and banks shuttled more money back and forth from computer to computer—called EFT or Electronic Funds Transfer—the program makers thought, "why not individuals?" Electronic-bill-paying appeared, as described in Chapter 4.

Also, people have other accounts and assets, such as cash, savings, credit cards, and even mutual funds and Certificates of Deposit. So the checkbook register programs expanded with registers for those accounts. And they added analysis tools for those various assets.

Categories Let You Budget and Plan for Taxes

The next step was assigning each outgoing or incoming transaction a particular category. This is different from the account. The account tells you where each pile of money is coming from or going to—checks, cash, savings, credit card or whatever. The category tells you the reason for the incoming or outgoing. Was it salary coming in or gambling winnings? Did that check go for groceries or business supplies?

Each income or expense has both an account and a category.

By sorting expenses by accounts, you end up with balances showing how much is in each account.

By sorting expenses by categories, you end up with sums showing how much has been spent on each type of thing. In other words, you see your real budget.

And by collecting those expense category sums that affect taxes—such as legal deductions and business expenses—you can estimate and then actually prepare income tax calculations (see Chapter 6 for more details on this).

Most personal finance programs use categories to let you see what you've actually spent, and then use that as a base for molding the budget you actually want to follow.

Timing—Calendars and Flows

Another aspect of each income or outgo is when it happens. By attaching a date to each transaction, you automatically get a chronological list of history—what you did each day. But the program can also use this information to create a future—a projection based on the past. How will your cash flow? Are there low spots you can adjust for?

That flow can become a calendar, if the program offers, where you can see what regular payments are due, and even be alerted that it is time to pay or receive. This is particularly helpful if you're running a small business using personal finance software. You'll need to estimate what you're getting, what you're spending, and when the taxes are due.

Cost of Personal Finance—A Few Dollars and More Hours

These programs cost only $20 to $50, or may even be free, bundled on the hard disk of that new computer you bought.

The bigger cost associated with these programs is that of time and commitment. For these programs to do you any good, you need to fill them with your financial information, down to the last receipt for checking, savings, credit cards, and even the coins in your pocket. And you need to keep entering any new transactions in your life. It isn't easy. I spread my initial entries over a couple of weeks, and that meant many evenings of digging through receipts just for the current year. It also meant sometimes backtracking to redefine my expense categories.

A word of advice: first think thoroughly about how you want to categorize your spending for tax deductions and for budgeting. You'll want to know what to call each expense as you enter it; the program you buy can help. Most offer predefined official tax categories, but you may need some categories or subcategories of your own for your particular situation. Don't worry too much, though: you can go back at any time and change them.

If that seems like too much work for you, and it will be for many people, then don't waste your money on one of these programs yet. Try the tax preparation programs or perhaps skip straight to the investment software. Remember, though, that some of these programs can handle basic investments as well, and then you'd have the organizational tools ready if and when you decide to thoroughly organize.

Don't abandon all hope of using these computer organizers just because you've never been organized before. I was the worst organized (or perhaps I should say the best disorganized) person ever. But the allure of the computer—allowing me to enter information only once, and then knowing it would show up for banking, taxes, investments, and more—finally turned me into my own personal accountant.

Incidentally, if a computer is too big for you, Panasonic has come up with an interesting pocket machine called the Check Writer. For $350 this calculator-sized device will keep track of two bank accounts (such as for personal and business use), ten credit cards, and cash transactions, as well as ATM transactions. It even has a phone log and calculator. Uniquely, though, it prints on your standard wallet-sized checks, right there at the store—the printer is built-in. It can speed check writing by storing up to 25 frequent payees and can print reports on activities. I don't know any way to link it to a more complete home finance program, yet. This chapter also mentions some other portable devices that let you track what you're doing, though they don't necessarily let you print checks while you're out and about.

What to Look for in Recording (Accounts and Categories) Software

There are almost a half-dozen major personal financial recording programs. There are many other minor competitors, with fewer features and a smaller number of sales. You'll even find some shareware and public-domain programs. I don't advise using any of these, however, because they have far fewer features yet only slightly lower prices than the commercial big names.

Here is what you want in such a program:

💰 Compatibility with your hardware—it should run on your computer, naturally.

💰 Compatibility with your software—it should work as a partner with your other financial software choices (which means you may need to skim the rest of this book before choosing one), such as exporting information to your tax prep program (Chapter 6), downloading information from your on-line service (Chapter 10), and sharing information with your portfolio analysis programs (Chapter 7).

💰 Ease—it should look and feel easy to understand, or at least as easy as possible.

💰 Appropriate—beyond the standard features that any such program has, it should have the special features that fit your situation, such as the links to portable electronic organizers in Quicken, the investment management in Managing Your Money, the electronic bill-paying in Novell Money, or the nonprofit business categorizing in MoneyCounts.

Example Programs

Here are the best-known programs for personal financial organization. Each has its strengths, from Quicken's ease and widespread use to Managing Your Money's investment advice.

Quicken

Quicken is the best-selling personal finance program in the world, with an estimated seven million users. The latest version comes with a Getting Started tutorial and on-screen "Qcards" that help tell you want to do for each account and window.

Quicken's first claim to fame was as an easy way to computerize the checkbook—with an on-screen display that looked like a typical check, a check register that was easy to fill out, and a patented system for lining up the blank checks to print. It is still strong at all of these. The QuickFill feature makes data entry faster by immediately guessing what you're typing by looking at past entries. If it is wrong, you can just keep typing through it. If it is right, you can stop typing and confirm the full entry (see Figure 3.2).

Now, with the CheckFree program thrown in, you can also choose not to print checks at all, but to send payments electronically. Chapter 4 shows this in more detail. Quicken also handles assets and liabilities, rental properties, and even small business accounting.

Quicken's built-in calendar schedules bill payments and monitors cash flow. Using the mouse, you can simply drag payments from the check register to any day on the calendar on screen. The calendar will alert you when it is time to pay one of these bills (see Figure 3.3). (You can also note birthdays on the calendar.)

Figure 3.2 The QuickFill feature in Quicken guesses ahead at what you're typing to speed recording.

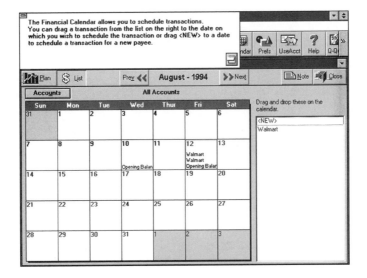

Figure 3.3 Quicken's Calendar schedules bill payments.

Uniquely, Quicken moved beyond simply letting you record credit card transactions with the IntelliCharge credit card. This Visa card, which you may apply for when you get Quicken, has on-line records you can dial into with a modem for monitoring your balance and reconciling your computer records (you can also get the records on floppy disk if you don't have or use a modem). Some competing programs are hoping to avoid the need for a special credit card such as this in the future, by offering on-line information for any credit-card.

Quicken also holds your portfolio information on securities such as stocks and bonds. Previous versions were weak in this area, depending almost entirely on the Quicken Companion program (described below) for investment features.

However, the latest version is beefed up, with more sophisticated record keeping for investments and even some investment tutorials. There's a portfolio view with 18 measures of performance and value. You can generate reports on capital gains, plus they're all illustrated with graphs.

Quicken is good at making budgets (automatically from historic spending patterns) and graphically demonstrating how you are sticking to or exceeding them. Naturally it will also show where you're not reaching budgeted amounts, but few of us worry about that or expect it. The expense categories it uses for making budgets are also useful for exporting to a tax preparation program. More tax programs accept Quicken data directly than that of any other personal finance program because it is so popular. In general, Quicken has become more graphic over the years, and the latest version can produce graphs showing your income and expenses. Double-clicking on an element of the graph or report will bring up the details behind the chart.

Quicken does not have as much planning or strategy capability as Managing Your Money or WealthBuilder, although it has improved on the planning capability from previous versions. It now helps you figure the differences between fixed- and variable-rate loans, showing payment schedules, and calculating refinancing details. It will also help you calculate what to budget for college and retirement.

Quicken does not yet have complete on-line banking, other than the IntelliCharge card, but is working on this with banks such as Banc One Corp., First Bank Systems, First National Bank of Omaha, Meridian Bank, and Wells Fargo Bank. The plan is to offer account balance information and financial transactions such as transfers and bill payment.

The Windows, DOS, and Macintosh versions of Quicken differ a little from one another in the way they look on screen and in particular features. The Windows version tends to have the most and latest features. Always check to see just what is in the version you're buying. The Mac version of Quicken has the same foundation as the Windows version (see Figure 3.4).

The CD-ROM Deluxe Edition of Quicken for Windows teams Quicken 3 for Windows and Quicken Companion 2 with on-line documentation and several other financial programs. There's enough room on a CD-ROM for many programs. The extras include:

💰 CheckFree for electronic bill paying.

💰 Your Mutual Fund Selector (for more information, see Chapter 7).

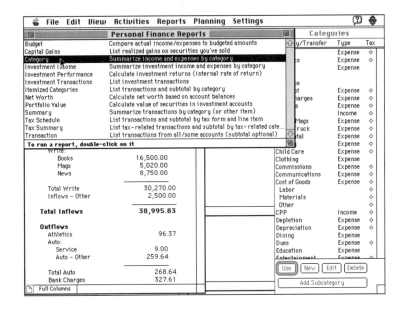

Figure 3.4 Quicken for Macintosh is quite similar to the Windows version.

🐷   The Wall Street Journal Personal Finance Library with interactive articles contains built-in calculators and answers to questions on investing taken from the famous newspaper (this also uses the ActiveBook format, and can be bought separately).

🐷   Tradeline Electronic Stock Guide with one-page snapshots on over 6000 stocks. It includes details such as week trends, price/earnings ratios, yields, returns, and more (this can be updated monthly or quarterly using the Tradeline Update Service, and details on this accompany the program).

🐷   US Government Personal Finance Publications consisting of twenty brochures on disk about buying life insurance, planning retirement, and so on.

🐷   Home inventory to list your belongings for insurance.

🐷   Insurance planning to make sure you have enough insurance.

🐷   Net Worth, which adds the value of your belongings to the net worth stored in Quicken.

💲 Quicken Quotes for dialing out through a modem to get on-line the latest prices on 11,000 stocks and mutual funds and to update your Quicken portfolio.

💲 Tax Estimator for estimating your current and soon-to-pay taxes, using TurboTax calculations.

💲 Tips for tracking frequent flyer miles in Quicken, prepaying mortgages, preparing expense reports, monitoring children's allowances, and more.

💲 Manuals, which are the complete books for Quicken and the extras with hot link cross-referencing to make finding the right information easy.

Pocket Quicken

In a quest to put Quicken everywhere and to make it easier to enter transactions immediately, Intuit has created Pocket Quicken, a version that appears in the Tandy/Casio Zoomer handheld computer (also known as a PDA or Personal Digital Assistant). Pocket Quicken is in other PDAs too, such as the HP 200LX, Apple's Newton MessagePad 120, Motorola's Envoy, and General Magic's Magic Cap (a portable software operating system). These all operate without a keyboard. You use a small stylus to write, draw, or point on the surface.

This does not have all the functions of Quicken, but does contain the basics for recording and categorizing expenses in checking, credit card, and cash accounts. With Pocket Quicken, you point to a graphic object in the wallet (such as a credit card) and then record spending information on electronic receipts. With the connectivity pack, you can later merge that data with your Quicken for Windows transactions stored on another computer (see Figure 3.5).

Managing Your Money

Andrew Tobias' Managing Your Money has long played second fiddle to Quicken's best-selling status. However, investors preferred Managing Your Money for its portfolio management strengths, leaving Quicken far behind. The latest versions of the two programs bring Quicken closer in portfolio management. At the same time, the latest version of Managing Your Money has a much more realistic-looking checkbook for entering transactions, matching or even bettering Quicken's traditional strength.

Figure 3.5 Pocket Quicken sample display.

As Quicken adds more investment strengths, and newcomers such as Novell Money challenge, Managing Your Money has a new look. Not yet in the DOS and Macintosh versions, the latest Windows version leaves behind some of the specialized features of previous versions and adds a new interface to make itself easier to use. It's called the SmartDesk, and you see a graphic cartoon of a small office on the screen (see Figure 3.6).

Figure 3.6 Managing Your Money's SmartDesk.

Instead of looking through menus for commands, you just click on the graphic representations of what you want to do. Need to pay a bill? Click on the check register on the desk. A realistic-looking checkbook will appear where you can type payee, amount, and so on. The register will be immediately above, and will instantly reflect whatever you type (see Figure 3.7). As with any of these sophisticated programs, the software will think ahead, trying to remember previous checks to the same payee, and suggest how to complete the transaction so that you may not even have to type more than a few letters.

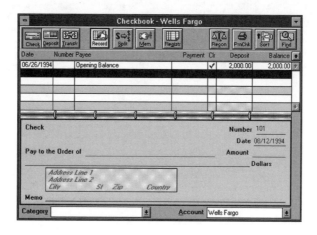

Figure 3.7 Managing Your Money's checkbook.

There are pictures of the Thinker sculpture (for help) and books on the case labeled Home, Mortgage, Tuition, Goals, Retirement, Insurance, and Analysis. Charts on the wall are labeled Investments, Reports, Graphs, and Reminders. There's also a tickertape, a notepad on the desk, a calculator, and desk drawers labeled *Accounts, Loans, Tax, Categories, Payees, Memorized,* and *Preferences.* If you prefer, you can still use the mouse, menus, and mini-toolbar for standard Windows operation of the program. This interface may follow the fate of many interface experiments—attracting newcomers, putting off experienced hands, and eventually lending some of its features to all personal finance programs. Personal finance programs can still intimidate first-time computer owners; perhaps this interface will ease their fears and get them started.

Managing Your Money still has banking, investing, tax estimating, planning, property management, and stock portfolio features. This program has been famous for being the best for tracking investments. It is still strong in this area from simple and annual appreciation and yield to far more sophisticated features.

For taxes, Managing Your Money includes tax planning and can export to TaxCut or other programs using the .TXF file format. And Managing Your Money has more tax planning built in than most tax-preparation programs because it is able to show you how your finances are affecting your 1040 and other major forms. For planning, there are many features such as three-year budgeting, comparison of budgets to actual expenditure, SmartPlanner analysis windows, and of course, the Andrew Tobias advice (see Figure 3.8).

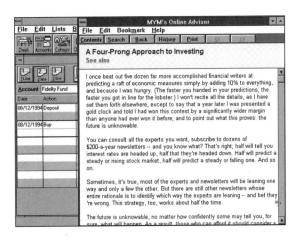

Figure 3.8 Andrew Tobias's advice is a key strength in Managing Your Money.

Tobias is a best-selling author of financial advice books, and his lightly humorous but quite clear advice permeates Managing Your Money and is one of the key reasons it is chosen over competitors' programs.

Managing Your Money generally goes beyond Novell Money and Quicken in helping you understand your investments, though Quicken is much closer than it used to be. Managing Your Money can even help you plan investment allocation, the way more expensive programs such as Allocation Master do (see Chapter 7). You can run what-if scenarios with it, putting your money into types of investments, then asking what would have happened during historic periods to that investment (the early 1980s bull market, the early 1970s bear market). And it can handle all the various Schedules A, B, C, D, E, F, and SE for income taxes on investments.

Block Software is the company behind Managing Your Money and CompuServe—the same company running the H&R Block Tax preparation retail stores. This firm bought MECA, the previous home of Managing Your Money. There have been plans to have other software developers make add-on utility programs for Managing Your Money, which would extend its power. Until one of these arrives for on-line banking, Managing Your Money is clearly behind Quicken and Novell Money in that area.

Microsoft/Novell Money

Money is a personal finance program for PCs running Windows. It used to be Microsoft Money but was sold to Novell as part of Microsoft's deal to acquire Intuit, manufacturers of Quicken.

Features in Money include investment management, financial-planning *wizards* (utilities that show you how to work the program), and on-line banking. It can import and export Quicken files. The AutoBudget feature creates a budget from your spending records. AutoReconcile compares your transaction to your balance. SmartFill and SuperSmartFill make data entry easier by remembering past entries and suggesting new ones. Future Transactions automates regular payments. It is compatible with popular tax programs such as TurboTax.

The wizards exemplify a trend in consumer software: tutorials are no longer something to study before you use a program but are built-in guides to stick with as you work. The wizards in Money pop up in windows telling you, step-by-step, how to make the program do what you want (see Figure 3.9).

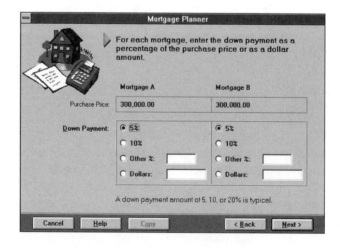

Figure 3.9 Money's planning wizards lead you through calculations.

There are reports with tables, charts, and graphs on transactions, budgets, loan payments, taxes, investment transactions, investment market value, income and expense, net worth, summary, capital gains, performance, and price history. The views let you see income and expense by category, payee, or time period. You can customize the reports to show only what you need.

Money will print standard or custom checks. Bank On-Line (see Figure 3.10) lets you transfer funds, check your balance, look at credit card transactions, and download transactions from your bank account directly. Pay On-Line lets you pay bills electronically. Quotes On-Line lets you check your investments through the market prices of securities. All of the on-line services require monthly fees, typically in the $10-per-month range.

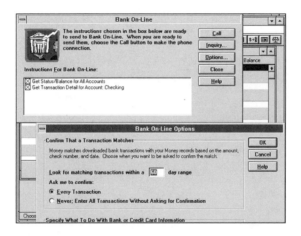

Figure 3.10 Money's Bank On-Line feature lets you check balances through the phone.

Like most personal finance programs, Money comes with expense categories for both home and small business, as well as letting you create your own categories (see Figure 3.11).

You don't need to spend extra on communications software—that's built in—and the calls are local. Bank On-Line is new and available only from a few participating banks, including First National of Chicago, Michigan National Bank, and U.S. Bank. More banks should sign on in the future. But if you use one of those, you can download bank statements, transfer funds, and update securities information. The planning feature includes simple calculations for retirement, mortgage, loan, and savings, with wizards to tell you how to use the calculations.

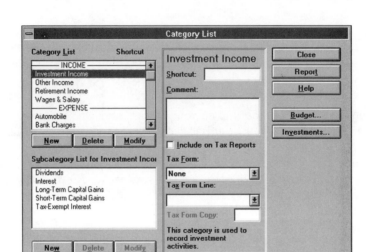

Figure 3.11 Money's expense categories list.

CA-Simply Money

Computer Associates is one of the world's largest software companies. It makes software for computers ranging in size from PCs to huge corporate mainframes. For PCs it has several well-known accounting programs. Computer Associates is now getting into personal finance programs with CA-Simply Tax (see Chapter 6) and CA-Simply Money.

Simply Money is a complete personal finance program, like Quicken or Novell Money. You can enter savings accounts, checking accounts, credit cards, credit lines, mortgages, and even 401(k) plans. It lets you store and recall transactions, print checks, keep lists of accounts and payees, and even create payroll checks (if you want to use it for running a small business). Other small business features include cash flow, balance sheets, accounts receivable, and accounts payable reports. You can pay on-line through BillPay USA.

The appearance of CA-Simply Money can be baffling at first, with all sorts of graphic icons on the screen that you must choose among and click on to help you through learning those icons (Figure 3.12). The program imports Quicken data if you're changing over from that program (see Figure 3.13).

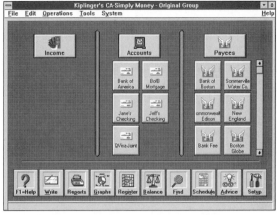

Figure 3.12 CA-Simply Money offers icons and buttons for control.

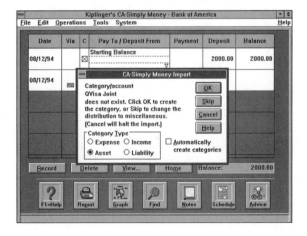

Figure 3.13 Simply Money can import Quicken files.

The Financial Advisor in CA-Simply Money tracks your financial moves and offers recommendations on how to improve your money management. The Financial Schedulers handle repetitive or planned payments. The Budgeting feature offer a dozen reports and graphs to let you see where the money goes, handling fixed expenses, variable expenses, and priorities. AutoBudget lets you create a budget from your history, so you don't have to guess in each expense area. Quicken, Managing Your Money, and Novell Money have similar features.

Along with CA-Simply Money you get several calculator programs for planning and precise figuring (see Figure 3.14).

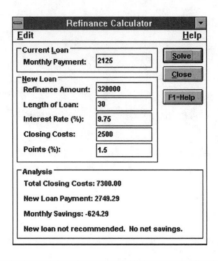

Figure 3.14 Simply Money offers specialized calculators, such as this one for refinancing a loan.

You should consider getting a CompuServe subscription if you use CA-Simply Money. There's on-line technical support where you can ask questions about the program. You can automatically load quotes into your CA-Simply Money data to keep current on your investments. Updates and fixes to CA-Simply Money also appear there; use the CompuServe command **GO CAIPRO**. Although these deals change over time, in 1994 CA-Simply Money came with a free introductory subscription to CompuServe, along with one month's basic service. The latest version comes with BillPay for on-line bill paying.

For investments, CA-Simply Money records buying securities, updating prices manually, tracking expiration dates, selling stocks, selling short, share transfers, stock splits, and even capital gains distribution on mutual funds. IRA custodial fees and tax-free accounts fit in too. There are financial calculators for planning such as refinancing, loans, interest conversion, dividends, and investments.

Kiplinger's CA-Simply Money is a special version of CA-Simply Money. It comes from the Kiplinger company famous for its books, videos, and newsletters on personal finance. They take the main CA-Simply Money program and add more advice, tips, and hints.

MoneyCounts and Money Mate

Parsons Technology offers an inexpensive personal finance program called MoneyCounts for both Windows and DOS. The Windows version offers typical checkbook abilities as well as the sophistication of electronic bill paying. It is the only personal finance program that comes not just with home and business expense categories, but with categories for farm, church, and rental property. The manual that comes with it explains accounting to the non-accountant. And you also get an Address Book/Mail List Manager program to keep track of the contacts involved in your daily life (and presumably in your bookkeeping as well) (see Figure 3.15).

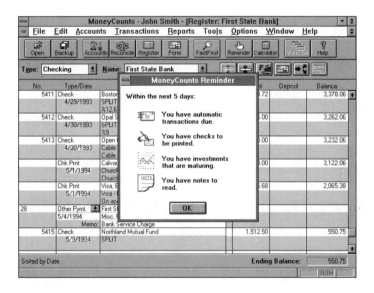

Figure 3.15 MoneyCounts offers expense categories for nonprofit groups.

MoneyCounts does not handle investments. You could use it for small-business accounting, though it doesn't have payroll or invoicing.

For even less—for only $8 shipping and handling—you can get a simplified version called Money Mate. It still has the basic accounts, net worth and transaction analyses, charts, budgeting, and tax estimation (see Figure 3.16).

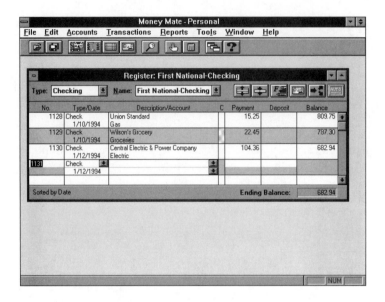

Figure 3.16 Money Mate gives you the basics of MoneyCounts at a very low price.

Tutorial Example: Using Quicken to Record Your Income and Outgo

Quicken is the most popular checkbook-register program and there's a demo version of Quicken for Windows on the CD-ROM with this book. So I'll use Quicken as an example for setting up and recording your financial transactions.

1. First you install the program. Typically that means starting Windows and then using the File menu's **Run** command to run the INSTALL.EXE program on the Quicken disk.

2. Press the **Enter** key each time you're asked where to install Quicken—the directory it chooses should work OK.

3. When Quicken is installed, you can double-click on its icon to start the program.

In order to load Quicken, make sure to use **INSTALL.EXE**, and not SETUP.EXE, which is more common in many Windows programs.

N O T E

Then you'll need to set up Quicken for your own use. You'll need to make a new:

💰 **File**—this is the name Quicken uses to store your information on disk (and it is actually stored as a group of disk files).

💰 **Account**—these are the names of your various financial areas: Checkbook, Credit Card, Wallet, Mutual Fund, and so on (with a separate account for each one).

💰 **Categories**—these are the names of your expense and income types: Rent, Gas, Insurance, Entertainment, and so on (because that's how you follow a budget and allocate tax deductions).

Don't worry about any confusion between Accounts and Categories. You need both, and after a few entries you'll see what they mean.

1. With Quicken running, you can start making these new necessities (File, Accounts, Categories) by choosing the File menu and then the **New** command. You'll see the window where you click on **New File** and then on **OK**. (The full, new version of Quicken leads you through this with some helpful questions.)

2. Next you'll see a window for naming that file. Type a name, but before you click on **OK**, choose either or both of the categories options at the bottom right of the window. This will start you out with home, business, or both kinds of categories. (If you don't choose these, you'll have to create all of your own categories. That's not so hard, but the ready categories here are a good start for just about anyone.) (See Figure 3.17.)

3. Now click on **OK**.

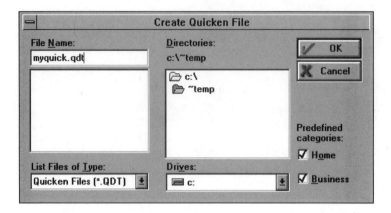

Figure 3.17 When starting with Quicken, create a new file and accept the ready-to-go categories (they're a good start and you can always change them later).

Setting Up Accounts

Now that your new file is ready, with categories ready too, you need some accounts. Everyone has some kind of cash, usually in a purse or wallet, so let's start with that. Notice that window in the bottom right of the screen? That's a Qcard, Intuit's way of guiding you through Quicken. Why not follow it? If the advice bothers you, you're free to turn it off so no more Qcards appear. Even without them there's a guide through account creation—make sure the little box is checked for that—and a **Help** button always at hand (see Figure 3.18).

1. To start with that Cash account, click on the **Cash** button.

2. You'll be asked for an Account Name (anything you like—I call mine W*allet*) and a description (not necessary, but useful if you set up multiple cash accounts, such as one for your home business petty cash and another for personal items). Just type them in, then click **Next**.

3. You'll be asked if you know how much cash you have. Find out; otherwise you'll just have to find out later. Then answer **Yes** or **No** and click on **Next**.

4. In the next window, type the current date and the amount of money you have in that account. Click on **Done** this time.

You'll see your new account appear (the $131.50 is just my example amount in this cash account) (see Figure 3.19).

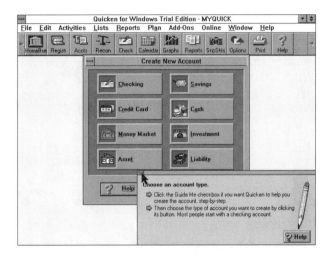

Figure 3.18 Create accounts using these choices, with the guide of Qcards if you want the help (as shown in the window at bottom right here).

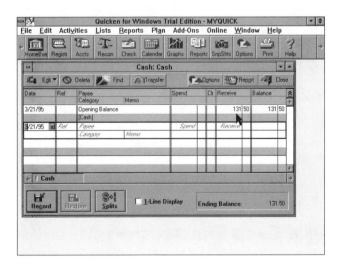

Figure 3.19 Your new account has its own register.

Most people have a checking account too. Make one for yourself now choosing **Create New Account** from the Activities menu, then step through the same process again, offering name, description, amount, date, and confirming **Done**. You'll see another register appear on screen. Continue this way with any other accounts you may need, including Credit Cards. (On Credit Cards you'll be asked if you signed up for the IntelliCharge card, a new credit card through Intuit that lets you check your account through on-line modem calls. See more details on this in Chapter 4.) Then click on the **Accounts** button to see a list of your accounts. Within that list you can add more details, such as the interest rate on credit cards or the phone number to call for information on the bank accounts, by clicking on the **Info** button (see Figure 3.20).

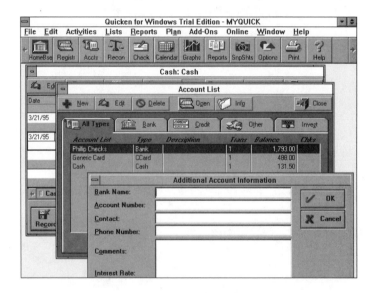

Figure 3.20 Quicken's Account List with window open for adding background information on the account.

Entering a Cash Transaction

Now that you have accounts, you can enter transactions. If you have a lot of time and energy, you can even go back and enter all your past transactions. But that is definitely a lot of work. You may be better off just starting now, and religiously keeping your transactions in the computer.

The first step is just to use Quicken as a recorder, not to have it print your checks. So let me show you how you would enter some example transactions.

1. It's the end of the day or week and you have receipts in front of you. (Keep receipts whenever possible, unless you're carrying your computer everywhere with you.) Here's a receipt for $15.47 for groceries. Double-click on the **Cash** account line. When the register for it appears, type the date, then press the **Tab** key twice.

2. You'll see the highlighting move to the Ref column and then to the Payee column. (If it isn't in the date column to start with, just click the mouse on that column to get started.) Type the name of the market, such as **Safeway**, and then press **Tab** again.

3. Type the amount of money: **15.47** (don't bother with a dollar sign—it appears automatically).

4. **Tab** again and you'll see the list of expense categories open up.

    You can choose from the categories on this list—which includes Groceries, by the way—or you can type a new category name. (When you create a new category you see another window for specifying whether it should be sent to your tax forms come April 15th. The categories built-in are already prepared for that.) You don't have to click on the category name. Just start typing it and Quicken will guess ahead at your spelling. I just typed **Gro** and the full Groceries appeared. That's what I want, so I press **Tab** again.

5. That moves me to the Memo area where I can add detail, such as **ice cream**. I can look up transactions later by amount, payee, or these notes.

6. Now press **Enter** or click on the **Record** button. You'll hear a double-beep meaning *got it* and see your balance automatically recalculate.

7. You can then enter the next cash receipt, including any deposits. For those, just remember to **Tab** to the Receive column before entering the amount (see Figure 3.21).

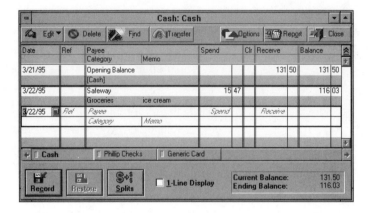

Figure 3.21 Example of entering a cash transaction.

You don't have to save your transactions to disk. Quicken does that automatically for you.

Entering a Check Transaction

Here's an example of entering a check transaction. Let's pretend you're going to pay a cable-TV bill.

1. Write the check out by hand as you normally do.

2. Then double-click on the **Checking** account line in the Accounts window. (There are also shortcuts all over Quicken, such as clicking on the **Checking** account button near the bottom of the Cash register window.) Type the date.

3. Press **Tab**. You'll see a list of payment methods appear, such as check number or ATM operation. Type the check number.

4. Press **Tab** again. Type the payee (who you're writing the check to).

5. **Tab** and type the amount.

6. **Tab** again and you're in the categories slot. A list of categories will drop down from there, and you can click on any of them, scroll through them using your mouse, or use an arrow key to move through the possibilities.

Also, as you type the first letter of the category you want to use, the list will jump to show what it has starting with that letter. Choose one of these—such as **Utilities**—or type your own new category, such as **Cable TV**.

7. **Tab** to the Notes section and enter any details that will help you remember the transaction.

8. Press **Enter** to record the payment. The balance will change, and that's all there is to it.

As you leave Quicken, you'll sometimes be asked if you want to back up what you've done. It's a good idea to do so—which means letting Quicken make a copy of all your records to a floppy disk, which you can then hide away in a safe deposit box or other safe place. Don't keep it with your computer or other backup copies. When they're all together, any single disaster can get them all. Keep them separate. But keep them private too. Remember, all your financial secrets are in here.

Summary

The first step to computing your finances is to get one of these recording programs.

The second step, and just as important, is to actually use it.

You'll need to develop a habit of entering all your expenses and income weekly (a good pace), monthly (could mean trouble—you might forget details), or daily (a bit overdone, unless you have lots to record). Keep your receipts and set up a regular time for the chore, then stick to it. Few things are more painful than trying to do it every three or six months, with a pile of receipts and probably a bigger pile of related paper for all those cash expenses you now don't remember.

Start paying your bills through the program. At least print them, then consider paying them electronically through CheckFree or whatever bill paying feature comes with the program. Use the automatic reconciling and balancing to get your accounts right with the bank. Enter your credit card accounts, and perhaps even get one of the linked credit cards, to keep those in balance. That's the next chapter of this book.

Then create a budget. Use the expense categories to see where your money really goes. That's Chapter 5 of this book.

Exercise the advanced features of the program. Try exporting your records to a tax-preparation program, and start planning your budget for next year and on into retirement. Chapters 6 and 7 detail that process.

The programs keep leapfrogging and copying one another, but the best for those investing in stocks, bonds, and so on is still Managing Your Money. It is also the most visual—in the latest Windows version—and entertaining, with Tobias' advice. The best for those wanting a simple setup for printing checks and keeping track of regular bills is Quicken. It is also by far the best-selling software, and using it puts you in the best position to get advice, find books, and exchange files with others. For example, its link to the on-line bill paying service CheckFree makes for the simplest paperless accounting. Its link to StreetSmart, Schwab's investment program, could make the best investment team of programs.

Microsoft/Novell Money has the best on-line payment system so far, but it isn't complete because it is only available for a few banks in the Midwest. CA-Simply Money is not only competent in most areas but is quite inexpensive, available just for shipping and handling (at least until the company withdraws that offer).

If you have a home business and want to stretch beyond personal finance into accounting, go with Quicken and its sibling QuickBooks. Money Counts is uniquely well-suited for handling accounting for small, nonprofit organizations such as churches, and comes in a lite version called Money Mate for the cost of only shipping and handling.

CHAPTER 4

Pay

Personal finance programs offer up to three ways to pay your bills:

- 💰 write a check by hand and then record it
- 💰 print a check from the program, with automatic recording
- 💰 pay electronically, with automatic recording

All offer check writing and check printing; many offer electronic bill paying, built into some and available as an option in others. I'll show how your program can also help with bill payment timing, scheduling and notification. Only the best programs so far offer a full calendar and payment alarm feature.

After paying, you need to balance your accounts, to reconcile your records with the records held by banks, mortgage companies, and so on. Most programs help you do this with automatic calculations. A few add on-line features, such as account inspection or even linked credit cards, to make balancing more sure and easy.

In the previous chapter you saw how to record transactions, such as deposits, cash expenditures and hand-written checks. In this chapter I'll repeat and expand on the hand-written check process, then show how printing, electronic payments, and linked credit cards can automate and simplify your bill paying chores.

This next section continues where the example tutorial at the end of Chapter 2 left off. Think of Chapters 3, 4, and 5 as one big subject broken into three easy pieces. For the examples of Chapter 3 I started a few new accounts from scratch. For the examples here and in Chapter 4 I'll use an example family's accounts, courtesy of Intuit.

Manual—Write Checks, then Record

When you write a check by hand the old-fashioned way, you should record it directly in your personal finance program or on some paper register which you can later transfer to your program.

Using our Quicken demo as the example program, you start your personal finance software (install and then double-click on it), open the Accounts list (click on the button in Quicken), and then double-click on the Checking account within that list.

Then you type the date, **Tab** to move to the next column, type the check number, **Tab** and type the payee (who the check is to), then **Tab** and type the amount. As you're typing the payee you'll see a list of past payees appear. At the same time, Quicken will try to guess which one you're typing—most of us write most of our checks to the same small group of payees, and often for the same amount each month. If Quicken has it right, showing the payee you intend on the line, just stop typing and **Tab** on to the next blank. If Quicken is wrong, keep typing. The highlighted guesswork will disappear (see Figure 4.1).

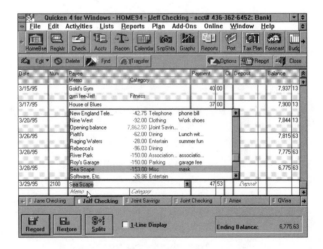

Figure 4.1 When you record a check, most programs remember your previous checks and try to guess which you're paying again. This saves you typing time and trouble.

Another **Tab** brings you to the Category column, where you can type what sort of expense it is. Try choosing from the categories already provided: you can choose from the Lists menu to always have the categories available from their own window. Then **Tab** to any notes blank where you can add details, and finally **Tab** to the Record button and click on it (or press **Enter**) to confirm and save the transaction (Figure 4.2).

Figure 4.2 When you write a check by hand, be sure to enter it in your account register, with an appropriate category.

If you're not happy with the transaction you've entered, you can click on the **Restore** button to undo it. If you want to see more of your transactions at a time, you can click on the **1-Line Display** box at the bottom of the register (see Figure 4.3). Don't like that? Click on it again.

Sometimes you'll need to click on the **Split** button. That's for expenses that don't belong in just one category. For example, when you pay for an airplane ticket for a trip that's half-business and half-pleasure, you should use a Split payment. A window will open where you can give any number of categories, assigning a certain amount of the total to each (see Figure 4.4).

Religiously enter all your check transactions and you won't even need that paper register. Plus, with the information in your computer, you can later reconcile, balance, budget, and even forecast taxes. But now let's see how to make bill payment even easier by eliminating that step of writing checks by hand.

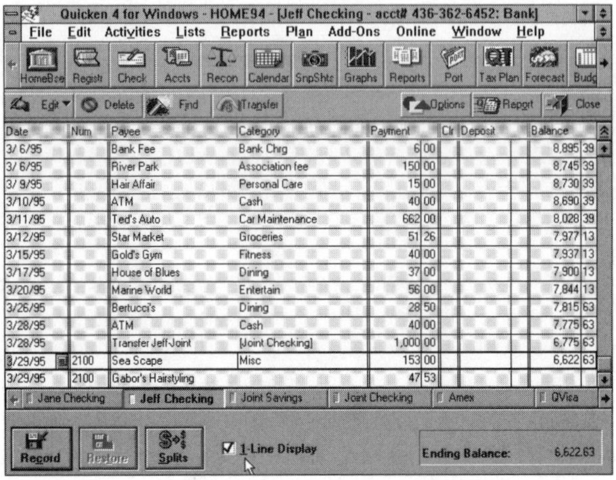

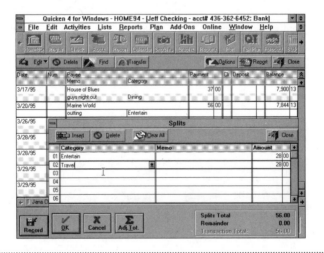

Figure 4.3 Most programs let you customize the on-screen display, such as this 1-Line Display choice in Quicken, to see more transactions at once.

Figure 4.4 The Split button is for dividing a payment into multiple categories.

The **Find** button lets you search for any transaction. The **Options** button lets you change the way the register looks. And the **Transfer** button lets you directly move money from this account to one of your others. You can also do this by writing a check to the other account and then recording it, using the other account as the category (see Figure 4.5).

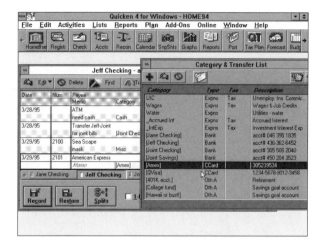

Figure 4.5 When you write a check to pay a credit card account, you use the card as your category.

Print Checks—with Automatic Recording

If you have a printer and blank checks for that printer, you can tell your program to print the checks and record them at the same time. All that's left for you is signing.

This doesn't prevent you from writing checks by hand. You still may need to do that when you're out and away from your computer and printer. Then you just remember to record the transaction as described above. But having your program print your checks will simplify writing those same sets of checks you probably dole out every month: rent or mortgage, car payment, and so on.

The first step is to get a printer connected to your computer. Look back at Chapter 1 for advice on this.

The next step is to get some blank computer-printable checks. You can't just slide your regular checks into the printer. Your personal finance program should have come with some order forms for such checks. Dig it out and order some. If you can't find the order form, look in the program itself. Personal finance software companies—such as Intuit and Computer Associates—are eager to sell you checks, because they make regular and profitable money on them. If none of that works, then call the tech support people and ask them where you can get checks (see Figure 4.6 and 4.7).

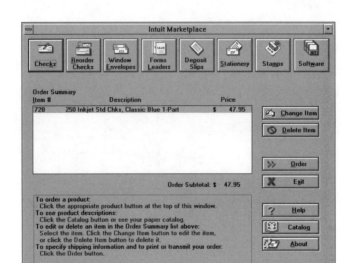

Figure 4.6 To get blank printable checks, look with
or in the program for order forms or commands.

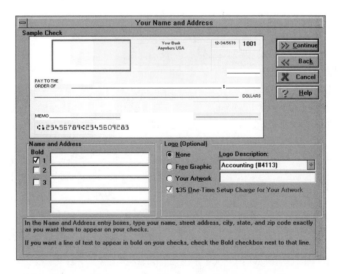

Figure 4.7 In pursuit of your dollars, personal finance companies like
to sell you lots of forms, envelopes, labels, and more, along with your blank checks.

You put the checks in your printer, then go to your accounts program (in our demonstration case, Quicken), and tell it what you're doing. Most programs have some kind of Printer Setup or Printer Configuration command. Here you tell what size checks you're using, any special images or words you want added to them, and so on (see Figure 4.8).

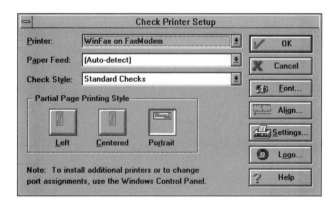

Figure 4.8 Tell your printer what kind of checks you're using.
Quicken does this through the File menu's Printer Setup command.

Now that your checks are hovering in the printer eager to get printed and your program knows how to handle them, you just need to tell the program which checks to print. Each program has a different command for this, which specifies checks by number, date, or other characteristic (see Figure 4.9).

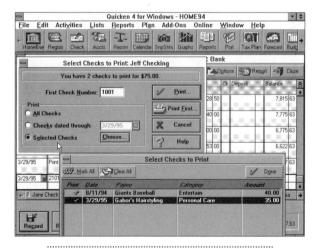

Figure 4.9 Give the command to print checks.

Your checks will print and be ready for your signature. Some programs will also print envelopes for you to stuff them in. Or you can buy window envelopes which won't need any addressing (the check's own addresses appear through a clear or open area).

What could be easier?

Actually, you could just skip buying the check blanks, printing them, putting them in envelopes, and rooting around for stamps, then taking the trip to the mailbox or post office. Pay electronically and you've cut off even more steps.

Pay On-Line with Automatic Recording

If you have a modem connected to your computer—see Chapter 1 for details on that—most checkbook programs let you pay bills through that modem. That is, using the modem, your computer dials out through the phone lines, connects to another computer at a bank or payment center, and transmits your payment details and official OK. The bank computer then either electronically wires the money to the right accounts—(which is called Electronic Funds Transfer) or prints checks and sends them.

You then receive a monthly statement from the bank or payment center, charging you for all the bills you've paid plus some service charge. This can be automatically taken from your checking account—more use of EFT—or you can pay it once a month by check or credit card.

Some programs come with electronic payment features built-in. Some other programs offer them as an add-on service. And some of those services can be put to work even without a checkbook program.

The most famous of these electronic payment services is CheckFree, which claims to process 30 million payments a year for 2 million consumers and thousands of businesses. Available for DOS, Windows, and Macintosh, it works with any checking account or checking program, though it has been integrated into some more than others. It lets you organize your finances, track your expenses, and pay anyone. (Watch out for services which only let you pay particular companies—they're better than nothing, but not as flexible as you can and should get.) If you're not happy with CheckFree, the company even offers a 90-day, money-back guarantee (see Figure 4.10).

Figure 4.10 CheckFree's on-line bill payee list shows who you've set up for payments.

CheckFree uses the Automated Clearing House (ACH) network or MasterCard's RPS to electronically transfer payments. For those companies or individuals who can't accept EFT, a laser-printed check is sent.

You have a personal security code, much like your bank ATM PIN number, which you must use when authorizing payments. All records of payments are kept in your own computer.

Timing can be a concern with electronic payments, so you need to know that checks are mailed two to three days before you schedule a payment, but your checking account is not charged until the date you asked to pay.

The service is available 24 hours a day and comes with automatic updating of your check register and reports on the categories and even budgets you set up.

Novell Money doesn't depend on CheckFree, instead having its own on-line banking abilities built-in. These include a link to the National Bill Pay service for electronic bill payments (see Figure 4.11).

Pay On-Line isn't as widely available as CheckFree, but does have more power for those who can reach it. A big plus is that it only needs a single day to get a check out, rather than the minimum of five demanded by CheckFree. Also, it lets you pay bills from two different accounts without paying twice the fee.

If you use Quicken, as with the disk demo in this book, you choose the **CheckFree** options from the Activities menu (see Figure 4.12).

Figure 4.11 Novell Money's on-line banking options.

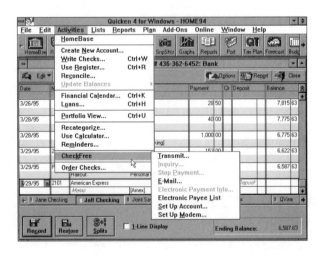

Figure 4.12 Quicken's CheckFree menu.

As you can see, there are commands to set up your account, make a list of payees, transmit or stop payments, and E-mail messages to the CheckFree support people.

That's the three ways to pay with your personal finance program: manual, printed, or electronic checks.

Timing—Calendars, Schedules, and Alerts

It's not enough just to pay bills; you have to pay them on time. The latest twist in some checkbook programs, even newer than electronic payment, is a calendar. This keeps track of your regular payments and lets you enter specific dates to pay—or at least be reminded to pay—bills.

Quicken, as in the demo for this chapter, has a calendar with reminder alerts.

The first element is the Billminder. This appears in Windows: you don't even have to start Quicken. It alerts you that there are Quicken actions to perform — such as payments due (see Figure 4.13).

Figure 4.13 Alerts, such as Quicken's Billminder, can keep you from missing payment dates.

When you do start Quicken, you'll see Reminders (see Figure 4.14). These detail what's due.

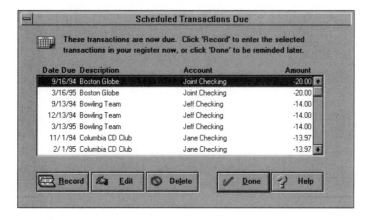

Figure 4.14 Quicken Reminders on startup detail what the Billminder summarized.

If you want, you can also view Calendar notes in Quicken. These don't have to be financial, because Quicken's Calendar lets you schedule personal and business activities unrelated to money (see Figure 4.15).

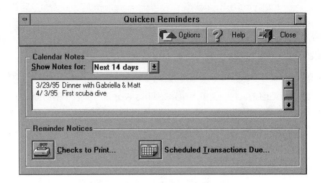

Figure 4.15 Calendar notes aren't always financial.

The Calendar lets you drag-and-drop events. That is, you can find them on screen, click the computer mouse pointer on them, hold the mouse button down while moving the mouse, and then release the mouse button when the pointer and event reach their destination. Visit the Calendar in our demo by clicking on the button. Then choose to view both Register events (when you wrote certain checks) and Scheduled events (things you've dragged from the list on right to the Calendar). The little colored squares in the corners of some days are written notes. Read them by simply clicking on them (see Figure 4.16).

By the way, you might keep an eye out for counterfeiting. Ironically, computers have made check counterfeiting easier than ever—even easier than cash counterfeiting. With a computer, a laser printer and a scanner you can capture the image of a check, clean it up, replace the check number, date, and payee, and print a new one. The American Bankers Association Check Fraud Task Force says that from 1991 to 1993 bad checks increased by 43%, even though the average bad check amount dropped from $1058 to $643. Checks are easier because there's no standard design. And laser printed checks are common. Even magnetic ink isn't a problem—you can buy cartridges with it for most laser printers.

This counterfeiting may diminish if the idea of special check stock comes true. Until it does, you can fight counterfeiting of your own checks by destroying canceled checks and keeping your ATM receipts. Those who worry about the security of electronic payments may take a second look as real checks become risky.

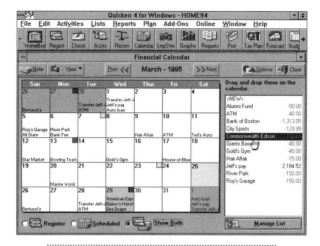

Figure 4.16 Calendar for scheduling payments.

The next step—now that you're keeping track of your transactions, and paying your bills with your program—is to balance and reconcile your accounts. You need to make sure that your results are the same as the bank's, and the credit-card company's, and the mortgage company's, and so on.

Reconciling/Balancing Your Accounts

You've written your checks. You've recorded and categorized the expenses. Now it's Balance time. Time to make sure you have the right sums.

Typically you do this when a monthly tally comes in from charge-card company or bank. In the Quicken demo, you would open the account then click on the **Reconcile** button. You'll see a window open for entering the ending balance, interest, and service charge on the account (see Figure 4.17).

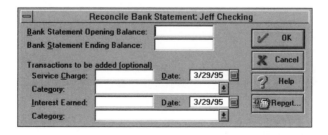

Figure 4.17 Quicken's reconciliation starts by asking you for balances, charges, and interest.

Then you see a window where you can mark those transactions appearing on the official accounts. You can change any that appear in your list by double-clicking on them. And you can add any that you missed (and believe the bank that they happened). As you mark them off, you'll see the reconciliation difference move toward 0 (naturally you hope it reaches 0, meaning no difference exists between your records and the official records) (see Figure 4.18).

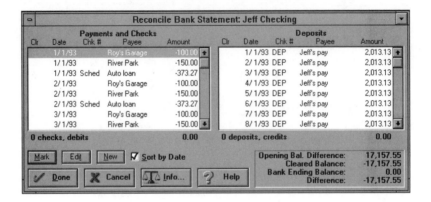

Figure 4.18 In reconciliation, you read from the official record to compare it to your own records.

When you're done marking items, if there's still a difference, you'll be asked if you want to enter an amount to adjust the difference to 0. And if you're working with a credit-card account, you'll be asked if you want to write or print a check for the outstanding amount.

That's certainly easier than doing all the arithmetic without computer help. And reconciliation alone might be enough reason to computerize your checkbook.

But let's keep pushing to make it easier. And what would that be? Not having to compare the tables of information at all. Not having to enter the transactions at all. The way to do that is to get your information on-line.

On-Line Banking

Banks send most of their funds from one account to another electronically. Transfers between banks are handled that way, too. And you're at home planning to computerize your finances.

It seems like all of these computers should talk to one another. And you've seen how they're starting to, with electronic bill-payment services. This scheme is comfortable because it works with standard accounts, simplifying the amount of setup necessary. There are several programs and services aimed in this direction, including CheckFree and BillPay USA (associated with the Prodigy on-line service).

Now a few banks let you dial into their computer systems to check your account balances and even transfer funds. Some have their own special software – ask your bank. Others are linking to personal finance programs. As mentioned above, Novell's Money Pay On-Line is a leading personal finance program in this area, in cooperation with a few regional (midwest U.S.) banks including First National of Chicago, Michigan National Bank, and U.S. Bank. It lets Money owners with a modem check their balances and more funds. More banks and more programs will surely follow (see Figure 4.19).

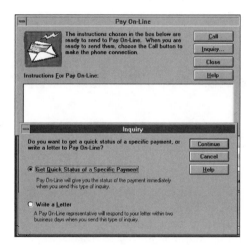

Figure 4.19 In Money, you can check the status of your payment on-line.

In a very few cases, this on-line access extends to credit card accounts. Credit cards are such a large part of our financial lives these days, but haven't been integrated much into the personal finance programs. Most of the programs will let you record credit card expenses and payments, but there hasn't been a good way to go on line with credit card information.

This has changed since Quicken's IntelliCharge feature appeared in late 1993. This is a Visa card you can apply for after getting Quicken. Any charges you make are recorded and can be downloaded later or received on disk for automatic categorizing, reconciling, and balancing in your Quicken accounts. The card has no annual fee and a low variable interest rate with a credit line up to $10,000, and typical gold-card benefits such as purchase security, extended warranty, and collision damage waiver protection for rental cars. It takes only about ten seconds to bring in new transactions. The card comes from Primerica Bank. Other personal finance programs are following suit, though some—such as Novell Money—are looking to link your personal financial accounts to your current credit cards, rather than forcing you to get a new card (see Figure 4.20).

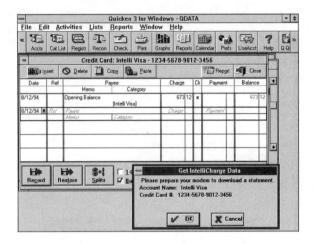

Figure 4.20 IntelliCharge acts as a credit-card account in Quicken, though one with on-line records.

More recently, in early 1995, Intuit made a deal with Travelers Bank to offer a Visa Gold Card with the IntelliCharge feature. Again you can get a record of all charges on disk or on-line. In fact, this could become a fourth way to pay bills, without writing, printing, or even sending checks on-line.

The Internet and Money

The Internet, the worldwide interconnection of computers mentioned in Chapter 1, is seen as a new world of business by some. That will require sending and receiving money on-line. But making that practical means making it secure, so the money only goes to the right place, and only when authorized by the appropriate person. It's mainly talk so far.

There are some examples appearing, though, of Internet buying and selling. For example, the Capital One Bank has recently started testing its own Internet Web site for Visa cards.

Summary

After you've created accounts and categories, and then entered any past transactions into them, you can start paying today's bills and recording them in your personal finance software. You can write checks and record them, print them and have the program record them automatically, or even pay on-line with automatic recording. Then you reconcile your accounts and the official accounts. This too is easier when you get an on-line banking feature or even an on-line link to your credit card accounts. Eventually this on-line buying, selling, and tracking may become the standard.

Now that you know what you've spent and what you're spending, it's time to cut that spending where it isn't getting you what you want. In other words, it's time to budget.

CHAPTER 5

Budget

For many people, the best way to make more money is to spend less of what they already get. For most people, it helps to budget, whether spending $20 on movie tickets or $2,000,000 on land purchases.

Now that you've got your transactions in the computer, why not have the computer sort 'em and organize 'em and tell you something about the results? Why not have the computer help you budget?

Ironically, no program yet does a *complete* job of helping you budget. They'll categorize and project and compare, but they won't advise, suggest, or trim for you. Still, let's look at what they *can* do and leave the thinking and deciding up to you.

Budgeting means seeing what you spend in each category each month (or week, or year) and then planning what you want to plan in those categories.

Personal finance programs are mastering that first step; someday surely they'll help with the second.

CA-Simply Money, for example, has a Budget Editor window where you can set amounts for each category for each month (see Figure 5.1). You can start your work here by using the **Autobudget** command to create a budget from past spending patterns. Then you can choose from a variety of reports and graphs on the budget, and see a graphic chart on how well you're sticking to plan. Figures 5.2 and 5.3 show sample screens from this program.

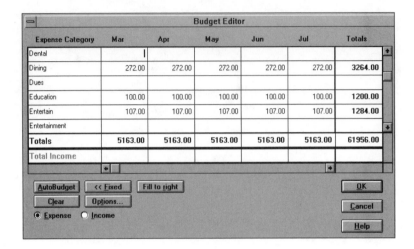

Figure 5.1 Simply Money's Budget editor window.

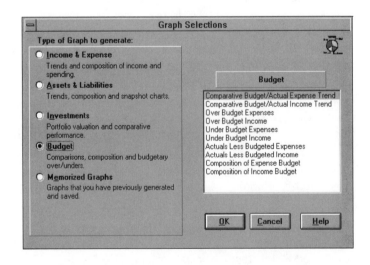

Figure 5.2 Simply Money offers many budget reports and graphs.

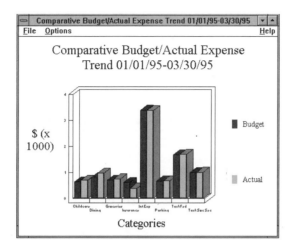

Figure 5.3 Example graph of budget variance in Simply Money.

Managing Your Money has a similar approach. Though it doesn't automatically budget as easily, it does let you compare this year's expenses to last year's. Again it offers reports and charts on your performance (see Figures 5.4 and 5.5).

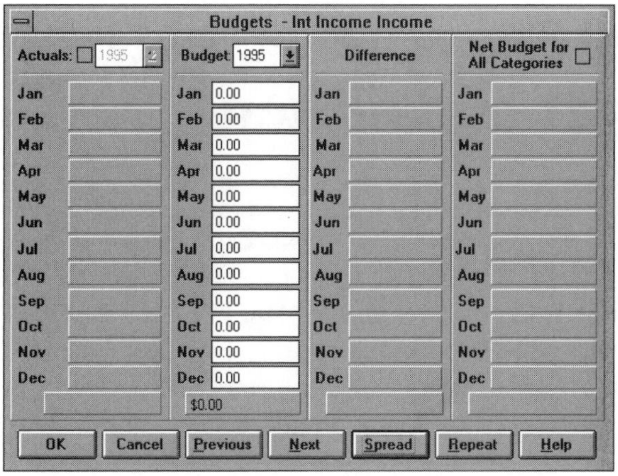

Figure 5.4 Managing Your Money lets you compare expenses from month to month or even year to year.

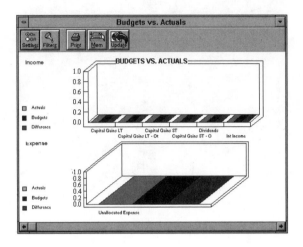

Figure 5.5 Managing Your Money can also create planned vs. actual budget charts.

Let's turn again to that demo version of Quicken on the CD-ROM with this book and see how its budget feature works.

Tutorial Example—Create a Budget in Quicken

In previous chapters you saw how to record what you get and give in Quicken. Then you stopped writing checks by hand and had Quicken print them or send them out through your modem. This tutorial shows how the records in Quicken let you budget. You can see what you *have* spent; you can plan what you *should* spend.

Using the sample data from the last chapter, here's an example of Quicken budgeting. Have that Quicken file open and go to the Plan menu. Choose **Budgeting**. (Or you can click on the **Budget** button just below and to the right of that.)

You'll see the Autobudget feature quickly lay out how much you've been spending each month, by categories and *supercategories*—combinations of related items. Figure 5.6 shows a calculated budget. When there's a + sign beside a super-category, you may click on that symbol to expand the details. Or click on a − symbol to hide details.

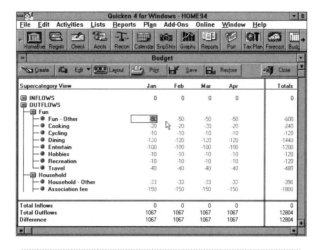

Figure 5.6 Quicken automatically prepares a budget from your history—showing what you spend monthly by categories.

Anyway, you can now save this budget to disk or print it, if you just want to keep spending at the same rate. Just click on either of those buttons.

But any *real* budgeting means adjusting planned spending from historic patterns. There's a lot of spending in here for fun. A savings plan would probably cut back in that category.

First let's learn what really happened month-to-month. Didn't it seem suspicious that every month had the same spending? Those are *averages* across the year. This option is one of the neat calculations that makes creating a budget much easier on computer than by hand.

Let's glance at the *actual* amounts by clicking on the **Create** button. Then from the window that appears, click beside **Use Monthly Detail**. You could also click the **Categories** button to exclude certain types of expenses from this budget. Figure 5.7 shows the options available when customizing your budget. (They're all included for now. Let's leave it that way, especially for this limited sample data.) You can see additional months by clicking on the vertical or horizontal scroll bars at the bottom of the screen or the far right of the screen.

The **Layout** button lets you see quarterly or annual amounts, instead of monthly. Oddly, the **Edit** button lets you switch to two-weekly budgeting. It can also copy the entire budget, in case you want to put it into a spreadsheet for more complex operations. And it lets you clear or change anything in the rows and columns. For example, let's change that $234 in the Dining category to $50. One night out a month should be OK if we're truly tightening our belts. Then use the

Edit button's **Fill Row Right** command, and **OK** to the end of the year, to see that $50 fill all the way across (see Figure 5.8). You can go on to change any of the amounts in this budget. If you don't like the results, click on **Restore**. If you do like them, click on **Save** and the budget will be on disk.

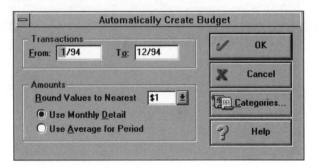

Figure 5.7 To customize the automatic budget, the Create command offers these options.

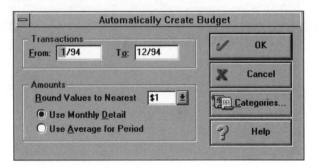

Figure 5.8 You can start with the historic budget amounts in Quicken, then change them to your desired amounts.

You can then view a Budget Variance chart to show in which months and which categories you spend more or less than planned. Click on the **Graph** button, select any options (such as **Supercategories**), and the graph appears. By clicking on the **Next 5** button, bottom right, you can see more categories. The overspent areas appear in red; the spending that matches or slips under budgeted amounts are green (see Figure 5.9).

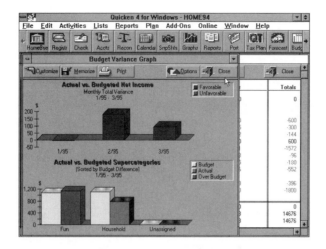

Figure 5.9 A Budget Variance graph shows danger areas in red (assuming you have a color monitor)—where you're missing your planned budget.

This graph can be printed or saved or customized, leaving out certain categories as you wish. You can print and save on disk both the numbers and the graphs, to keep your budget goals in mind, and to periodically compare to your recorded real spending.

Forecast—Cash Flow, Savings, and Taxes

You've budgeted and watched how your past and current spending compares to plans. Most personal finance programs let you look at future budgeting too, in the form of cash-flow forecasts (see Figure 5.10). These show you how your income and outgo will play against each other, following the scheduled payments and regular income.

In our Quicken demo, you can see this under the Plan menu as the Forecasting command. This creates a chart where you can watch for any dangerous dips to 0 or below. You can create different *scenarios* for dealing with such troubles, and have them appear on the chart at the same time for direct comparison.

A specific item in forecasting is seeing how your savings are stacking up. Eventually this will come directly from your financial planning software, but for now you're lucky to find it as an added feature inside a checkbook and accounts program. Quicken, for example, lets you create accounts you regularly save to for particular needs: vacation, education, etc. As pictured in Figure 5.11, Quicken's Plan menu lets you see how far your savings have reached toward a goal.

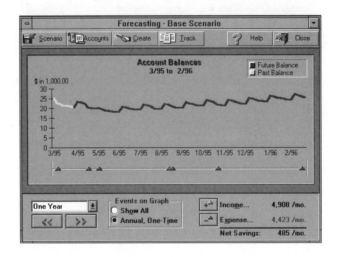

Figure 5.10 The Forecasting feature in many checkbook programs is a form of future budgeting—so you can watch for cash-flow troubles.

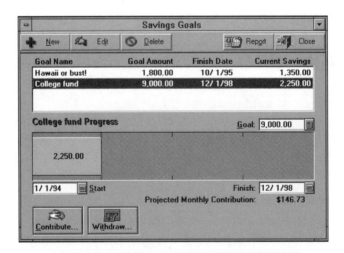

Figure 5.11 As part of forecasting, Quicken lets you see how your savings have progressed toward goals.

To summarize all the various forecasts, Quicken has a Snapshot feature that combines them all—minus the detail—on screen at once (see Figure 5.12). If you want to see the detail, you may click on any and it will zoom into closer focus.

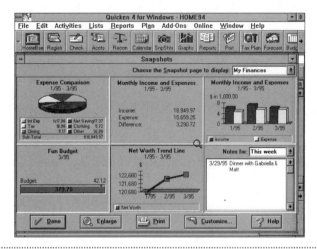

Figure 5.12 Quicken's Snapshot command quickly creates summary graphs of your budget, forecast, and other financial status facts.

You'll notice Tax forecasting in some checkbook account programs. This forecasts what your income tax will be based on the historic and current spending and income patterns. As seen in Figure 5.13, Quicken, for example, puts this in the Plan menu.

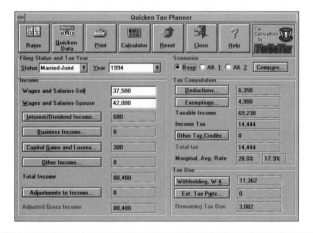

Figure 5.13 Tax forecasting is part of your cash-flow future, and some programs include a quick look at what taxes your current spending and income will generate.

Summary: Budgeting is More Important than Investments

We all track our expenses sooner or later, even if it's just by looking into an empty wallet. Paying bills by computer printer or modem is sexy and fascinating. But budgeting really matters more than either of those steps. For most people, it is the *key* to improving personal finances. (And you could budget even with guesstimates at expenditures, without all the computerized precision.) Use the budgeting and forecasting features in your software, and push the companies to add more.

But don't think your budget or forecasts are complete until they include taxes. Taxes will certainly be an important factor in your financial scheduling and bill payments. Figuring how to pay the least legal tax and preparing the forms for paying are much easier with a computer handling both the calculations and the comparisons. That's the next chapter.

CHAPTER 6

Tax

Got a computer? Think about preparing your tax returns on it, especially if you have already entered your financial data into one of the programs discussed in the earlier chapters. You could save time and money with tax preparation software. Why? Because tax preparation software does the following:

- 💰   saves you from having to find paper forms
- 💰   makes sure your arithmetic is correct (calculating for you)
- 💰   saves you from entering information again and again
- 💰   helps you find deductions you might overlook
- 💰   keeps you up-to-date on the latest tax changes
- 💰   prevents you from leaving some important line blank
- 💰   can file electronically for faster returns
- 💰   can help you forecast future tax payments
- 💰   if you use personal finance software, can automatically fill in most of the forms, saving time and sweat

Tax software used to do little more than make your forms prettier—just accepting the values you typed, then adding and subtracting them and printing the result. But tax software changes every year to keep up with the changes in the laws and to compete with all those other tax preparation programs. They're becoming more comprehensive and easier at the same time. Today's tax software includes advice and more forms than you'll find even at the local library of tax preparation firm. And it tackles complex tax ogres, such as depreciation, that give even an experienced tax professional the willies.

However, if your taxes are at all complicated—beyond the 1040EZ level, that is—you should take your computer-prepared form to a tax accountant or attorney. You won't pay much for that inspection because the work will already be done. If the expert doesn't find any problems and your circumstances don't change much from year to year, you could probably reduce such checkups to every two or three years (or after any major tax reform).

Those using tax software already have more-complex-than-average returns. Where 25% of Americans file form 1040A, and 17% the simple 1040EZ, only 8% of TurboTax users (the most popular program) file either of those. And where a third of TurboTax owners use Schedule E for rents and royalties, only 4% of non-tax-software users do.

Retain some skepticism. Tax preparation by computer is not as easy as some people think. You have to buy the software (which is tax deductible, by the way), buy the state version, learn the program, enter the data, pay a professional to give the results a once-over, pay a service bureau (if you want to file electronically), and still send in some paper forms such as W2s. The expense and hassle can leave little margin, or even run you more, than just taking your accounts to a tax preparer.

In early 1995, as part of a bad string of problems, Intuit admitted that both TurboTax and MacInTax made math mistakes in some cases. Blocks' TaxCut admitted a similar problem. This is rare, however, even in those cases only affecting 1-in-100 at most. The companies immediately promised new, fixed copies of the programs free to anyone who asked. And in early 1995 Intuit admitted that some thousands of electronic returns filed through it had been vulnerable to either disappearance or even copying by unauthorized computer intruders (hackers).

Whichever way you go, don't use tax software on any taxes beyond the most simple without getting a good tax suggestions book, such as the popular one by J.K.Lasser, called *Your Income Tax*. Also, have a tax accountant or attorney give your computer-prepared tax forms the once-over, just to be safe.

If your taxes fit on the one-page form 1040EZ or if you have an accountant you love (and can pay), you don't need tax software. All other computer owners should consider it: it can dramatically cut the preparation time, complex-form confusion, deduction-missing, and math mistakes. These days most of the top programs have a Q&A interview session to determine your tax situation, ability to import financial records from personal finance programs, tips and advice on best strategies, audit checks to catch mistakes, promises to pay for any math mistakes, and printed or electronically-filed finished returns. Avoid 4Home's Simply Tax, available only for Windows, which has a confusing interview and no other special features. Intuit's TurboTax is the friendliest, for Windows or DOS, and offers especially tight links to the Quicken personal finance program. MacInTax is basically TurboTax for the Mac, with the ease but without the special links to Quicken. Personal Tax Edge is sometimes overlooked, but has the same features as its better-known competitors, at half the price. Tax Mate cuts that even further, offering the features and forms 75% of us need for only $9. But my favorite is TaxCut because it has support above and beyond: not just an 800 number for questions but a connection to the H&R Block tax prep service so you can ask tax questions for free, have a Block accountant accompany you to any audit, or even just give up on the software and get a discount for its price toward the Block service. Dedicated Quicken PC users should get TurboTax. Personal Tax Edge for Windows has the best multimedia with video explanations of each step. PC owners with simple needs and tight budgets should get Tax Mate. All other PC owners, and all Macintosh owners, should use TaxCut. I am. That H&R Block connection can't be beat, even if TurboTax and Personal Tax Edge match TaxCut's features and TurboTax is a shade easier for beginners. Whatever you choose, make sure you're getting a final version, not some left-over "headstart" or "early bird" box. And buy a state form if your state has complex income tax rules, such as in California and New York.

Comparing Tax Programs, Accountants, and Tax Preparers

If you can afford an accountant, that's probably your best choice. They don't just know the specifics of the tax law, but how the IRS is interpreting them. It will run at least several hundred dollars. The precise amount depends on where you live and how complex your taxes are. Ideally this same accountant keeps your books all year, so you don't have to keep tabs on which expense falls into which category. But that ideal, again, costs the most.

The tax preparer, such as from the famous H&R Block firm, can't keep your books all year but can prepare your itemized return for about $100. You'll have more responsibility for keeping receipts organized.

The tax preparation program knows the details of tax law and math cold. It can print final forms beautifully, to look just like traditional forms or in a new "1040PC" form that is shorter and gets through the IRS quicker. It can even send them in electronically for a quicker refund, though this costs an extra fee of about $15. What it *can't* do is listen intelligently to your words, scan your receipts, and size up the best filing strategy for you. You'll only spend $20 to $35 on the program, plus somewhat less than that on a state version (unless you're one of the lucky few in a state without an income tax), plus the cost of the computer, of course. You'll also spend you own time and effort organizing receipts and choosing among strategies—2 hours instead of 8.

Recent Improvements in Tax Software

Not that the tax prep programs aren't trying hard to be smart listeners. Ten years ago they were mere calculators with rows and columns, much like spreadsheet programs. Then they began to show realistic IRS forms right on screen. Now they have colorful, numbered interview questions on screen which prompt you for vital statistics. They import your financial numbers either directly from the files of common checkbook programs such as Quicken, or from files saved in the generic .TXF format. Their IRS and accountant forms and jargon are organized by tabs, which look like notebook dividers on screen. They are hidden behind charts and arrows and just-plain-folks explanations. The latest CD-ROM versions even carry audio and video clips from tax experts on how and what to file. And if you liked last year's improvement of "auditing" your return for possible discrepancies—math mistakes, blank lines, deductions beyond IRS tolerance levels—you'll love this year's suggested solutions and tips.

Support is Crucial

A crucial factor is the telephone support you can get. You'll want an 800 number and someone answering the other end. (All of the companies offer computer bulletin-board and fax-reply tech support, but there are plenty of times you'll just want to talk to someone.) Each tax season I hear from people who swear their company never answers the phone, probably doesn't even have it plugged in. But I haven't heard that more about one company than another. In the TurboTax section I'll mention some of the support fiascos of 1995.

Features You'll Want

In fact, all of the programs look very much alike. And their commands and options are very similar too. Deciding which is easiest has become more a matter of personal taste than of clear differences.

Windows is the best place for tax preparation, with the latest touches for easy use and the only multimedia CD-ROM versions. Macs are still good, because of their graphic nature, but the Mac software and DOS software falls about a year behind the Windows in slick operation.

Here are the key features to look for in a tax preparation program:

⑤ **Support**—should have the most helpful, reachable, informed people behind it

⑤ **Compatibility**—it should run on your computer, naturally

⑤ **State version**—make sure there's one for your state, or that your state doesn't have income tax (unless you're in one of the states with a super-simple form, such as Utah)

⑤ **Forms**—includes the forms you'll need plus a lot more in case you find new needs (Intuit estimates that 85% of filers use Schedule A, 84% B, 43% C, and 55% D)

⑤ **Interviews**—asks questions to get the basic data

⑤ **Understandable**—you can understand the instructions, advice, and approach

⑤ **Importing**—pulls financial data in from your personal finance program

⑤ **Audit check**—flags omissions, inconsistencies, and other problems

⑤ **Comparisons**—tells you where you're claiming more or deducting more than the national averages

⑤ **What-if**—lets you try alternate ways of placing expenses and income and calculating results to find the least tax

💰   **Printing**—lets you print IRS-approved forms on your printer without more software or fonts (96.5% of tax software users file on paper)

💰   **1040PC**—prints this new abbreviated form that makes for quicker and more accurate IRS review (10.7% of tax software users file the 1040PC form)

And here are some lesser features, still useful, but not vital:

💰   **Headstart** (also called Early Bird) version—which comes out late in the previous year so you can start tax planning with time to make changes

💰   **Shoebox**—lets you enter disorganized information—expenses and income—and organizes them for you

💰   **IRS instructions**—the full text is available in case you need to refer to it

💰   **Calculators**—for arithmetic and complex math such as depreciation

💰   **Notepads**—for annotating figures and entries so you can remember later why you made your choices

💰   **Worksheets**—for making lists to back up entries, even when the forms don't demand a list, but when a list could be useful to explain or calculate the entry

💰   **Tips**—it suggests ways to save, especially by looking at your particular situation

💰   **Planning**—lets you get a jump on a future year's taxes, perhaps including charts to illustrate the numbers

💰   **Electronic filing**—lets you file via modem or by sending in a floppy disk without buying any or much extra software or paying a large fee (only 3.5% of tax software users file electronically)

💰   **CD-ROM**—it's not vital but a nice touch, because a CD-ROM version gives space for helpful video clips, more complete instructions, and companion programs for planning

💰   **Tech support**—it has people you can call for help, with a number that's easy to get through with a minimum wait at the most possible hours

💰   **Guarantee**—it guarantees that the company will pay for any arithmetic mistakes the program makes

Speed is not particularly important in tax prep software. Although a critical element in many computer programs, it doesn't affect tax preparation where ease, accuracy, and completeness are far more important.

Here are some details on aspects of tax preparation programs that might not be immediately obvious.

Prices

Tax preparation software companies sell most of their software between January and April, naturally—with April 15th being the personal income tax deadline. That makes it hard to spread their income over the entire year.

Unfortunately, the tax laws are often in flux until sometime in January. That means the tax preparation programs can't be finished until January, or even the beginning of February. At least they can't contain every little quirk and percentage until Congress makes up its mind.

The result is the head-start version of tax preparation software. Many software companies finish as much of their tax preparation programs as possible and market them starting in September or so of the year before, calling this an *early bird* or *head-start* version. Often the price for such versions is less than for the final version, or you get to buy the final version at a discount price either directly from the software company or from a software retailer by using a coupon from the head-start package.

Should you bother? Sure—if you want to get a good idea what your taxes will be, and want the extra time to analyze your strategies for avoiding too big a tax bite. In fact, for some schemes, such as Keogh savings plans, you must complete your paperwork by December 31st, and a head-start version can show you approximately what you'll save.

But you'll still need a final version of the software. You wouldn't want to file a finished tax return from the head-start version, which can certainly provide wrong numbers and conclusions.

Guarantees and Reliability

Some tax preparation software companies will even guarantee they'll pay any IRS penalties from computational penalties. That's not such a big guarantee but it is a nice addition to the value of the program. These programs do sometimes make mistakes.

ComputerLife magazine's Theresa W. Carey in February of 1995 put the same example tax situation—that of a $50K per year family—to 9 tax programs. The results ranged from a $310 refund to a $1484 bill. Readers found this a bit unsettling, as though mistakes were made. Even tax preparers thought it meant trouble in the programs. The editors came back to say that most of the calculation differences came in the Business Use of Home area, not surprisingly a favorite for audits. Carey just accepted the default calculations each program offered there. But some of the programs were aggressive with depreciation assumptions; others less so. Some, such as TurboTax, did a good job of allocating mortgage interest and other expenses between Schedule A and Schedule C. The more taken on C, the bigger the improvement in the final bill because those dollars aren't taxed at the self-employment rate for Schedule SE. Also, some programs did a better job of dealing with Schedule C expenses and with Schedule E Rental Income. Their conclusion? Taxes are an art.

Importing Data

Computing your taxes is much easier if you don't have to type all the data in from your receipts. How can you avoid that? By having already typed it in for a personal finance program. There is no magic way, yet.

If you have entered your financial data into a personal finance or accounting program, you should be able to avoid entering it again. Your tax preparation program should be able to import it. Most tax preparation programs have a command to do this. Don't expect it to be entirely easy or always complete. You will often need to clean up some details such as designating categories for particular entries, either in the tax program or in the personal finance program. But at least it's faster than typing all those numbers in from scratch.

Sometimes you'll import directly, which is possible if you've used a very popular personal finance program such as Quicken or Managing Your Money. Other times you'll import using the Tax Exchange (.TXF file format), which many programs now support. This is a standard format for personal finance computer information storage on disk. It is a way for programs to save and read from a standard file type. Good personal finance programs should have an option to save their data in this format on disk. Good tax preparation programs will be able to import .TXF files.

Don't expect the import to work easily, even if both programs—personal finance and tax preparation—claim to support .TXF. When programs have different expense and income categories, which most do, the import can be subverted and derailed. Add to that the need for all that information from the personal finance program to end up on the appropriate line on the tax form, and that tax forms change every year. You can see the complexity.

Interview

Once upon a time, tax preparation programs simply showed you lines on the screen with text labels, and you typed the figures you had collected from your various receipts. Then came graphics displays that looked just like the paper tax forms. You worked through them on the screen just as though you were filling out the paper forms. The latest innovation makes data entry even easier: the interview. The program starts by asking you questions and putting those into the appropriate lines on the tax form. You're still free to enter data directly, but the interview is more comfortable for most people. Your answers to early questions can even eliminate later questions from the list, if those questions don't apply to you.

Depreciation

Depreciation is one of the most difficult, but often quite important, parts of figuring your taxes. Computers are a real boon here. Depreciation doesn't let you immediately write off the entire value of something you buy or use for business in the first year. Instead, you can only write off that portion of its value you used in that year. This means you must calculate how much value is lost each year from standard determinations of how long the item is worthwhile and what fraction of it is then used up per year. If you have significant equipment to deduct for a personal business, make sure your program makes depreciation understandable— such as having special calculators for figuring the calculations.

By the way, if you file self-employment income, you can write off the portion of your computer and software used for that. But you must depreciate them.

Hardware depreciates in five years, though you may be able to write it all off at once time under Title 26 of US Code, Section 179 so long as the total is less than $17,500 for the year. Using this part of the code, you may be able to write off what's left of the value in a single year, even if you started depreciating it in a prior year.

Software also depreciates if it costs more than $200. Under that you can call it supplies and write it off right away. As an intangible asset it needs depreciation in a straight line over three years, or faster if you can prove it will be outdated in less time. Software bought before 1993 must be depreciated over five years. However, tax software can be written off in a single year. (When you're done with it, try donating it to The National Christina Foundation, which gives computers to the disabled. Call 800-274-7846. Then you can still deduct the undepreciated value of the system.)

Special Trouble Spot—The Home Office

Business expenses and deductions for a home office are an IRS focal point. This can easily trigger an audit, because it is so easily abused. That's too bad, because in this era of downsized corporations and personal computers, there are more home businesses all the time.

Before using home office expenses on your forms, especially if you hold a standard job as well, look into the law. You need to be sure that you:

💰 Use the office regularly

💰 Use it only for business

💰 Use it as the principal place of your business (unless it's a separate structure)

💰 Produce your goods or services or meet customers there

If you want to claim the home office while having links to business elsewhere, you need to prove that:

💰 This home office is essential to your business

💰 There is no other available office

💰 You spend substantial time there (relative to other places)

💰 If the deductions exceed 2% of adjusted gross income, you must file form 2106

You can take the home office deductions even if you have a full time job elsewhere, if you work at home for your employer's convenience and not your own.

If you meet all of these criteria, there are plenty of possible deductions, from the rent or mortgage percentage (depreciated) to the utilities and property taxes, phones, advertising, and furniture, home insurance, general maintenance (house-cleaning), carpet cleaning, painting, electrical work, plumbing, and even a new roof (depreciate over years), related supplies and materials, and outdoor land-scaping if the office is used for client visits, all on Schedule C (Profit or Loss from Business).

The toughest to figure is the mortgage depreciation. First, most people can deduct mortgage interest on their home anyway. Second, if you do use it as a home office expense, and then sell the home later, you need then to recapture the depreciated amount and pay taxes on the capital gain. You may be able to avoid this by not taking the home office for a couple of years before the sale. The rules are sure to change year to year. Few tax prep programs properly split the mortgage monies between personal deductions and business expenses. Part III of the IRS Form 8829 is the place to see. If you're renting your home and have an office, Part II is for you.

IRS Instructions

Most tax preparation programs come with not only their own help information but with some of the actual IRS instructions. There are too many instructions to fit on a typical floppy disk, or even three or four floppies. When that happens, you can often get more of the IRS instructions—the "full text" as it is called—from an on-line service connection of the program company. For example, MECA software has put the full-text on its CompuServe forum, where you can read it or download it (import it to your computer for reading at any time).

Electronic Filing

Starting in 1985, the IRS accepted electronic tax form submissions. That year only 25,000 were filed electronically. By 1993, 12 million filed electronically. By the year 2001, the IRS expects 80 million. Because the results feed directly into the IRS computers, you can get your return sooner. An electronic filing can get a refund in as little as three weeks, while filing a paper return takes four to eight weeks.

Electronic filing is done by modem or disk. Your program must be able to save to the electronic file format. For modem filing, you'll need the modem itself and a program that contains the telecommunication software. You'll also need a filing service—an Electronic Return Originator (ERO)—to send the file to. You don't send your return directly to the IRS. Instead you send it indirectly to the filing service, which forwards your return in a batch with others to the IRS. You send the forms via disk or modem, mailing the filing fee and the completed Form 8453 U.S. Individual Income Tax Declaration for Electronic Filing (which the tax software will produce). You must also send Copy B of your W-2, W-2B, or W-2G as paper. If you want the direct refund to an account, you must include that bank account number. You must also send any of these forms if you use them: 8332, 2120, 8283, Schedule R.

The fee for this is typically $15. (Some tax software firms act as their own filing services.)

You can't file electronically if you have more than the following:

- 30 Forms and Schedules
- 3 Schedules C
- 5 Schedules E
- 15 Rental Properties on Schedule E
- 2 Schedules F
- 1 Schedule SE (two, if married and filing jointly)
- 20 Forms W-2
- 30 Forms W-2G
- 10 Forms 1099-R
- 8 Forms 1116
- 1 form 2106 (two if married filing jointly)
- 4 Forms 4562
- 1 Form 5329 (two if married filing jointly)
- 3 Forms 6198
- 3 Forms 6252
- 2 Forms 8283
- 1 Form 8606 (two if married filing jointly)
- 3 Forms 8814
- 1 Form 8829 per Schedule C

After you send the electronic return, you need to send the paper documents with the necessary signatures. (Electronic signatures aren't possible yet.) You should specify with your electronic return if you want any refund deposited directly to your bank.

An Intuit deal with AT&T will let TurboTax users file electronically using AT&T's EasyLink E-mail system. TurboTax will have the software for doing this, and TurboTax users will get return receipts via E-mail. At first this will only work for state tax returns for businesses, but eventually it will be used for personal income tax. Microsoft's planned network will probably have a similar feature. Filing through on-line services such as America Online, Prodigy, and CompuServe is also becoming a reality. You file, get a confirmation within 24 hours, get a printed confirmation later, and are billed about $20.

States are getting into the act too. California first offered electronic filing in 1995, issuing refunds within 7 days.

Some of the original excitement about electronic filing came from the Refund Anticipation Loan. Some lenders gave these loans to almost anyone in return for assigning the refund to the lender. The IRS would provide an indication within hours if the return would be accepted and wire the money to the lender almost immediately. That wasn't true in 1994, though. The IRS discovered that some returns had liens against them—such as for back taxes or delinquent child support—which didn't end up being refunds.

Another problem has been that the IRS computers seem to lose some electronic returns. With all the imperfections still encountered with electronic filing, the paper forms won't disappear as soon as some expected.

For more information on electronic filing, the IRS number is 800-829-1040.

By the way, if you're worried that the 1040PC raises your audit probability, the IRS says not. The forms don't matter as much as the complexity of the results.

1040PC

1040PC is a new tax forms paper-printing format, introduced by the IRS. It is meant to let the IRS take advantage of computer preparation to process returns more accurately. The 1040PC eliminates all liens that have no entry—all the zeros on your return. That makes for a return that is shorter, easier to read, and more quickly processed by the IRS. It's good for you to get this feature in your program, though a complex return may not be able to use it. Check the law: the IRS may offer the option of filing the 1040PC early but waiting until April 15th to actually pay. All of this encouragement comes because the IRS likes the 1040PC. It is easier for the service to process, cutting their costs.

Tax Preparation Programs

Here are descriptions of most of the tax preparation programs available for PCs and Macs. Note that big changes can take place each year, though the top programs are relatively stable from year to year, even as the companies that make them are swallowing one another. For example, in 1993 Intuit bought ChipSoft, H&R Block bought MECA and Legal Knowledge Systems, and CA bought the rights to EasyTax from SoftKey.

After that frenzy all of the companies with leading personal finance programs also have tax preparation programs. Intuit has Quicken, TurboTax, and MacInTax. MECA, now Block Financial Software, has Managing Your Money and TaxCut. CA has CA-Simply Money and CA-Simply Tax. Parsons has Money Counts and Personal Tax Edge. Microsoft had only personal finance, not tax, with its Money program. But in 1994 Microsoft tried to buy—the Justice Department hasn't okayed the deal yet—Intuit, and so would have TurboTax and MacInTax. Microsoft sold its Money program to Novell, and will keep Quicken as its personal finance program, pending approval.

TurboTax

TurboTax, the best seller for several years, also has some impressive connections. It comes from Intuit, the same company that makes the top-selling Quicken checkbook and personal finance program. (You'll probably see some deals selling the two together at a discount.) And this latest TurboTax focuses on that connection by not just importing Quicken data but, like Block's link between Managing Your Money and TaxCut, by helping you direct any questionable details to the right places. It will even change the settings inside Quicken if you need. (Import features often run into trouble sorting your expenses completely.) Another connection is the Tax Planner program you can buy to estimate your taxes and schemes to minimize them over the next five years. Competing programs have some what-if strategizing built in, but not this much planning power. In '96 and beyond you may see connections between TurboTax and new on-line banking services, because Microsoft, the world's largest software company, is waiting for final government approval to buy Intuit. And Microsoft is openly interested in on-line transactions that would pay bills and taxes, balance accounts, and shop, all through computers and phone lines.

Inside TurboTax you'll start with an EasyStep interview that has clearer and simpler steps than any competing program's interview. It does a better job of adjusting future questions based on your past answers. There are tax tips and advice, a deduction finder, what-if strategizing, and an audit of your results to make sure nothing is missing or questionable. The File Cabinet helps organize your receipt information, tax graphs show where your money is going (if you really want to know), and the result can be printed or filed electronically. The CD-ROM version for Windows adds 60 IRS tax publications and audio and video clips from author Marshall Loeb and ex-IRS auditor Mary Sprouse explaining what to do and what to avoid. These are livelier and less technical than the clips in multimedia TaxCut. The Macintosh version is called MacInTax (it used to be a different program) and looks entirely like the Windows version, though without the special Quicken link improvements. The CD-ROM version of Quicken comes with a Tax Estimator that estimates your current and soon-to-pay taxes using TurboTax calculations so you can do something about your taxes before it's too late. You can import data from Quicken for the estimation and printing results if you like. This covers quarterly estimated tax payments and should also help you avoid penalties for under-withholding or lost interest from over-withholding. It tracks the latest tax rate changes with a phone number to call for the latest details, and helps you figure the tax results of large transactions such as buying a home or selling stocks.

Perhaps to compete with TaxCut's link to H&R Block Tax preparers, TurboTax and MacInTax users got the *Professional Partners* program in 1995. They could dial Intuit's toll-free number to get referrals to local tax professionals, who would then take $25 off their tax-prep fees.

Intuit also makes a TurboTax for small businesses now, alongside its QuickBooks accounting program for small business.

The DOS version of TurboTax has similar features but is without the latest ease and tip changes: it is pretty much like last year's DOS version, but with this year's tax laws and numbers inside. TurboTax also has an Uninstall feature, but tech support is not a toll-free number (see Figures 6.1 and 6.2).

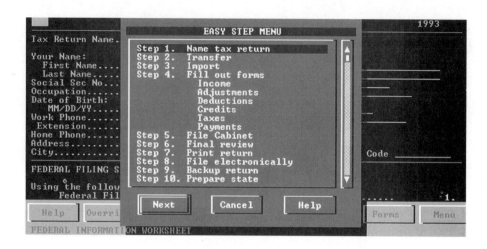

Figure 6.1 TurboTax's interview in the DOS version.

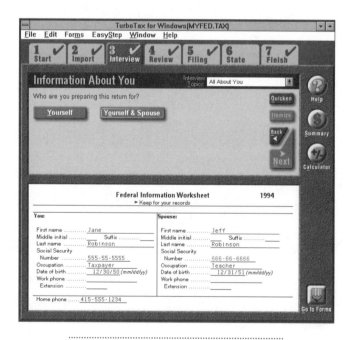

Figure 6.2 TurboTax for Windows' interview.

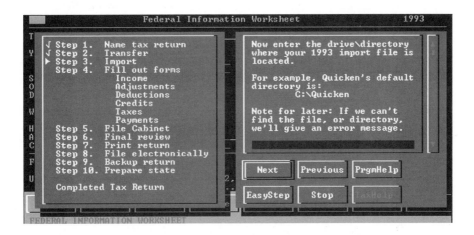
Every kind of help you might want is in TurboTax. It has tips, verbatim IRS instructions, and directions to IRS publications, to what-ifs for this year and tax planning for next year. There's phone and fax support as well as an on-line forum for support (see Figure 6.3).

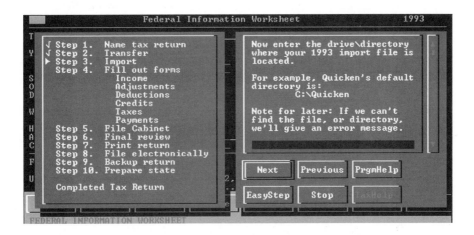

Figure 6.3 A TurboTax strength is direct import from Quicken, shown here in the DOS version.

For more details on TurboTax, turn to the tutorial example at the end of this chapter. There I'll show you how the TurboTax for Windows works. (There's a copy of the Headstart version on the CD-ROM with this book.)

MacInTax

MacInTax is Intuit's Macintosh tax preparation program. It used to be a very different program from TurboTax but is now almost identical to the Windows TurboTax, though without the special new links to Quicken.

TurboTax Tax Savings Guide and MacInTax Tax Savings Guide

TurboTax Tax Savings Guide and MacInTax Tax Savings Guide from Intuit offer more than 250 tax-savings tips with examples to illustrate the ideas. You can get them by looking through a topic index, searching for keywords, or answering questions (see Figure 6.4). You don't have to own TurboTax to use the guide. The tips include:

💲 Income and expense strategies to shelter income and time expenses to minimize tax liability, defer income, exercise stock options, and create nontaxable rental income.

💲 Investment strategies for stocks, bonds, mutual funds, real estate, and how to calculate the investment base for these including which shares to sell.

💲 Year-end tax strategies through simple steps to take at the end of the year to reduce tax liability for the whole year, such as charging charitable contributions at year end and still deducting them.

💲 Retirement strategies such as methods for reducing taxes while preparing for retirement, including diverting tax dollars to retirement savings, knowing when to invest in a retirement plan, what the benefits of a 401(k) plan are, and when you can withdraw retirement funds before retirement.

💲 Estate and gift strategies such as how much you can give away tax-free.

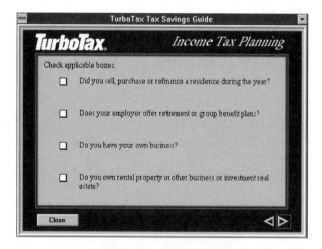

Figure 6.4 TurboTax Tax Savings Guide.

TurboTax Tax Planner for Windows and MacInTax Tax Planner

The Tax Planner program is from Intuit and comes in DOS, Windows, and Mac versions (see Figure 6.5). This program helps you analyze your finances and estimate your tax liabilities for a five-year period. It has an interview to determine your situation. The 1995 version included the new tax laws for that year and helped planning through 1998. For each year you can set up five different scenarios. Tax Planner will import data from Quicken and Managing Your Money.

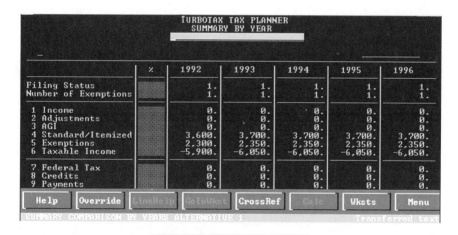

Figure 6.5 TurboTax Tax Planner.

TaxCut

TaxCut from Block Financial Software has the best connections this year. It comes from the same company that sells Managing Your Money, the second-best-selling personal finance program. (It also imports from Quicken, .TXF, and other common programs. The Mac version even imports from MacInTax, if you want to use that competing program's previous-year results as a starting point.) That means you can track your expenses all year on your computer and then import the results directly to the appropriate forms and lines in TaxCut. Better yet, the same company runs the more than 8000 H&R Block tax-preparation service offices around the country. In fact, if you're not happy with TaxCut, you can call your local Block office for free tax advice (the phone numbers are in the program), or even take it and your receipts to your local Block office and have them prepare your returns, at a discount for whatever you spent on the software (bring that receipt at least). Even if you are happy with the returns, but later the IRS isn't—auditing you—a Block expert will accompany you to the audit (see Figure 6.6).

You can work through the Q&A interview or go directly to the forms. The Shoebox organizes your tax documents; you still organize receipts. There are tax tips, an auditor flags for out-of-line and inconsistent entries, What if? options to try alternatives, and deduction suggestions. It prints or files the return electronically, comes with a short (only 15 pages, which will thrill some and disappoint others) but funny manual and on-line help, and has an 800-number for free tech support. Here's a new fine feature: the program un-installs itself when you're done, so it won't eat up that 10MB of your hard disk while doing nothing the rest of the year. The program comes in versions for Windows, DOS, and Macintosh versions and add-ons for most states. A special Windows CD-ROM version, for the same price, adds audio and video clips to talk you through the return plus some related (mortgage, insurance, legal, on-line membership) software. The program "Kiplinger TaxCut" (800-235-4060) adds advice from the popular Kiplinger Tax Letter newsletter. A CD-ROM of Kiplinger also has video clips.

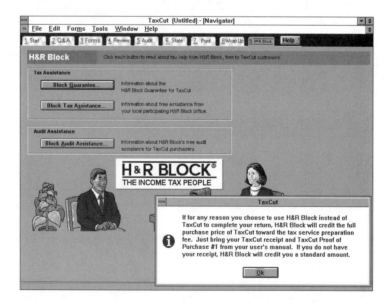

Figure 6.6 TaxCut offers a unique connection to the H&R Block Tax preparation service.

Personal Tax Edge and TaxMate

Personal Tax Edge has some decent connections too. First, the company also makes a personal finance program called Money Counts. Tax Edge can import information from that as well as from Quicken or .TXF files and other standards. Intuit, maker of TurboTax and Quicken, bought Parsons Technology last year, including Personal Tax Edge. That connection doesn't mean anything yet—PTE is still sold separately, often through the mail—but could in the future, especially now that Microsoft is buying Intuit. (It gets pretty confusing.) But the best connection is PTE's "lite" version called TaxMate, which you can have for only $8.95. What makes it lite is offering only 6 forms instead of the 80 and more in PTE and competing tax programs. But according to Parsons, the IRS says those 6 will fill the bill for 75% of Americans.

Inside the program you'll find all the state-of-the-art features: import, interview, tips (including from the well-known J.K.Lasser tax guides), audit, planning, paper/1040PC/electronic filing, and state versions. You'll find unique calculators for depreciation and interest (see Figure 6.7). A Tax Guide works to make the interview easier, though it is not as comforting for beginners as the interviews in TurboTax or TaxCut. And I had some trouble moving around in the actual tax forms. But the CD-ROM multimedia version for Windows has video clips to explain everything, step-by-step, down to what each button means. For my money this beats the video tips that make up most of the other multimedia tax preparers. The DOS version is nearly identical. The Macintosh version lacks the Guide you'll find in Windows and some of the other extras, such as some of the tips and calculators. Tax Mate (see Figure 6.8) lacks most forms, as noted above, as well as the importing of data, depreciation and interest calculators, the Lasser tips, even the Organizer for keeping track of your receipts and forms. Parsons does not have a toll-free tech support line.

Parsons claims to have given away 250,000 free copies of Tax Mate (they charged for shipping and handling) in 1994, no doubt hoping people would buy state versions to go with it (you buy the Personal Tax Edge state versions), next year's Tax Mate, Personal Tax Edge (upon discovering that they needed more forms or abilities), or even some other product Parsons Technology makes. Tax Mate can handle basic tax returns, such as those with a 1040 form, deductions, Schedule A, and other fundamentals. It has 1040, 1040A, and 2441 forms and Schedules A,B,D,R, and EIC. It has an interview, a forms list, an audit check, a tax-at-a-glance display, comparison to averages, tax saver tips, printing, and electronic filing (including Form 8453-Tax Declaration for Electronic Filing and Form 9282—Electronic Payment Voucher).

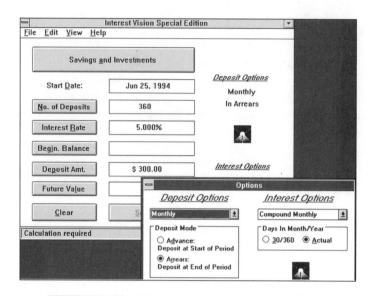

Figure 6.7 Personal Tax Edge has powerful calculators for loans, annuities, savings, investments, and depreciation.

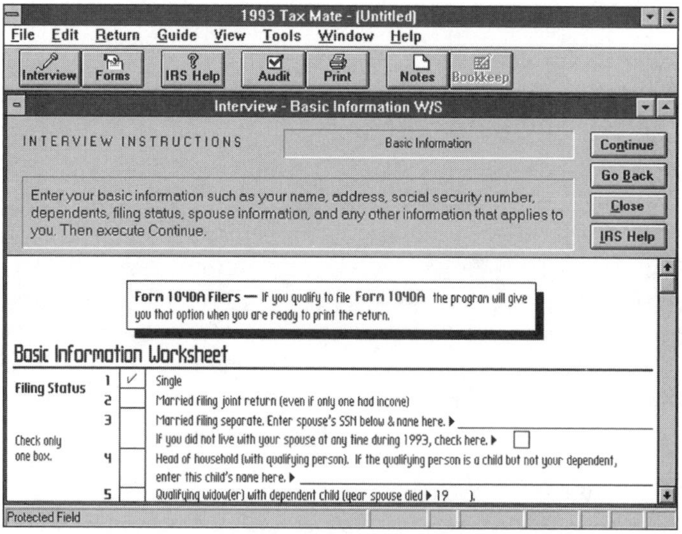

Figure 6.8 Tax Mate has the key features of Personal Tax Edge, but with only the basic forms and at a very low price.

Novell's Taxsaver

This program for DOS and Windows is part of Novell's new WordPerfect Main Street consumer software division. TaxSaver has 79 forms, schedules, and worksheets. It has a Tax Coach that guides users through filling in the forms, a sort of interview. It will then check for errors and jump to any that it finds. A "what if" feature lets you explore the different results from filing jointly or separately. And the audit compares your results to averages and to your previous year. It can import from standard personal finance programs.

CA-Simply Tax

Simply Tax has few connections. That surprises me because it comes from one of the world's largest software companies. 4Home is part of Computer Associates. That same firm also makes the personal finance program Simply Money, but is more experienced with minicomputer and mainframe software—programs for those $100,000 and $1 million machines. Simply Tax has many of the same features as the competing program: importing from standard finance programs, a "PathFinder" interview, tips from the famous Ernst & Young guide, audit alerts, and state versions. It does a good job organizing your forms. And it has a unique feature I like that alerts you to imminent tax-form deadlines (see Figure 6.9).

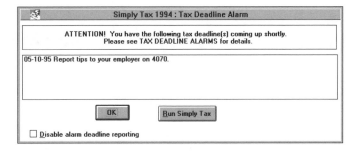

Figure 6.9 CA-Simply Tax has a unique feature that alerts you to tax deadlines.

There's just about every kind of help imaginable, including the interview, tips by syndicate columnist Gary Klott, IRS instructions (which have hypertext definitions and cross-references), and on-disk context-sensitive, telephone, and on-line forum support. There is no fax support. There is what-if and next-year analysis.

But the interview confused me, with too many windows, icons galore, and directions I couldn't follow (see Figure 6.10). And it was slow. And there was no manual at all. Don't even ask for toll-free tech support. Or a DOS or a Macintosh or a CD-ROM multimedia version.

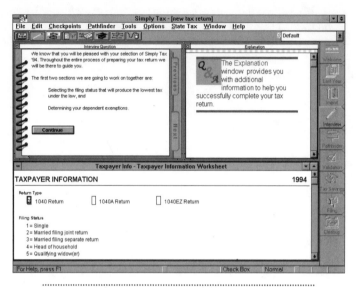

Figure 6.10 CA-Simply Tax's interview can be confusing.

Lesser-Known Tax Preparation Programs

TaxDollars is a tax prep program for the OS/2 operating system. From BT&T Consumer Technology, it is so far a minimal thing, with only 14 forms: 1040, 1040PC, A,B,C,D, and E, and W2. But then, it only costs $7.95 (for shipping and handling) and is very easy to use. It does have help information on both the program and several dozen tax topics. It doesn't support .TXF importing.

AM-Tax Personal 1040 from AM Software is one of the simplest tax preparation programs, even though it changed quite a bit and added a lot of power in 1994. It is a DOS program that now has what-if and audit checks. As you work it checks for 100 omissions or inconsistencies and compares to national averages. It has on-line help and a tax summary window. You won't find an interview, special calculators, tax tips, or data importing from personal finance programs. An option lets you file electronically through NELCO (National Electronic filing service). If you want to print IRS replica forms, that too is an option, as are state forms. The results will print on dot-matrix inkjet or LaserJet printers, but not on PostScript printers or on a 1040PC form. A unique feature lets it print blank forms. Support is through fax or phone, but there's no bulletin board. Unlike most competitors, it doesn't need a hard disk drive. In fact, it will run on PCs with only the original 8088 processor—from way back in 1984. There's a lite shareware version available on the company's BBS at (816) 741-7668 that will handle Forms 1040, A, B, C, D, E, EIC, F, R, and SE.

TaxPerfect from Financial Services Marketing does not import personal finance data or shoebox disorganized data. You have to enter the numbers manually. Nor are there tips, IRS instructions, or an on-line forum. It can import last year's TaxPerfect entries and you can call or fax for tech support and use the pop-up calculator while working in the 48 forms. TaxPerfect will calculate your return, audit it, and then print it on dot-matrix inkjet or LaserJet printers. It doesn't offer 1040PC or PostScript printing but can file electronically.

Tax Preparer from Howardsoft could be used by an individual, and it does work on a PC with only DOS and a single floppy disk drive. But this program is aimed more at professionals who want to prepare taxes for others. It costs $300 the first time and $100 to renew each year.

Tax Solver from Intex Solutions is not an independent tax program. Instead, it is a collection of tax preparation templates for the Lotus 1-2-3 or Microsoft Excel spreadsheet programs. A *template* is a collection of equations in spreadsheet form, just waiting for you to enter numeric amounts that it can calculate. In other words, you'll need to have and understand a spreadsheet (and your computer will need lots of memory to load large spreadsheet files) to use Tax Solver. But if you are in that class, this is a powerful collection without much help but with lots of what-if power. There's an audit feature, a checklist and the ability to print IRS-replicas of all 147 IRS forms.

Tutorial Example with TurboTax for Windows HeadStart Version

Here's an example of using a tax preparation program, in this case the TurboTax for Windows HeadStart version which comes free on the CD-ROM in the back of this book. TurboTax is the best-selling tax program. And because it comes from the same company that makes Quicken, the two work together well.

1. Your first step is to install the program. Follow the instructions in our CD-ROM chapter.

2. Start TurboTax by double-clicking on its icon. Soon you'll see the opening display (see Figure 6.11).

Figure 6.11 When you start TurboTax for Windows, this is what you see first.

As you can see, you control this program by clicking on the buttons such as those on the right, and notebook divider tabs across the top.

Follow the suggestions unless you have a specific reason to step out of the track. Click on the **Next** button when that's suggested.

If you're a pro, go straight to the forms. Most of us should use the EasyStep process, which is TurboTax's interview.

You'll be asked to save your work each time you finish a section. Save more often than that to be safer. Just give your file a name, as in Figure 6.12.

Now that you're rolling, those who suffered all year entering their financial data into a program such as Quicken can now take it easy. Let TurboTax import that data. Also, if you used TurboTax last year, you can save even more time by importing those old results. TurboTax this year won't use your actual amounts from that year, except for comparisons, but it can learn from the categories you used (see Figure 6.13).

Remember that the .TXF choice is for importing from other personal finance programs.

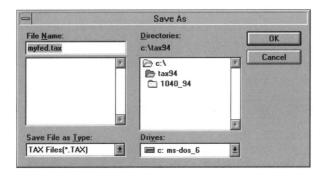

Figure 6.12 Save your tax work often.

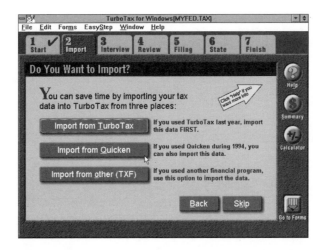

Figure 6.13 Import your financial data to save time and avoid mistakes.

The latest Windows version of TurboTax has a Tax Link feature to get more precise information from Quicken. (This is a good reason to buy TurboTax if you're a committed Quicken user.)

If you're a beginner, just let the Link do its job. If you're an expert or curious, though, you can view what it does (see Figure 6.14).

Figure 6.14 The Tax Link to Quicken lets you see
what numbers are coming in from your finances.

The interview will explain what you need to enter, with help information always on
hand, and show you the form where the information lands. You just click the buttons and answer the questions to proceed (see Figure 6.15).

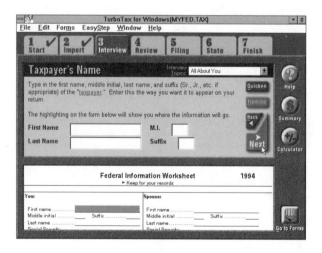

Figure 6.15 TurboTax interview.

If you think you made a mistake at any point, click on the **Back** button to return to the previous question. Then answer it as best you can.

If you have a home business and are planning to deduct the very computer you're using, TurboTax will help you through the depreciation gamut. It includes categories for the different rates of depreciation. It will even offer the Section 179 deduction to write it all off in this first year, if you qualify.

Home office deductions come up during the interview as well. You can either enter the numbers alone, or be guided through the questions that qualify a home office.

After answering more questions, lots and lots more questions, you'll finish the interview. Then you can use the Review to see any problems in the form s — things missing, things inconsistent, things likely to get the IRS all excited.

When it finds a problem, or a spot for improvement, it will explain the thinking and display the relevant form (see Figure 6.16).

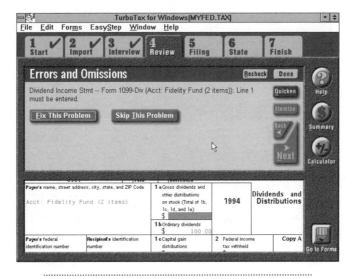

Figure 6.16 The Review shows where change can help.

TurboTax will also use this opportunity to suggest tax planning for the next year. In these displays, when you see a highlighted and underlined section, you can click on that information to jump to more details.

The final part of the Review, the Audit check, shows where TurboTax thinks the IRS is most likely to question a return. In this example case, the only hot spot was the Home Office deduction, as explained (see Figures 6.17 and 6.18).

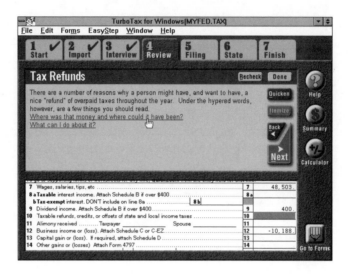

Figure 6.17 Underlined and highlighted text means more details available at a click.

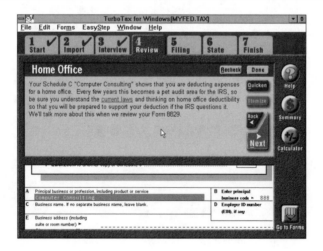

Figure 6.18 The Audit Flag points to possible trouble spots in the return.

In the Filing step you get to choose just what to print or send electronically. This is the HeadStart version, though, which doesn't print a return you can file (nor would you want it to, because it uses old tax law). See Figure 6.19.

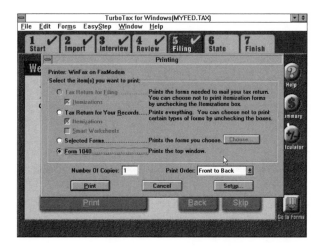

Figure 6.19 Filing lets you print a standard return, a partial return (for your files), a 1040PC return, or send the return electronically.

Done with the Feds? Now you can tackle the state, which often depends on a completed federal return.

And as you work, remember that you can see a summary so far by clicking on that button on the far right. The Tax Graphs choice in the Window menu is another way to see what you owe and why (see Figures 6.20 and 6.21).

Tax Summary	
Tax Summary	
► Keep for your records	
Total income	38,715.
Adjustments to income	
Adjusted gross income	38,715.
Itemized/standard deduction	12,320.
Personal exemptions	7,350.
Taxable income	19,045.
Tentative tax	2,854.
Total credits	
Other taxes	0.
Total tax	2,854.
Total payments	12,373.
Form 2210 penalty	
Refund	9,519.
Balance due	
Tax bracket	15.00 %

Figure 6.20 The Summary button gives you a quick read on your tax status so far.

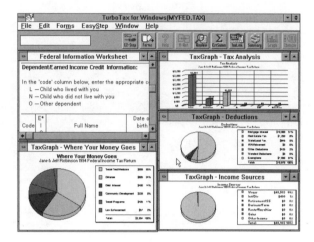

Figure 6.21 Tax Graphs in TurboTax.

When you go directly to the Forms, you get to choose any particular form or worksheet for making entries. If your entries conflict with what TurboTax is automatically trying to feed from previous entries, you'll see a warning.

The Plan Mode worksheet lets you project what your taxes will be in the current year, information you can then feed to the next filing season's version of TurboTax. The history table lets you see how your taxes have been changing over the past several years (see Figures 6.22 and 6.23).

Tax History Report   **1994**
▶ Keep for your records

Name(s) shown on return
Jane & Jeff Robinson

Social Security Number
555-55-5555

Five Year Tax History:

	1991	1992	1993	1994	1995
Total income				38,715.	
Adjustments to income ...					
Adjusted gross income ...				38,715.	
Tax expense..........				1,895.	
Interest expense				10,000.	
Contributions				425.	
Miscellaneous deductions					

Figure 6.22 The Tax History worksheet.

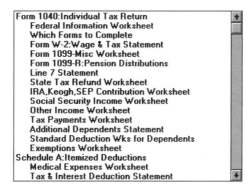

```
Form 1040:Individual Tax Return
    Federal Information Worksheet
    Which Forms to Complete
    Form W-2:Wage & Tax Statement
    Form 1099-Misc Worksheet
    Form 1099-R:Pension Distributions
    Line 7 Statement
    State Tax Refund Worksheet
    IRA,Keogh,SEP Contribution Worksheet
    Social Security Income Worksheet
    Other Income Worksheet
    Tax Payments Worksheet
    Additional Dependents Statement
    Standard Deduction Wks for Dependents
    Exemptions Worksheet
Schedule A:Itemized Deductions
    Medical Expenses Worksheet
    Tax & Interest Deduction Statement
```

Figure 6.23 Going directly to forms lets you enter information anywhere at any time.

There is also tax planning built into personal finance programs (see Figure 6.24). Managing Your Money, for example, as a summary form 1040 right in the program. Quicken has a tax planner.

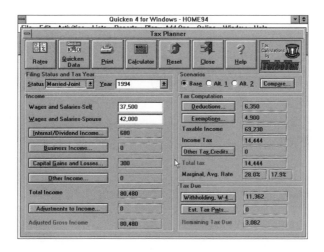

Figure 6.24 Tax Planning in Quicken.

Here you can play with the values as you go, experimenting with different withholding rates, and seeing how much you need to save to pay your taxes.

Now that you're done, use the **Uninstall** command to take TurboTax off your disk drive. Or wait until you've filed your taxes to do this. There's no reason to keep it on your drive all year, eating up disk space. That's especially true because next year you'll get a new copy of the program anyway. Keep the floppies, though, because you might want them later for looking at your results.

To use Uninstall, just double-click on that icon in your Windows Program Manager.

On-Line Help

Did you get a modem and an on-line service when you set up your computer system? If so, here's a chance to use it with your tax prep software. There's lots of on-line help about the ins and outs of tax law and software.

For example, if you have an Internet Web Browser (such as Netcruiser or Mosaic), the IRS has its own home pages at:

💰   http://www.ustreas.gov/treasury/bureaus/irs/irs.html

💰   http://www.ustreas.gov/treasury/bureaus/irs/questns.html

In the first you'll find a multimedia site with a color photo of IRS Commissioner Peggy Richardson and a description of how she's only the second woman to head the IRS since it started in 1863. In the second there are common questions with answers.

Not too exciting?

How about an FAQ (Frequently Asked Question) file full of just what the name implies? How about links to on-line catalogs of IRS forms? Both of those are practical. You can download (copy into your computer) the forms in .PDF (Portable Document Format) which your programs can then use if you have an Adobe Acrobat reader program. These are available free from the FTP (File Transfer Protocol) site at

💰   ftp.adobe.com/pub/adobe/Acrobat/Applications

They'll take a while to download because they're so big.

Frank McNeil's Income Tax Information home page on the Internet's Web is also helpful, with explanations on finding tax information. Try

💰 http://ftp/netcom.com/pub/ftmexpat/taxsites.htm

Or get the text version using FTP at

💰 ftp.netcom.com/pub/ftmexpat/html2text/taxsites.txt

Or via E-mail by sending a request asking **SEND ftmexpat/html2text/taxsites.txt** to

💰 ftp-request@netcom.com

with text.

Tax Site on the Net is a web page with links to tax mailing lists, newsgroups, and taxform libraries.

There are discussion groups—news groups—on the Internet, such as *misc.taxes*, with lots of answers from experts and amateurs.

On CompuServe you can find H&R Block's Income Tax Calendar (**GO HRB**). (Block owns CompuServe.) The Executive Tax Service there is for complex tax questions. The Investor's Forums (**GO INVFORUM**) for financial planning. You'll also find the Working At Home forum (**GO HOME**) with an Accounting and Tax section, and even details on tax law in the Tax Notes Today documents of the Legal Research Center (**GO LEGALRC**) though this is a premium (added-cost) service. CompuServe is home to lots of software company support bulletin boards, so you can look to Parsons' (**GO PTFORUM**) or Block/Meca's (**GO MECATAXCUT**) or Intuit's (**GO INTUIT**) forums. Tax forms are at **GO TAXFORMS** and electronic filing is at **GO TAXRETURN**.

America Online has a business forum called Strategies for Business (KEY-WORD BUSINESS) which also covers tax issues, and in the Personal Finance section you'll find a Tax Message Board (KEYWORD INVESTOR) chat area for sharing tax stories. Genie has a Tax and Accounting Round Table (KEYWORD TAX or PAGE 1040) for answers from CPAs and tax-preparers, as well as tax forms in .PDF and PostScript formats. The BIX on-line service has a taxes topic; Prodigy has a twice-monthly column by Juliana Block on taxes (JUMPWORD BLOCK) and a Money Talk board (JUMPWORD MONEY TALK) with plenty to read.

Tips for Using the Tax Programs

Here are some tips for using these and any tax preparation programs:

💰 Buy the Headstart or Early Bird version of your program in the late months of the year. That will give you time to estimate your taxes for the year and a chance to do something about them other than just writing a check. Perhaps you can change income or expenses before the end of the year.

💰 Organize your finances with a personal finance program. Then import the data directly to your tax preparation program. You might buy your tax preparation program with that in mind—ask which personal financial programs it is most compatible with. This will save you a lot of time and minimize mathematical errors when preparing taxes.

💰 Make sure you've printed all the forms you worked on and send them all in. Leaving forms out is a perfect way to get audited.

💰 Look up the IRS details on depreciation, amortization, medical deductions, and retirement income if you have significant money in any of those areas. The law is complex.

💰 Annotate your entries if you can. Add notes that explain why you put the amount you did in each area.

💰 Use the built-in calculators for most arithmetic.

💰 Use the what-if feature of your tax preparation program to see which way an expense or income item is best entered. The law is flexible enough so that many items, such as home office expenses, can be entered in more than one place on all the forms.

💰 Remember to deduct the cost of the tax software itself. This fits in Schedule A, Line 20 for Other Expenses, Miscellaneous Deductions.

💰 If you're going to deduct your computer hardware, or part of it, be sure to look into the latest depreciation schedules and rules.

💰 Use a state tax module—you've already entered most of the information in the federal forms anyway.

💰 Use the audit feature and give yourself enough time to go back and clear up any omissions or problems it finds. If it suggests that your expenses are unusually high in some area, make sure you've got receipts to back them up.

💰 If your printed return doesn't look right, make sure your computer has all the necessary fonts.

💰 Seriously consider whether it's worth your while to file electronically. Most programs can now do it, but filing that way will cost you a fee of $20 or more, and you'll still have to mail in some paper forms. All you earn is a refund in three weeks instead of four to eight weeks.

💰 Plan ahead for next year's taxes. Use the planning feature of your tax package, or a specialized tax planning program for estimating what next year's tax will be. Then use those results to minimize your tax, such as by opening a new Individual Retirement Account (IRA) or Self-Employed Pension (SEP).

Summary—Tax Preparation Programs

First you'll want to get a personal finance program and enter your financial data in it. Then find your tax preparation program. Remember to look for these basic features:

💰 It runs on your computer

💰 There is a state version for your state

💰 The tech support is there and helpful (try calling the help line even before you buy)

💰 It will import the data from your personal finance program, directly if at all possible—importing as a .TXF or ASCII file is distinctly more difficult

Remember that although multimedia tax programs on CD-ROMs with sound and video are flashy, they don't help most people much with the truly difficult parts of the process—keeping records and working through the questions. In fact, the added help information on the CD-ROMs is sometimes quite useful, and so more important than the video.

Then choose a particular program.

💰 Personal Tax Edge gives you the most for the least money on PCs.

💲 AM-Tax could be best for those with older, less-powerful PCs, such as with only a floppy disk drive but no hard drive.

💲 TaxCut offers the best connection, with its link to the H&R Block Tax Preparation service, for Mac or PC.

💲 TurboTax is the most popular and has the best links to Quicken as well as to tax planning software.

Then do some tax planning for next year and the years after with the what-if facilities in your tax preparation program (giving decent results), with the planning abilities in your personal finance program (if there, these may do an even better job), or with a planning program, such as those mentioned earlier in this chapter.

Finally, if your taxes involve much money at all, pass it all by a tax professional.

CHAPTER 7

Invest

Use money to make money. That's supposed to be the secret of the rich, right? And of the successful middle-class folks who manage to afford kids, houses, college for those kids, vacations, and retirement.

But you're already using your money to make money. You probably already have a savings account. It's probably an interest-bearing checking account, too. Many people own at least some treasury bonds if not mutual funds, stocks, and more exotic pieces of paper.

If you want to save enough for kids, college, and retirement, you'll have to invest, whether that investment is a totally secure, low-return bank account or a risky, high-return derivative.

So how do you know where to put your money for saving and investing? There's only one safe way: *learn*. You'll have to read, listen, follow the news, and learn many new terms. Your only other choice is to trust some investment advisor, and that can be a big mistake if you don't know enough about investments to question and monitor his or her advice and actions.

And it's not computer learning I'm talking about. I mean *financial smarts*, discovering the difference between bonds and stocks, options and commodities, and how the world and psychology affect their value and price.

What do computers have to do with all of this learning and choosing? Plenty. They can help you do the following:

- 💰   Learn about finance.
- 💰   Calculate how much you need and want to save.
- 💰   Analyze, select, buy, and sell all those pieces of paper

Computers do this when they are armed with the right software, such as:

- 💰   Planners that suggest goals
- 💰   Portfolio managers that track what your investments are worth (built into some of the personal financial managers and available in some investing programs)
- 💰   News and quote sources (on-line or disk collections of historical and current prices, reports, and other company and security specifics)
- 💰   Fundamental analyzers to filter the right investments from the tens of thousands of securities by looking at profits, industry outlook, and other such details (listed in this chapter)
- 💰   Technical Analyzers to filter the right investments from the tens of thousands of securities by looking at price history (these are listed in this chapter).
- 💰   Traders to let you buy and sell through a modem connection without having to call or visit a broker

This chapter surveys what's available in investment software. The summary at the end of the chapter suggests what to start with and where to go from there.

Steps to Computer Investing

The first step is to get a portfolio manager. If you have only a few investments and you check prices only occasionally, you should stick with one of the personal finance programs mentioned in Chapter 3, such as Managing Your Money or Quicken. Each includes portfolio management—recording what you own and how much it is worth—as one of the many features. These programs also help you plan when and where you should invest more. The planning programs in Chapter 2 can contribute to this work, such as figuring how much debt you have, whether you should refinance your home, how much to save for retirement, and so on. The best programs will also help you calculate your gains and losses based on prices, as well as figure the tax implications.

But computers cannot be trusted to know you and your situation. They cannot tell you just how much risk is involved, how much savings, or which securities fit your lifestyle.

The general personal finance programs won't satisfy the serious investors, those who check prices daily, watch a ticker on CNBC, and listen to the "Lous" (Dobbs and Rukeyser—the famous television financial pundits). Although their portfolio manager portions may stretch to fit, those programs won't do anything to help you filter through the tens of thousands of stocks, bonds, mutual funds, and other securities to find those that meet your risk and reward goals. For that you'll need an on-line connection: a modem, a subscription, and a program to let the modem tap that subscription. This on-line connection will let you track investments and update your portfolio as you trade. All the major services offer such connections: America Online, Prodigy, and CompuServe. You'll also find lesser-known computer entities through the financial world, such as Dow Jones News Retrieval and Morningstar. Remember, too, that some of the on-line connections are included in other programs. Some are independent services you can link to common programs.

The next step is to dig deeper into the analysis of investments. You have all this data downloaded and updating your portfolio. How can you improve that portfolio to find the best investments and keep finding them as conditions change? *Analysis*, that's how.

Fundamental analysis programs help you look at the numbers behind a stock: how much debt it carries, what the inventory levels are, how quickly it is expanding, what new products are on the way, and where the general economy is going.

Technical analysis programs—also known as *charting programs*—don't care about all that. They see only the historical record. Where have the highest, lowest, and last prices been? How can you trace lines between the peaks and valleys, detecting patterns to know when they'll recur so you'll know when to buy or sell or hold? These programs graph the numbers, draw the lines, and issue the buy and sell orders, but they are based only on the built-in schemes or your own custom schemes. There is as much art to technical analysis as there is science.

Both fundamental and technical analyses win some and lose some. In either case, you'll need to learn a lot to know how to put these tools to work.

The final step is to use trading programs. Instead of running all your software, then dialing a phone number to tell a broker what you want to buy and sell, you can use a trading program to make those deals directly through a modem.

In fact, many programs have a mix of capabilities. Many on-line connections also contain some portfolio management. Many analysis programs have some fundamental and some technical analysis abilities.

A few programs combine it all. WealthBuilder, for example, is an unusual program that you should consider because it combines on-line information with portfolio management (including some of the better advice for investing) and it provides fundamental and technical analyses. Link it to the Reuters Money Network and it can trade too. Destiny from Comtrad combines portfolio management—and even asset allocation—with retirement planning.

As you're shopping, look for bundled deals. For example, you might get a personal finance program for free with a new computer, and a free month's subscription to one of the on-line services as well. Or your technical analysis program might be discounted if you buy it with an on-line subscription.

As you look at investment programs, you'll notice two trends. First, there are many more programs than there were five years ago—more than 500 now, double the number in just the past two years. Second, most of them are for PCs, not Macs. If a program description doesn't mention which computer it is for, you can assume it runs on the PC.

Are you a Casual, Serious, or Semiprofessional Investor?

If you used the full gamut of software tools, you'd have just as much power at your fingertips as the banker in a 50th floor office on Wall Street. Personal computers can put you on a level playing field with those pros. You would run regular technical and fundamental analyses based on your own rules of thumb, watching where the market was moving and sifting through funds, bonds, stocks, and commodities to find the best mixes and hedges. Since you're not actually getting paid for such play, I'll call that *semiprofessional investing*. As an alternative, you can simply use your personal computer to add some mutual funds to your checking and savings account, and then to automatically calculate the taxes you'll owe and the profits you've made on that investment. That's *casual investing*.

In between are the *serious investors*, who regularly check stock price quotes, buy and sell their own securities on-line, and occasionally use an analysis tool to scope out their next move. Remember when using these programs that most are *tools, not intelligent advisors*. Don't think of them as aspired contractors ready to build your investment house. Think of them as hammers, bulldozers, and building codes that can take your plans and convert them into a stable structure.

Few of the programs even give advice. Those that do may give bad or out-of-date advice. Stick to what you've learned, and talk with professional investment advisors to figure out what you want. Then use these tools to get there.

The first step is to get a portfolio manager. Serious investors will then add a quote service and some fundamental analysis tools. They may even want on-line trading ability. Semiprofessionals will want all of those plus the latest technical analysis software. The rest of this chapter shows you which programs fit into those categories.

Portfolio Management and Asset Allocation

Keeping track of your investments—what they are and how much they're wort h — is easy if you don't have many. The first generation of portfolio managers, such as those built into such programs as Quicken and Managing Your Money, handle this quite well. These programs keep your checkbook, record your stock purchases or sales, and calculate the value of your portfolio.

For more serious investors, those who are in the more than 35% of the 160,000 members of the American Association of Individual Investors who say they use computers to manage their portfolios, more serious software is appropriate. These are people who trade more than once a month and who own mutual funds, stocks, bonds, and more. They read the *Wall Street Journal*, business magazines, and probably a newsletter or two. They dig into more details of their investments. For example, more than 17% of those members like to use their personal computers to analyze mutual funds. They don't just buy the top-rated fund in the latest magazine comparison. In the past, these folks might have plotted price charts by hand. Now they drink coffee while the computer plots. The ease of this process is causing more and more amateur investors to challenge the professionals. Who needs a broker's expensive advice when you have your own ideas and can track the market yourself?

Second-generation portfolio managers, such as WealthBuilder, don't just track finances. They help you create a portfolio, suggesting the mix of risk and reward you should seek. They search through mutual funds, stocks, and bonds to find those that are right for you. They can even set alarms to let you know when a security hits some specific target, such as a stock finding a particular price/earnings ratio.

Semiprofessional investors could also use these although they may want to look at the portfolio management built into trading programs such as Schwab's StreetSmart, discussed later in this chapter.

Quicken

Quicken's strength is in checkbook and credit card accounts. It has only recently come to have real portfolio management (see Figure 7.1). Still, the latest version does record your stock, bond, and mutual fund holdings. Links through the Quicken Companion or the Reuters Money Network (RMN) can add on-line information searching. That means portfolio updates and some fundamental analysis. Also, Quicken can link to some of the sophisticated fundamental and technical analysis programs listed in this chapter. When it comes time to trade on-line, Quicken owners should consider RMN or StreetSmart from Schwab.

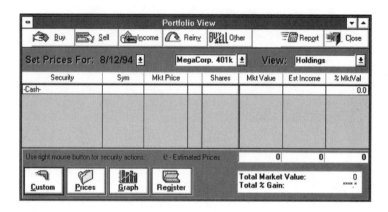

Figure 7.1 Quicken's portfolio management.

Managing Your Money

Managing Your Money has always been a force for investing. While competitors such as Quicken focused on the basic checkbook, Managing Your Money made it a point to record portfolio information, calculate the latest value and net worth from it, and figure capital gains and tax results (see Figures 7.2 and 7.3). It follows stocks, bonds, mutual funds, puts and calls, and even dividends, tax status, risk levels, expiration dates, strike prices, and other details. This lets you get the exact status of any investment, including simple and annual appreciation and yield. For trading, Managing Your Money owners should consider Fidelity Online Xpress (FOX) from Fidelity Investments. It was developed by the same company that makes Managing Your Money.

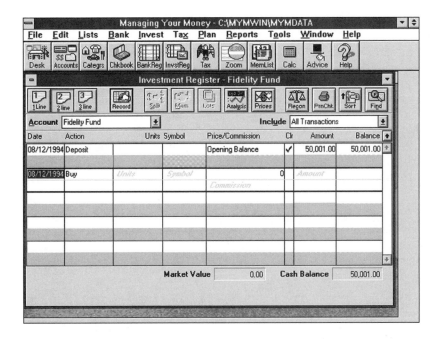

Figure 7.2 Managing Your Money's investment register.

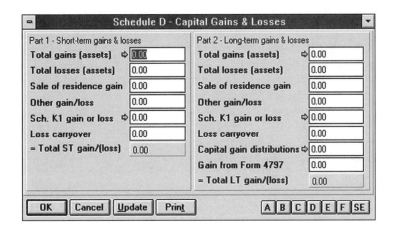

Figure 7.3 Managing Your Money's capital gains calculations.

WealthBuilder

One of the best portfolio managers for novice investors is in WealthBuilder by *Money Magazine* (sold by Reality Technologies). It includes financial planning, asset allocation, and even strategy suggestions. When you use the Reuters Money Network (also from Reality Technologies) linked to it, you can automatically update your portfolio and receive alerts on buying and selling. Better yet, it can educate you about investing from its on-line help to its manual. Reality claims more than 150,000 users of WealthBuilder.

Inside the program you build a Personal Profile after answering questions about net worth, risk tolerance, and investment preferences. There's a WealthAdvisor to suggest investing strategies including specific investments. The Research Databases let you sort, filter, and graph fundamental data on 18,500 investments from Standard & Poor's (S&P), Morningstar, Bank Rate Monitor, *Money Magazine*, and others. The Financial Calculators handle loan comparisons, mortgages, buy versus rent, and so on.

WealthBuilder can import and export data to Quicken and Managing Your Money. It produces Tax Schedule B and D reports and exports to TurboTax. The latest version comes with Pond's Personal Financial Planner ActiveBook (see Chapter 2 for details).

WealthBuilder comes with a free subscription start (you then pay the monthly fee) to the Reuters Money Network. That lets you look up quotes, news, fundamental research data, and even on-line brokers. WealthBuilder can help you create custom alerts so that your trading continues to show intelligence even when you're not available for answering questions.

In early 1994, Reuters bought a majority stake in Reality Technologies. It has a joint marketing relationship with Time Inc.'s *Money Magazine*. Reuters is used by 200,000 brokers, traders, and portfolio managers around the world. The Reuters Money Network used to be called Reality's Smart Investor by *Money Magazine*.

Windows on WallStreet Pro

Windows on WallStreet from MarketArts manages your portfolio and adds both fundamental and technical analysis (see Figures 7.4 and 7.5). It has built-in software for downloading information from services such as Dow Jones, Dial Data, and CompuServe. It has easy tools for charting that data. Uniquely, it also explains much of what it can do. This is one of the few programs that can be a useful and educational tool.

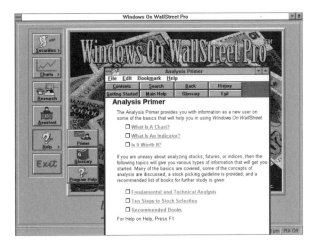

Figure 7.4 Windows on WallStreet can be an investment education tool.

First you can use the data to screen securities to find those that meet your criteria. Then you can learn the fundamentals about promising prospects using company reports and late-breaking news. You can view a stock in several windows at once or overlay one window on another to compare different charts. You can tell the program to alert you to exceeded limits by issuing warnings when the price rises or falls by 10% or more or when the volume reaches a certain level. Chart settings can be saved and applied to other security charts. Windows on WallStreet can be set for unattended operation, such as to save money by downloading at night when rates are lower. It can work with TC2000, MetaStock, Computrac, ASCII, AIQ, and CSI data.

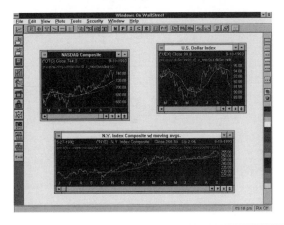

Figure 7.5 Windows on WallStreet manages a portfolio and adds analysis abilities.

Windows on WallStreet gets its ease from the context-sensitive help, the learning mode, and the integration of all elements. The Personal Investment Assistant helps too; it can automate tasks such as charting. And when you're charting, you can work with an unlimited number of securities per chart.

Want sophistication? Windows on WallStreet has moving averages and Bollinger bands, linear and semilog scaling, a library of 500 custom indicators, profitability testing, and more. It can connect to on-line information for fundamental or technical research. Even here, the ease rules, with hints on what price reversals mean, for example. The downloading comes through Dow Jones News/Retrieval, Dial Data, or CompuServe. Windows on WallStreet can even run other Windows programs and keep a list of your appointments—reminding you when the time comes.

Allocation Master

Allocation Master from Frontier Analytics is for the professional financial planner with a Windows PC. It helps balance the various investments that can bring you the return you want with the minimum risk (see Figure 7.6). A graph charts risk versus return. You simply move a red dot to the point you want on the risk/return line, and a pie chart shows the program's recommended allocation of various securities. There's an additional charge for quarterly updates.

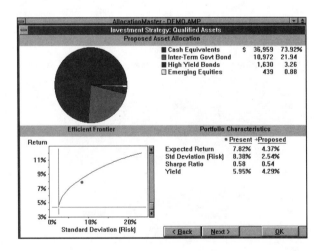

Figure 7.6 Allocation Master balances up to 22 different types of investments.

The program uses long-term financial market relationships to optimize and find the best alternative portfolios for investment. It tries to find the highest return for the chosen risk (volatility) while considering diversification needs, liquidity needs, income needs, time horizon and age, and tax status. In all it balances up to 22 different investment categories including large and small capitalization stocks, intermediate and long-term government bonds, T-bills, CDs, international stocks and bonds, and real estate. And all of this is done with the Modern Portfolio Theory, part of recent Nobel prize economy theory. Projections can run up to 75 years and consider both inflation and taxes (see Figure 7.7). Market indices followed include S&P stock indices, Dow Jones Stock Averages, AMEX, NYSE, NASDAQ Stock indices, Salomon Brothers Bond indices, Lehman Brothers bond indices, Merrill Lynch Bond indices, Federal Reserve money market yields, economic indicators, Mutual Fund returns and averages, real estate, precious metals, commodities, international stock indices, and international bond indices. The 300-page manual explains all of this. The company also makes other software for Asset Optimization Model, Endowment/Foundation model, Defined Benefit Model, and Defined Contribution Model.

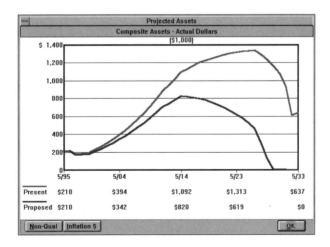

Figure 7.7 Allocation Master can project up to 75 years, correcting for inflation and taxes.

Destiny

Another planning program with a built-in portfolio manager is Destiny from Comtrad Industries. Besides the calculations for savings, retirement, and tuition, this DOS program helps you balance asset allocation to reach your goals. It will adjust the suggested balance as your wants and age change. It comes with a 30-day money-back guarantee.

FolioMan 1.3

Although it doesn't have any graphics yet, this DOS portfolio manager is famous for its thorough tracking of the cost basis of investments in your portfolio in order to figure your capital gains for taxes.

Investment Basics

This Mac program from Competence software manages and tracks investments. It is planned to be the first in a series of seven investment tutorials about stocks, bonds, mutual funds, and futures.

On-Line Quotes and News

Every major on-line service has continuously updated financial news and data. Members can get at it, sometimes for free, sometimes for added fees or surcharges depending on what the information is. Stock market quotes are usually subject to the 15-minute delay—they are only updated every 15 minutes—with immediate quotes costing extra; delayed quotes are always less expensive. (Check to see what quote service comes with any analysis or trading program you get. For example, you can get up-to-the-minute quotes for free with a Charles Schwab account on Genie.)

The on-line services also have information such as company annual reports, pundit opinions, economic indicators, earnings statements, industry analyses, tax information, and the latest business news. They have bulletin board areas with discussions and arguments about investments. Prodigy, for example, has a MoneyTalk bulletin board with more than 300 topics on stocks and bonds.

Personal Journal is a new on-line service from Dow Jones that delivers personalized news and quotes.

Reuters Money Network

The Reuters Money Network from Reality Technologies is an on-line service that comes through a program on your PC as a personal financial newspaper. You choose what's important to you and your portfolio, and each time you sign on to the network, a new edition of your paper will appear with the relevant prices and news filled in on the screen (see Figure 7.8). The information includes databases on more than 18,000 investments; 15-minute delay quotes from NYSE, AMEX, and NASDAQ; news; fundamental stocks; bonds; a complete Standard & Poor's Research database on 500 stocks and 6000 bonds; the best of Morningstar on mutual funds, historical pricing charts, and even broker access (discussed later in this chapter) (see Figure 7.9). The software, which runs on PCs with Windows, will sort, filter, and graph those securities by your own criteria. The integrated portfolio manager will let you know how you are affected.

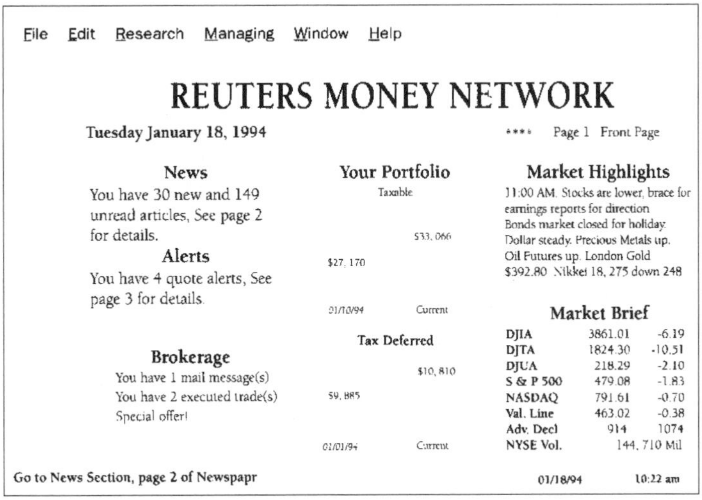

Figure 7.8 Reuters Money Network offers quotes.

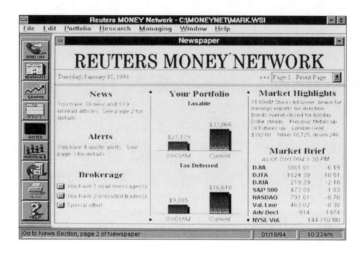

Figure 7.9 Reuters Money Network offers securities screening and a clipping service.

CompuServe

CompuServe is the world's largest consumer on-line service. It has plenty of financial information including access to databases, opinions, and research tools. The Company Analyzer (which is called Ticker Retrieval) gives information including current quotes, Value Line statements, forecasts, Standard & Poor's reports, security information from MicroQuote, and recent company news sent over all major news wires. The Investor's Forum contains discussions on financial topics.

The Company Analyzer program (use the command **Go Analyzer** to get it) summarizes company ownership, price, and financial information from many databases including Standard & Poor's. It costs $1 to $30 depending on how long you browse and what you get. The **Go Trend** command will generate price/volume graphs, but you can only view these with an interface program such as the CompuServe Information Manager or Procomm Plus for Windows or by paying $1 per chart to see them on screen. The **Go Screen** command will screen stocks by book value, market value, growth rate, debt/equity ratio, market/book ratio, earnings/share ratio, price/earnings ratio, and yield. This costs $5 per screen plus $0.25 per issue. For current quotes, you can use the **Go Basicquotes** command (see Figure 7.10). Historical prices can be had with **Go Prices** for $0.05 per quote. *Money Magazine*'s mutual fund database appears with **Go Fundwatch** to screen funds by type (growth, balanced, or income); performance periods; loads; expense; and other variables. **Go Invforum** takes you to the investor discussions. There are specialty areas here devoted to analysis programs such as MetaStock, which is described later in this chapter. In addition, CompuServe can analyze securities (see Figure 7.11).

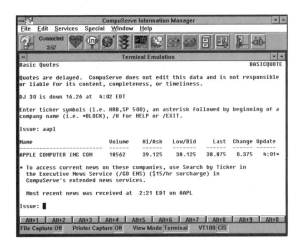

Figure 7.10 CompuServe offers stock quotes.

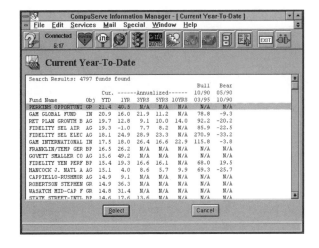

Figure 7.11 CompuServe can analyze securities.

America Online

America Online is the fastest growing on-line service. One reason is the software that you can get for free from many sources, including most computer magazines. This software contains some intelligence that resides in your computer, and it makes the service easier to use than a simple telecommunications program and simpler than some bare-bones interfaces such as CompuServe's used to be.

Along with all its other information, you can use America Online to get stock summaries and financial data (see Figure 7.12). You can even use the America Online interface program as a portfolio minder (see Figure 7.13). You look up prices by typing the first few letters of the name (AOL will look it up). You are then asked if you want to include them in future portfolio updates, and you'll be prompted for the number of shares and their original purchase price. When you dial into America Online, you'll see the closing prices and how they affected your portfolio's value. The keyword *Morningstar* will take you to the Morningstar Mutual Funds area, where the famous financial information provider rates funds.

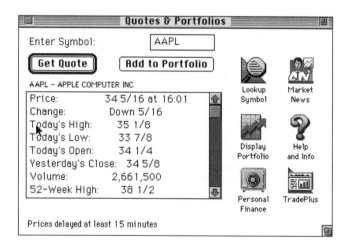

Figure 7.12 America Online offers stock quotes.

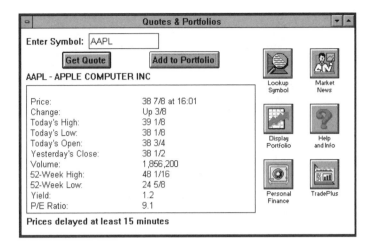

Figure 7.13 America Online has a portfolio manager.

Dow Jones News Retrieval

The Dow Jones News Retrieval service can be reached through several on-line services. One other way to get to DJNR is via MCI Mail's E-mail service. In Dow Jones News Retrieval, you can download the latest prices and volume data and scan the news wires. The software can do this automatically, saving you on-line time. Then you can use the Market Analyzer Plus software to look at moving averages and smoothing swings and to watch for rising volume, falling volume, and more exotic indicators such as relative strengths.

Market Manager Plus is a portfolio manager for those using Dow Jones News Retrieval for quotes and news. It includes a calendar for financial dates such as bond maturities, dividends due, and option expirations.

Other On-Line and CD-ROM Sources of Quotes and News

Quicken Deluxe for Windows comes with a Quicken Quotes utility (see Figure 7.14).

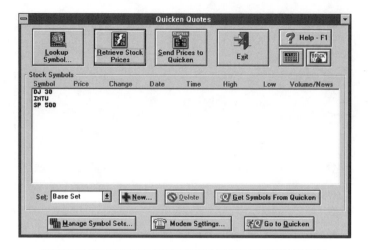

Figure 7.14 Quicken on CD-ROM has a stock quotes utility.

U.S.Equities on Floppy from Morningstar holds 200 variables for 6140 stocks. You can search through them by market performance or review individual profiles. Then you can create custom reports that rank the stocks by the criteria you choose.

The Disclosure SEC database of public companies includes current and historical financials, profile information, and full-text management information and analysis on more than 11,000 public companies. You enter the name of the company or search by any of 20 criteria, including current ratio, sales, market value, and cash flow. You get to it on CompuServe, with the command **Go Disclosure**. Then, for a demonstration, type **HRB** for a free record on H&R Block.

StockTracker is an automatic stock quote service that depends on CompuServe. Use the **Go Virgil** command for a demo; use **Go Oli** for information on the service. You'll find stock prices, news, company reports, and price/volume charts. You can retrieve current stock, mutual fund, or option prices and immediately calculate the value of your portfolio from them. The software makes many tasks into one-button click operations for company news, reports, charts, and histories. The Standard & Poor's report includes information on historical earnings, dividends, market action, and fiscal history. You can create a schedule for the program, which will then automatically update your portfolio. If you have the Basic Services plan in CompuServe, all the current quotes are free. The software costs $60 and runs on PCs with Windows.

Global Report is a service of Citibank. It offers quotes and prices U.S. Treasuries, international money markets, global indexes, interest rates, equities, and currencies. You'll also get commentaries by analysts. The program lets you build your own custom tickers. The Autosearch feature lets you find information such as company profiles, country reports, calendars, and breaking business news for the global market. The foreign exchange, major secondaries, and exotics are updated as the trades occur 24 hours a day.

Knight-Ridder is one of the largest newspaper chains in the United States (I write a column that is syndicated by the Knight-Ridder-Tribune newswire.) The Knight Ridder End-of-Day Prices and News service provides final market results, end-of-the-day futures prices, options volatility, and cash data for more than 360 markets. You'll find daily open, high, low, and close prices and total volume for U.S., European, and Asian markets. There are a variety of costs, depending on which sets of information you choose, starting at $20 per month; you can try it with a free five-day demo.

Track OnLine from Track Data Corporation provides real-time quotes and news that you can set up in pages with scrolling headlines, alerts, and interactive quotes. To help you, there's a command to search for the ticker symbols for particular stocks. You can review the time and sales for stocks and search a database full of fundamentals, including insider trading from Vickers. It costs $95 per month but you can start with a two-week free trial.

Dow Jones Market Monitor on-line data is frequented by professional brokers and traders. It carries news and information on companies, markets, industries, stocks, bonds, mutual funds, and insider buying and selling. You can use it to compare fund performance, view historical quotes, access buy and sell recommendations, and read articles from the *Wall Street Journal*. It costs $30 per month for access from 7 p.m. to 6 a.m. You may be able to get the start-up fee waived, and you may get a month free when you sign up for a four-month subscription.

The Data Transmission Network (DTN) offers electronic quotes and news for $40 per month. The quotes are on a 15-minute delay for stocks and bonds, but are immediate for indices, futures, funds, government issues, interest rates, currencies, metals, petroleum, commodities, and news. You can use DTN with a stand-alone terminal or on your own PC or Mac; the start-up fee differs, depending on which you choose. There's a 30-day money-back guarantee.

Signal is a PC-based quote system from Data Broadcasting Corporation. It uses on-screen graphics to make the data look like 3-D objects—supposedly making it easier to search through and use. The quotes come in via radio, so you can hook your PC up to Signal almost anywhere.

The Stock Data Corporation packs five years of U.S. stock market data on CD-ROM for $500. Or you could download it by modem, getting about 9000 issues in 1.5 minutes.

StockQuoter 2 from Advanced Wireless Communications moves stock quotes as a hidden part of the TV signal. This doesn't require a modem. You get

15-minute-delayed stock market quotes on more than 15,000 stocks and real-time market indices on the NYSE, ASE, NASDAQ, and OTC exchanges. You also get the USA Today Decisionline electronic newspaper and NewsWire services. It's a little complex—you have to plug a circuit board into your PC, attach the antenna, pay your $25 a month, and then download your quotes, perhaps even exporting them directly to Excel.

You can get the full text of *Money Magazine*'s 1990s' monthly issues, as well as full-motion video clips on financial subjects on the *Money Magazine* on CD-ROM. From Laser Resources, it includes a text-search utility that will help you look up anything of interest in those articles. It is available for either PC or Mac.

Fundamental Analysis Programs

Fundamental analysis of securities means predicting future prices from factors including quality of company management, prospects for company products, and prospects for the company's industry as a whole. Fundamental analysis does concern itself with price statistics such as price-to-earnings ratio, but it also takes into account the impact of world news on the company. Unlike technical analysis, which tries to predict prices solely from mathematical patterns in historical prices, fundamental analysis tries to understand what's happening in business and the world.

Here are some programs that specialize in fundamental analysis. Remember that some will also have technical analysis features.

The Telescan System and Telescan Analyzer 3.0

Telescan combines on-line information gathering and analysis, although to get the whole bag of tools you'll pay a lot extra. Using Telescan you'll find both fundamental and technical data—more than 200 variables and screens—and you can use up to 40 at once. It retrieves news from Reuters, UP, Business Wire, and more; insider trading filings; Standard & Poor's reports and MarketScope; Wall Street Week; Dan Dorfman's writings; and 22 sample newsletters. Of course, there are also quotes from NYSE, AMEX, NASDAQ, and the Canadian Exchanges, which are updated on a 15-minute delay. There is a surcharge for Morningstar and Macro*World stock data. The price and volume information goes back to 1973 on more than 77,000 issues.

The built-in stock evaluation program combines more than 80 technical charting tools with fundamental analysis to confirm buy/sell decisions (see Figures 7.15 and 7.16). It can weight the criteria you choose and construct searches off-line to save you on-line charges. You can run on-line at up to 9600 bps.

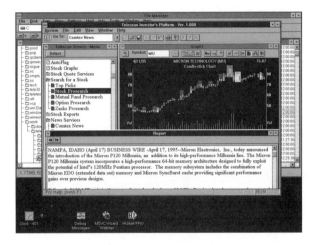

Figure 7.15 Telescan has fundamental analysis tools.

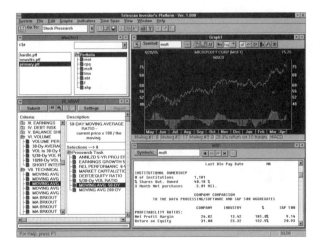

Figure 7.16 Telescan also has technical analysis charting.

Options include the Options Search program, QuoteLink (for downloading current and historical quotes), Mutual Fund Search, Profit Tester/Optimizer, Portfolio Manager 3.0, and Options Analyzer.

Macro*World Investor

Macro*World Investor correlates economic and financial trends to the history of a stock's price. It is full of advice on national and international trends that could affect a stock. Although you could learn these things from reading magazines and newspapers, the program lets you correlate the data to the price histories. You might think of it as technical analysis for the world. The program can show you what has historically predicted the stock's price. Of course, there's no guarantee that the same factors will continue to predict, but there's hope.

Macro*World Investor runs on a PC and needs a 9600-bps modem and comm software—it isn't built-in—to get data updates. It costs $700, which includes six monthly updates; additional updates are $40 each.

Money Maker 2.0 for Windows

This program from Q-West Associates combines fundamental analysis and portfolio tracking with a communications module for automatic security-price downloading via CompuServe. It also has a charting module for technical analysis of stocks, bonds, options, futures, mutual funds, and real estate. The advanced features cover hedging strategies through puts, calls, and straddles.

There are a dozen reports including transaction details and price histories for individual securities. You can print reports for average cost, with both realized and unrealized profits. The tax reports cover ordinary income and capital interest expenses.

Value/Screen III

This program comes with Value Line's stock rankings, statistics, and projections, and it contains more than 80,000 data items on more than 1600 companies. The data is updated monthly. This includes Value Line's Timeliness and Safety rankings and business summaries in text—not just numerics. It can export data to a spreadsheet, database, or word processor.

Here you can screen stocks using 49 built-in criteria and up to 20 more criteria you can add. These include checking equities with high appreciation potential, sales price below book value, financial strength, cash flow per share, and earnings growth. It comes in both PC and Mac versions. You can try it for two months for $60.

Quant IX 5.0

This PC program combines portfolio management with fundamental analysis. For $60 you get the ability to create six different models to estimate stock values suing methods such as earnings growth. A what-if function projects the effect of events such as earnings surprises on interest rates.

Stock Investor

You'll find 100 statistics on 8100 companies on this disk from the American Association of Individual Investors. But the windows are hard to read and the screening depends entirely on your own knowledge; there are no preset variables. There are details on buying shares directly from companies, and full addresses.

Mutual Funds Analysis

Mutual funds are collections of securities that are chosen and administered by professionals. You buy shares in the fund and are rewarded if the managers have chosen a mix that adds up to growth. Some funds are quite volatile; others are not. Some funds are riskier than others. Fund track records are pored over in magazines and newspapers and are the topic of many conversations. Most quote services and fundamental analysis programs include mutual funds, but there are some programs that focus on mutual funds by helping you dig through the thousands of funds to find the one that's right for you. Here are some examples of mutual fund analysis programs.

Mutual Fund Selector

This recent release from Intuit lets you filter through many popular mutual funds to find the one that fits your plans. A copy of Mutual Fund Selector comes on the

CD-ROM deluxe version of Quicken. There are eight chapters in the work. In Chapters 1 through 5 you define your goals by answering questions and watching videos of actors—typical husband-and-wife investors. The Investment Advisor asks your personal objectives and feelings and gives you information on investing. In chapters 6 through 8 your look into the database, finding the best funds for you based on their strategies and historical rates of return. The Database of 1000 mutual funds by Morningstar helps you select a particular fund. You get one free database-update disk or pay for a year of quarterly updates. There's no dial-up connection nor any link with Quicken.

Mutual Fund Expert

This program from Steele Systems helps you inspect and compare mutual funds. It is for PCs but doesn't require Windows; there's an OS/2 version. The funds—either 4200 in the pro version or 3300 in the personal version—are listed on the screen. This includes equity and fixed-income funds as well as flexible, municipal bond, international, global, precious metals, and even sector funds. The program can find any particular fund or value and filter and rank them with name, objective, ratings for return, and ratings for risk. You can compare performance, monitor your selected funds, graph and report the results, create sales presentations from these reports, and use the provided toll-free numbers to contact them (see Figure 7.17).

Figure 7.17 Mutual Fund Expert can give you a detailed report on any of its thousands of funds.

The data is current to the month of purchase or your most recent update. When you buy the programs you also buy either quarterly or monthly updates. You scroll through the list until you find the fund you're interested in, or use the **Locate** command to leap directly to it (by name), then choose a fund and ask for a report on it. In the report you see give-year return, year-to-date changes, and other such details.

You can also screen the funds, instead of looking at reports one at a time. Choose the screen menu, then highlight what you care about, and enter the values you want to **Screen** in or out. There are personal and professional versions of the program at different prices.

Morningstar Mutual Funds on Disc and Floppy

Morningstar is probably one of the biggest names in mutual funds. It is famous for its storehouse of information on thousands of funds (see Figure 7.18). Now you can get that information on CD-ROM or floppy disk. Either way you get a manual that explains what funds are, a complete listing of funds with proprietary ratings from one to five stars, at-a-glance performance tables, and a screening program. This can filter through funds by 49 criteria over 3, 5, or 10 years. When you find an interesting fund, you can turn to the extensive detail reports.

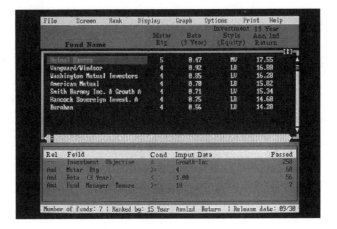

Figure 7.18 Morningstar Mutual Funds has a huge list of screenable fund ratings.

Monocle+

This mutual fund analysis program from Manhattan Analytics keeps a five-year historical database of every mutual fund and lets users dial in daily for fund updates. It can graphically analyze a portfolio of funds. You choose one fund or market index as a baseline and it compares them.

FundMap for Windows

The Charles Schwab discount brokerage, which also makes a trading program called StreetSmart, now has a mutual fund selector called FundMap for Windows. It offers the facts on thousands of funds and Windows program to screen through them. The program also offers some retirement planning and asset allocation abilities.

Other Mutual Fund Programs

Vertigo Development offers Your Mutual Fund Selector, a CD-ROM book and program for Windows. On it, you'll find Morningstar ratings of more than 1000 funds, as well as articles and video clips explaining mutual funds and mutual fund selection.

Markex II Plus version 6.0 is a mutual fund program from Huntington Associates. It keeps up-to-date information funds through downloaded information. The current version is for PCs running DOS, but a Windows version is coming.

The Mutual Fund Investor version 5.2 from American River Software is both a mutual fund database and a portfolio manager aimed at active traders. The current version is for PCs running DOS, but a Windows version is coming.

More than 2500 funds in 16 categories crowd Cauldwell Data CMFunds 2.0. It lets you compare up to 200-color coded funds on screen at once, ranking them by the criteria you choose.

Technical Analysis Programs

Technical analysis is the study of historic prices to predict future prices. There is no thought to the products the companies make, the management of the companies, the world diplomatic situation, or anything except the prices. It is entirely a number-crunching pursuit looking for patterns in the ups and downs of prices. The theory behind technical analysis is that you can predict the future if you find the mathematical patterns in past prices, even if you don't know why those patterns emerge. Technical analysis is also known as *charting*.

There are many technical analysis programs, full of obvious and obscure mathematics techniques, all looking to download data, calculate it, and then suggest buy and sell times according to past patterns. The following pages list some of the technical analysis programs you'll find for PCs and Macs. Remember that some of the fundamental analysis programs just discussed also have some technical analysis capability.

If you have an on-line connection to the Internet, you can find technical analysis discussions in the news group **misc.invest.tech**.

SuperCharts 2.0

SuperCharts 2.0 from Omega Research is perhaps the best-known and advertised technical analysis program. It claims superiority to the next best-known—MetaStock 4.0—because it runs under Windows (and therefore is easier), can chart more data, and has built-in features (such as downloading) that cost extra in MetaStock.

SuperCharts 2.0 has context-sensitive help and icons you can click on for common operations. Data downloading is built in. It can display and scroll through more than 13,000 bars of data. Indicators within can overlay on any chart or display in up to seven dynamically linked subgraphs. Color codes help you see what's important. The Automated Analyst feature alerts you to charts and conditions you're looking for and checks them daily. The System Optimizer is advertised as a "no-wait" feature that can immediately check for moving averages that could be most effective for a particular stock or futures market. It can tell you if the performance of a system you build would be helped or hurt if you add a protective stop or profit target. It can download data, reading standard formats such as MetaStock, ASCII, CompuTrac, Tick Data Inc., TradeStation, and Quotron, and TC2000. You can get a free demo by calling 800-556-2022.

Wall Street Analyst

This new program from Omega, the SuperCharts company, uses fuzzy logic with its charting and analysis to help your computer be not just precise but a helpful analyst. The techniques are sophisticated enough for professionals; the automation and explanations let beginners use it too.

For example, there isn't just on-line context-sensitive help, but actual bear and bull icons that appear with technical or fundamental analysis factors to show the market is headed in one of those directions. This program doesn't just show indicators, it tells you what they mean—you can click on highlighted words in those comments to learn even more. There's an on-screen slide show tutorial on the basics of technical analysis.

The Automated data downloader with scheduler can get information when it's most convenient. Analyst can export updated price data to Quicken for portfolio tracking. The Expert Outlook Window shows a quick summary analysis. Charting includes price, point & figure, candlestick, and volume histogram charts with an unlimited number of indicators per chart and up to seven dynamically linked subgraphs per chart. The Automated Analyst can scan hundreds of charts daily to alert you to potential buy/sell opportunities based on price and volume indicators such as new highs, unusually high volume, rapidly increasing volatility, moving averages, stochastics, relative strength index, Bollinger Bands, and others. Fundamental analysis isn't left out, with price-to-earnings ratios, dividend payout history, earnings history, and sales growth over last five years also grist for the mill.

MetaStock 4.0

Probably the best-known technical analysis program, MetaStock 4.0 from Equis International helps you study the trading patterns of stocks. MetaStock has 80 predefined indicators, can track moving averages, can draw tend lines for stocks or groups of stocks, and lets you create and use your own indicators. The system tester works with automatic optimization. The option worksheet handles volatility and price changes (see Figure 7.19).

The Windows version is Microsoft Office compatible—it even looks something like Office—and has drag-and-drop operation.

MetaStock 4.0 comes with enough documentation and help that it can be considered a course in technical analysis. It offers many optional add-on modules, which could end up costing you a bundle but focus on specific areas of analysis. All of them run on a PC with at least a 386 processor and 2 MB of memory. You'll need a modem—9600 bps is best—for current data. MetaStock 4.0 uses end-of-the-day prices; the more-expensive MetaStock RT uses real-time immediate prices. The Dial/Data single-feed download option costs extra, as does the multiple-feed downloader. The Pulse Portfolio Management System is also extra. There's a free demo disk available.

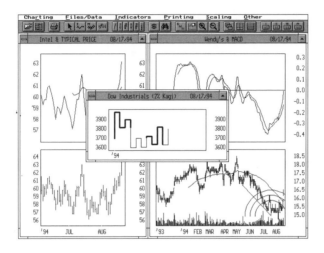

Figure 7.19 MetaStock 4.00.

Nirvana Add-Ons for MetaStock

Nirvana Systems makes software that adds to MetaStock. The Director can automatically test multiple trading systems to identify those that are most accurate for your particular stocks. The goal is to generate the most accurate trading signals possible using the best parameters. It runs tests using 80 systems that are built-in, or you can use your own systems. The Director will filter out stocks that don't meet the criteria you set. It comes with a free instructional videotape. There are four volumes of these trading systems.

TeleChart 2000

You'll see this program from Worden Brothers in many ads. A technical analysis program for stocks and mutual funds, TeleChart 2000 includes a downloading program, a comprehensive toll-free database (with 10,000 stocks and mutual funds), and an advanced charting program.

Other General Technical Analysis Programs

Personal Analyst from Trendsetter Software handles classic charts: Japanese candlestick, point and figure, and barline. It offers a range of technical studies: Gann Fibonacci, stochastics, DMI, CCI, RSI, MACD, and more. It can put these out for daily, weekly, or monthly periods, and put its own trend lines on the results. It can then issue trading recommendations for entry, exit, and stop-loss.

Business Cycle Indicators 1.0 for Windows will graph all sorts of business cycle indicators based on a variety of government numbers. You can zoom in and out, compare the charts smooth data, fiddle with the scaling, and display the Bureau of Economic Analysis business peaks and valleys. There isn't much analysis ability, just charting. You can export to ASCII files for more analysis in programs such as MetaStock.

Ultra Market Advisor 2.0 from Ultra Financial System is an index trading system and personal goal manager. It uses 19 technical indicators and 19 buy/sell/stop rules to give buy and sell signals for mutual fund and index investors. Ultra Market Advisor 2.0 is based on Steve Huter's trading techniques. For PCs, a math coprocessor is recommended. A free demo is available.

Relevance III is an advanced market technical analysis program from Duvall International. It lets you play with Elliott, Gann, Andrews, and Fibonacci schemes.

Q-Trax for Windows 3.0 from EDMS is a technical analysis and portfolio management program that creates comparison charts with up to 36 indicators. It produces trendlines, volatility measures, and candlesticks. The portfolio manager handles everything from buys to dividend reinvestments and updates itself from data files from CompuServe, Prodigy, Dow Jones, or Warner.

Stock Prophet is a general technical analysis program from Future Wave Software. It handles stocks, commodities, and mutual funds. It aims to give you clear signals days—or weeks—before necessary execution dates. There's an interface to BrainMaker for those who want to add neural networks to the mix. It can work with data in the CompuTrac or MetaStock format.

Fourcast Time Series Analysis & Forecasting Software from Engineering Management Consultants has a name that pretty much tells what it does. You can have this software as a demo disk for $5.

CandlePower 4.0 from North Systems focuses on the "candlestick" technical analysis for automatically producing trading signals. It can read data from MetaStock, AIZ-Stk/TEx, Tech Tools, Mega Tech, CompuTrac, Dow Jones RTR, TC-2000, N2/Apex, CSI, and even ASCII (123 PRN files). A free demo version is available.

Artificial Intelligence (AI) and Neural Network Technical Analysis Programs

Neural networks are computer programs that try to emulate the pattern-recognition abilities of the human mind. Given inputs (data from the real world of security prices, typically, or from any other factor a technical analyst might consider), the neural network looks for and "learns" a pattern. Theoretically, this allows a neural network program to learn the pattern of the market, even if the human operator doesn't know that pattern and can't tell it to the program. The learned pattern can then be used to predict the future of the market. There are a number of programs now devoted to using neural network technology to figure out where the market is going. They offer options for adjusting how the net learns. Most of these programs also offer some sort of interface to a more traditional analysis or trading program so the results can be put into practice.

Genetic algorithms are even more up-to-date than neural nets. These mimic natural selection by starting with a large number of possibilities—market movements—and then letting a "survival of the fittest" approach—those that are successful remain, those that aren't are killed off—thin the population of possibilities down to a few, or even one.

Neural nets, genetic algorithms, and other avant-garde mathematical machinations—such as chaos theory—make for exciting reading and plenty of computer-fiddling time, but they are certainly beyond the needs of any but the most dedicated amateur investors. Still, here are some examples of the programs you can try.

BrainMaker

BrainMaker from California Scientific Software builds neural nets. It can import data from Lotus, Microsoft Excel, dBASE, binary, or ASCII files and make predictions about where the data is headed. This can be used for trading strategies for stocks, bonds, and commodities. BrainMaker runs on DOS, Mac, and Windows. The professional version (3.0) has larger limits and more flexibility. It reads MetaStock and CompuTrac files. It lets you create four indicators, can handle six moving averages, and manages recurrence for automating historical data. Finally, it has better graphics and a runtime license so you can distribute trained systems.

There's also a new genetic training option for the professional version. There are standard and professional versions and a genetic option.

Evolver

Using a genetic algorithm, this program from Axcelis breeds a population of solutions. It can work with discontinuous functions, such as lookup tables and if/then statements, as well as with random or noisy data or complex macros. Evolver can handle an unlimited number of variables and constraints. The Evolver/VG toolkit lets you interface with Visual Basic.

Other Neural and AI Technical Analysis Programs

Talon Development's @Brain neural net works with standard spreadsheet programs.

NeuroForecaster/GA 3.0 from NIBS, Inc., puts both neural network and genetic algorithm schemes to work. It evolves and optimizes a network structure featuring hidden layers, hidden nodes, and learning and momentum rates that you can adjust. Pretrained forecasters for daily, weekly, monthly, and six-monthly market indices and stock prices come with it. There's a 30-day money-back guarantee.

Visual Solutions makes neural nets for indicating buy-sell points, fuzzy logic for indicating market trends, and chaos theory to access market predictability. There are even genetic algorithms to develop historical trading decisions. It runs on Windows; you can call for a free demo.

TradingExpert 2.5 from AIQ uses artificial intelligence techniques to generate a bullish-to-bearish ratio on stock analyses. The goal is to improve your risk management. A Profit Manager function lets you set up groups that will be automatically charted.

N-Train from Scientific Consultant Services is a neural net program that can be trained to converge on stock market data, using it as a real-time module for Omega Research's TradeStation program.

Neural Edge Index Trader from Teranet has a Standard & Poor's 500/OEX 100 that combines the pattern-recognition power of neural nets with expert system rules. It aims to identify market turning points using only a few minutes of your time to enter data at the end of each day or even to automatically download data from the Signal quotes system.

EOS from Man Machine Interfaces is a genetic algorithm application framework. You add specific investment rules. It was formerly called EvolvE.

The Outcome Advisor from Patrick Consult Inc. consists of Consult, Consult-I, and Consult Learning. This software analyzes stock portfolio data using not just classical statistics or neural nets but also next-generation analysis algorithms. It claims to outperform rule-based expert systems and fuzzy logic algorithms.

NeuralWare uses neural nets to model market timing and stock selection.

Options and Commodities Technical Analysis

There are a few technical analysis programs that specialize in *options*, those leveraged investments where you bet on the future price of more fundamental securities. *Commodities* are those natural resources—such as soybeans, oil, or pork bellies—that have future prices you can buy or sell short. Here are some examples of options and commodities programs.

Option Master from Option Research hopes to find underpriced and overpriced options on stocks, commodities, and indices. It doesn't require any downloading of information. Based on the book *The Compleat Option Player* by Kenneth R. Trester, it is available for PC, Mac, and the old Apple II computer.

Option Pro from Essex Trading is a technical analysis program for buying and selling options.

The Options & Arbitrage suite of programs from Programmed Press for the PC will analyze and forecast actual or fair values in addition to hedge ratios for investments. These programs use such techniques as Merton Black-Scholes and Stoll-Parkinson and can advise you on both puts and calls. You can get a 30-day free trial for $50.

The Dow Jones Telerate Software for PC or Mac can get on-line, real-time futures quotes 24 hours a day through Telerate. It then uses the CompuTrac technical analysis software to test your theories about those quotes. It handles daily, weekly, and monthly historical analysis for stocks, futures, bonds, derivatives, and cash.

Tick Data can give you all the daily data on 66 commodities and futures from 1968 to the present. You'll see open, high, low, close, volume, open interest, total volume, and total open interest prices. You'll also get a copy of version 6.0 of the Tick software for PCs. This lets you monitor current prices tick by tick via modem. It also lets you view, plot, and convert the data to standard technical analysis formats such as CSI, CompuTrac, ASCII, FutureSource, MetaStock, System Writer Plus, Master Chartists, and Lotus 1-2-3.

Trading Services

Most of the programs in this chapter merely let you analyze investments. For actual buying and selling, you must turn to a licensed brokerage company. You could do this by calling a broker or going down to the office.

Or you could do it through an on-line trading service, either as part of a larger on-line service or through a dedicated securities service. For this, all you need is your computer and a telecommunications program, or you could buy a trading program that includes links to an on-line trading service. This will add portfolio management and security screening to the telecommunications capability. Remember that there is a difference between the on-line trading service and the software that links you to it.

Although you have 24-hour access to the brokerage computer systems with an on-line service, the actual trades are only made during market hours. Still, this lets you upload your trade orders and download the results after hours, presumably when you're off work and the phone charges are lower.

On-line trading often has the advantage of being cheap. You'll find discount brokerage-level commissions and sometimes save another 5 to 10 % off of those. After all, you're using even less of the brokerage's time and personal help than if you call in an order. Several of these programs are profiled here.

Here's a tip, though, before you get started. *Trading costs money.* Commissions can easily drain any profit you make from the trading, or worse. If you're handling a small portfolio, stick to quotes in the newspaper and trade over the phone. The on-line software and time for downloading quotes will cost you more than they're worth. Remember to ask about the different commission schedules and trade availabilities. Acccutrade, for example, has fewer services so it may be cheaper than some of the other discount brokerages. On the other hand, Fidelity and Schwab can cost somewhat more, but they are the only two that give no-commission access to no-load mutual funds. Also ask about quote charges—are they for on-line time, per quote, or both?

Here are some of the companies involved in such trading:

- ⑤ Charles Schwab Brokerage Services (800-334-4455): You can reach Schwab through the Genie on-line service at keyword *Schwab* (or as explained in the next section, directly through Equalizer or StreetSmart programs). You'll get discounts of an additional 10% on orders for stock, bonds, options, and mutual funds.

- ⑤ QuickWay Online Brokerage Service on CompuServe at **Go Qwk** or through American Online is the discount brokerage services from Quick & Reilly (800-634-6214 or 800-541-6431).

- ⑤ Max Ule's Tickerscreen on CompuServe at **Go Trk-1** has a wide range of on-line brokerage services.

- ⑤ PC Financial Network (800-825-5723) on Prodigy at **Jump PCFN** is one of the largest on-line brokers, claiming nearly 10% of daily volume on the NYSE. It is a service of Donaldson, Lufkin & Jenrette. PCFN is available only to Prodigy or Reuters Money Network subscribers, but that makes it work with DOS, Windows, and Mac computers. There is a $40 minimum commission. OTC, mutual funds, corporate bonds, precious metals, U.S. government securities, unit investment trusts, CDs, municipal bonds, options, listed stocks are all available. Users can receive an execution report of the trade within 60 seconds. Market orders, limit orders, all-or-none orders, fill-or-kill orders can all be done on-line, without talking to a broker. Frequent traders get a 25% commission discount (Quote100 is a real-time quote service that works with it). Call 800-TALK-PCF.

- ⑤ Spear Rees & Co. Online is on CompuServe at **Go Spear**. It combines discount on-line brokerage services with a toll-free phone order system. If you place your order on-line or by phone, your on-line portfolio records are automatically updated.

- ⑤ TradePlus on America Online at **Stocklink** lets you establish brokerage accounts for buying and selling shares of stock.

- ⑤ E*Trade Securities (800-786-2575) can be reached through America Online or CompuServe.

- ⑤ Unified Management Corporation (800-862-7283) can be reached only through your own communications software.

- ⑤ Fidelity Investments (800-544-8666) can be reached only through the FOX program, described in the next section.

- ⑤ AccuTrade (800-228-3011) requires your own communications software for a direct connection. AccuTrade has been around for a while, even permitting stock trading via Touch-Tone phone; AccuTrade PC lets you trade through your computer. You may enter orders 24 hours a day, though they'll execute only during normal market hours. You may also view positions, balances, and open orders at any time, as well as receive stock quotes. Trading here costs $0.03 per share commission, no matter the share price, with a minimum of $48. There's no fee for the software, but you need at least $5000 to open an account.

💲 The American Association of Individual Investors (AAII) has a newsletter called *Computer Investing* and a product comparison of on-line brokers. You can call 312-280-0170 to reach the association.

Trading Software

The most integrated approach to on-line trading is to combine communications portfolio management stock screening, on-line information, and on-line trading in a single package. There are several packages to choose from.

Fidelity FOX

Fidelity On-line Xpress, known as FOX and developed by MECA Software (makers of the Managing Your Money personal finance program), is both a portfolio manager and a trading program. Through FOX you can get real-time quotes and send trading orders to the Fidelity brokerage, saving 10% more on commissions on stock and options trades, even below Fidelity's (a giant in mutual funds) discount rates. At times, Fidelity gives you a free first trade, saving up to $40 in commissions, after you buy FOX.

Easier than Schwab's old Equalizer, FOX is not as easy or comfortable as the newer StreetSmart. Nor can it sell short or trade corporate or treasury bonds. It does keep records on your trades, though. FOX also manages a portfolio, including tax lot tracking and instant research. Through FOX, you can reach the Dow Jones News Retrieval, Telescan, or Standard & Poor's MarketScope news and analysis services for historical and real-time quotes (on stocks, options, mutual funds, and market indicators), performance analysis, and company news. And if you're a Managing Your Money user, you may want to have FOX, too; the two work together well. FOX helps keep all the records you'll need and produces the forms for income tax filing.

You need a Fidelity brokerage account to place orders with FOX. The program needs a PC, but not Windows. A Windows version is on the way. FOX buyers get a 30-day free trial of the Telescan System investment information service with technical charting and fundamental analysis tools to screen stocks.

Schwab's Equalizer

Charles Schwab is perhaps the country's most famous discount brokerage house. Many who want to trade stocks at low commissions and with little broker handholding and advice than in traditional brokerages turn to Schwab. The firm was an early entrant into the trading software game with the Equalizer for PCs running DOS.

Now the Equalizer is obsolete, left behind by StreetSmart 1.0, a trading program with more features and flexibility. The Equalizer doesn't have the charting, customizing, Quicken link, or tax form Schedule D abilities of StreetSmart.

Schwab's StreetSmart

StreetSmart is a Windows and Mac program that links you directly to Schwab's computers, where you can trade stocks, bonds, funds, and options (see Figure 7.20). You enter custom orders by setting price or stop limits, price alerts, and short-sales if you like. You even set the timing for the order, such as good for a particular day or good until canceled, or fill or kill. You also set the order size with directives such as all shares must be available or order is null. The Schwab computer will estimate the cost, based on the current quote, and request a confirmation from you. You can tell StreetSmart to dial back later to check the order status.

Like FOX, StreetSmart tracks positions and can pull down research reports and stock and mutual fund prices. But StreetSmart's use of Windows means more menus, colors, and other on-screen elements to make trading easier and more obvious.

You can get up to 100 current quotes for free with each trade. These can be basic quotes with price and volume of the security or extended quotes that mention dividends, price/earnings ratios, and other such data. You can also dial directly into the Dow Jones News Retrieval Service for current and historical news. Or you can dial into the Standard & Poor's MarketScope service and order company reports. You can even read E-mail about your account.

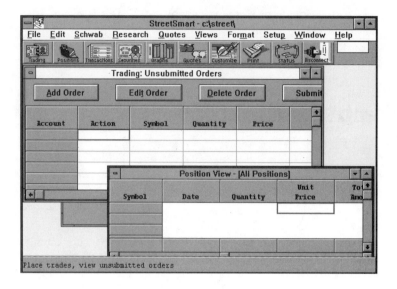

Figure 7.20 Schwab's StreetSmart trading software for Windows or Macintosh.

Within StreetSmart you can view your portfolio through custom views, including or excluding particular data as you like, and sorting the order of up to 18 different types of columnar data. You can graph asset allocation, gains, losses, and other such details.

The program is a decent partner with Quicken, able to import from there, though it would be improved if StreetSmart could also export to Quicken. StreetSmart is also missing a few other tricks, such as reinvesting dividends. It can can create a Schedule D for income tax from your trading results. You need a Schwab account to use StreetSmart. Trades cost about 10% less than a standard discount commission.

Walk-Through Example: Trading with StreetSmart

When you start with StreetSmart, as in this example, first you see the menus and a set of buttons for major operations (see Figure 7.21).

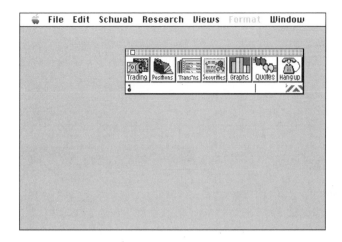

Figure 7.21 Schwab's StreetSmart trading software's initial display.

Perhaps your first step would be research. There's a menu option for that, and windows to hold your requests and the results. That's true for most types of information you want to get from or send to the Schwab brokerage. There are news windows where you can dictate what Dow Jones News stories to get, for example (see Figure 7.22). After you lay your guidelines here, those stories will be collected during your on-line time. Some of the news sources are free; others charge for your time and stories. Naturally you can also get quotes and assign the Quick Quote window for requests.

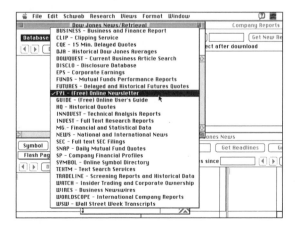

Figure 7.22 StreetSmart's news gathering windows.

Then there are windows to view your portfolio, in positions, and for Schedule D analysis figuring tax on capital gains. Finally, you can see how you would add orders to your list of pending work for Schwab's computers (see Figure 7.239). These would go to Schwab once you signed on to the service. Later you could check your order status and E-mail and see your current account balance.

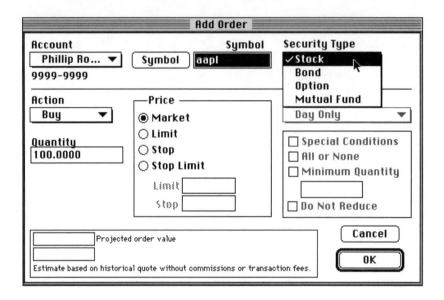

Figure 7.23 Adding a new security transaction order in StreetSmart.

TradeStation

TradeStation is another program from Omega Research; the company that makes the SuperCharts technical analysis program. It will automate any intraday trading system ("real-time," that is, while the market is open, not just after-hours for action the next day). It lets you customize your own indicators that will follow the market on a tick-by-tick basis to buy and sell opportunities, including protective stops and profit targets. There is a free demo.

Summary

If you want to invest via computer, start with the portfolio manager of your personal finance program. See what it can do for recording and tracking any investments you already have. Managing Your Money is probably the best personal finance program for this pursuit.

Then turn to asset allocation and how to divide those moneys you have for investment. WealthBuilder is strongest here, though some of the planning programs discussed in previous chapters can help.

Next, decide what type of investor you will be. Are you going to buy a few stocks, bonds, or mutual funds and hold them for a significant time? I strongly urge this course, because *churning* your portfolio (frequently buying and selling) can cost you dearly in commissions—and even more dearly in time spent watching the market and playing with finance programs. However, if you think you can outguess the market often enough, or are just fascinated by trading, you may decide to be a frequent trader, in some ways, a speculator.

Then analyze, screen, and filter securities to find the ones you want. Use a program such as Wall Street Analyst or Windows on Wall Street to learn about analysis. Your decisions here will differ if you're a long-term holder (you'll look for growth or income, depending on your financial planning) or a speculator (you'll look for quick movements up or down).

CompuServe has some good on-line tools for screening, and WealthBuilder has some built-in tools, too. These should fit the needs of the long-term holder. This type of investor is probably better off without an on-line information service—they'll be looking up prices infrequently enough that a glance at the newspaper now and then should do the trick—or an on-line trading program (just make a call to a discount broker).

Mac users don't have as many choices for analysis or trading, but there are some good programs. WealthBuilder comes in a Mac version, though this isn't as up-to-date as the latest PC version. StreetSmart's latest Mac version is very current. Mac owners should start with the personal finance program, take a look at WealthBuilder or StreetSmart, try some of the analysis programs such as Personal Analyst, and then turn to the on-line programs built into CompuServe or other services.

Speculators should sign up for some on-line information service; CompuServe and Dow Jones rank highly. And they should look for fundamental and technical analysis tools to aid in their quest against the professional money managers. Start with WealthBuilder, add to that perhaps Telescan Analyzer (which fits nicely with Dow Jones), Morningstar Mutual Funds on Floppy, Your Mutual

Fund Selector or FundMap, and SuperCharts or MetaStock (if you believe in charting). If you're a deeply serious analyzer, look to some of the more obscure tools mentioned in this chapter.

Finally, the frequent trader, the speculator, or just the investor wanting the most personal control, should get an on-line trading program. Choose one that fits with the personal finance program and on-line services you have, such as Schwab's StreetSmart for Quicken owners and Fidelity's FOX for Managing Your Money owners.

Update your portfolio, notice any changes in market conditions, then turn off your computer and go outside to play. The worst way to invest is to obsess over your holdings. Too much time sitting in front of your computer screen in your chair is a good way to injure your best investment—your health.

CHAPTER 8

Protect

What happens to your finances when trouble comes along: market catastrophe, illness, death? You should protect your personal financial plan with the right records, habits, insurance, and legal documents. Your computer can help you:

- 🤑 List and record what you have to protect.
- 🤑 Learn how to avoid ripoffs and scams.
- 🤑 Decide what insurance you need.
- 🤑 Create the legal documents you should have.

Keep Records and Inventory

You're using a personal finance program such as Quicken or Managing Your Money, right? That will track all your monetary accounts. Maybe you've added a portfolio manager, such as those described in Chapter 7, to keep more details on your securities. Just make sure you keep your data disks—the ones with your Quicken or StreetSmart or whatever files—backed up. That is, make copies of them regularly and put those copies in a safe place. Better yet, make a couple of copies regularly and keep each copy in a different safe place. For example, make a copy every week of your information and put it in a different room from your computer. Then make another copy every month and keep that in your safe deposit box.

But you also own physical properties, at least most of us do. You should insure those you would want replaced after flood or fire. But before you even consider insurance, you need to record what you have. What better place to keep that list than in your computer?

You'll find that some personal finance programs offer just such a feature.

Quicken

Quicken for Windows, for example, in its CD-ROM version, helps you keep records for backing up insurance claims (see Figure 8.1). (Make sure to create a backup disk and keep it someplace safe away from home.) This home inventory lists and describes all of your belongings (see Figure 8.2). You start with basics, which the program claims can be entered in about an hour, using its reminders, and then add details later.

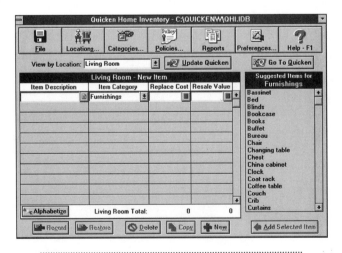

Figure 8.1 Quicken for Windows has a home inventory
program for insurance and estate planning.

Figure 8.2 Quicken's Home Inventory even helps you list where your insurance policies are.

Managing Your Money

Managing Your Money has a similar inventory feature, but instead of being a separate program it is built right into the main structure (see Figure 8.3). This inventory list lets you categorize your possessions in your own way.

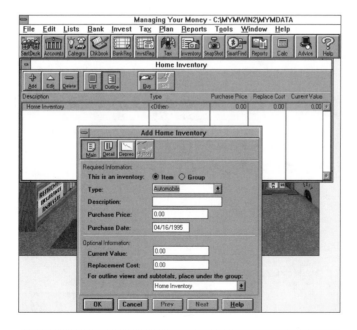

Figure 8.3 Managing Your Money has an inventory feature built in.

Personal Recordkeeper

Far more thorough is Nolo's Personal Recordkeeper 3.0. Available only for Macintosh (there was a DOS version, but it had a bug that lost information), this program gives you a single, organized place to list family, financial, legal, home inventory, medical, insurance and other vital data. It can even export its lists to Quicken, if you're in a mood to examine your net worth including real possessions.

To be more precise, in Personal Recordkeeper you can store: emergency information such as who to notify, child or animal care, living will, power of attorney, and available money; sources of current income; pensions and retirement accounts; securities; real estate; business interests; copyrights and patents; vehicles including boats and planes; home inventory and list of valuables; insurance; money, tax, and legal advisors; people/services/contracts; tax records; credit cards; what you owe; what's owed you; burglar alarms; locked places and where the keys are; hiding place; medical information; memorabilia; personal documents; personal information (including relationships and military record); your family; death plans; and estate matters and your will. That's 27 categories and 200 subcategories (see Figure 8.4). In addition, using that information, the program can compute net worth and print lists of insured property. You select from the categories and subcategories and fill in the blanks. The 200-page manual contains legal and practical advice on estate planning techniques, tax reduction, and probate avoidance. You can even use the Personal Recordkeeper to store some of the stories of your family's history. Figure 8.5 shows how Personal Recordkeeper tracks financial information, including any worker's compensation you may deserve, and Figure 8.6 shows the home inventory ability of the program.

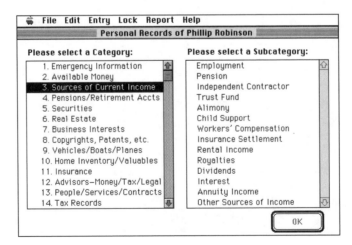

Figure 8.4 Nolo's Personal Recordkeeper offers 27 categories and 200 subcategories of blank forms waiting for details on your life.

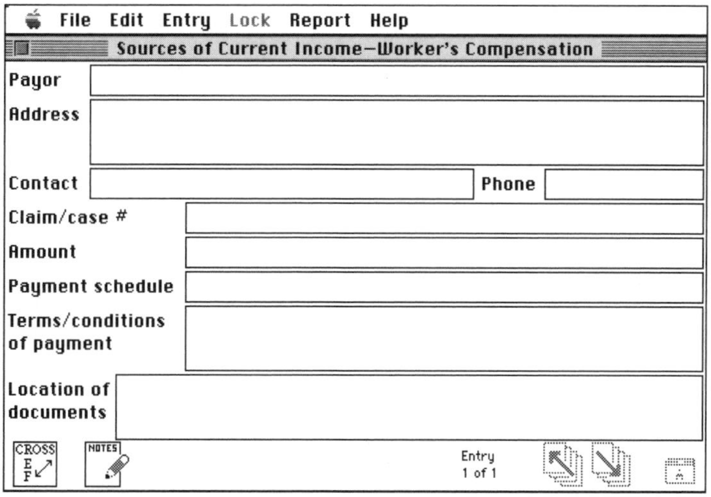

File   Edit   Entry   Lock   Report   Help

Sources of Current Income—Worker's Compensation

Payor

Address

Contact   Phone

Claim/case #

Amount

Payment schedule

Terms/conditions
of payment

Location of
documents

CROSS
E
F

NOTES

Entry
1 of 1

Figure 8.5 Personal Recordkeeper can store financial information, including the facts of any worker's compensation you deserve. This can be vital if you are incapacitated.

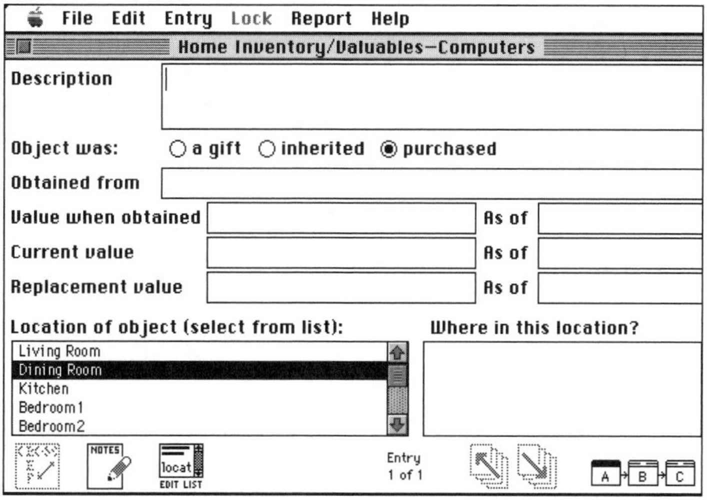

File   Edit   Entry   Lock   Report   Help

Home Inventory/Valuables—Computers

Description

Object was: ○ a gift   ○ inherited   ◉ purchased

Obtained from

Value when obtained   As of

Current value   As of

Replacement value   As of

Location of object (select from list):   Where in this location?

Living Room
Dining Room
Kitchen
Bedroom1
Bedroom2

NOTES

locat
EDIT LIST

Entry
1 of 1

A   B   C

Figure 8.6 Personal Recordkeeper also has a home inventory ability.

Insure

If it's worth earning and monitoring, it's worth insuring. Your financial plans and your budgets should include enough money to insure your:

- 🐷 life
- 🐷 health
- 🐷 work (disability)
- 🐷 house
- 🐷 automobile
- 🐷 possessions
- 🐷 computer

But how do you know how much insurance to get? I haven't seen software that will tell you all you need to know about insurance, but I have seen pieces of insurance wisdom tucked inside personal finance programs. Often you'll find these in the planning programs described in Chapter 2. For example, the ActiveBooks from Vertigo pack both text descriptions of insurance and resources for getting the most insurance for the least money.

Computers are sometimes covered under homeowner policies—sometimes not. It depends on your insurance company, the policy you choose, the total value of your computer hardware and software, and even whether it is primarily for personal or professional use.

Wall Street Journal Personal Finance Library

The Wall Street Journal Personal Finance Library from Vertigo offers general information of many types of insurance (see Figure 8.7). It is an ActiveBook with a built-in calculator that gives tips on many financial matters, including insurance (see Figure 8.8).

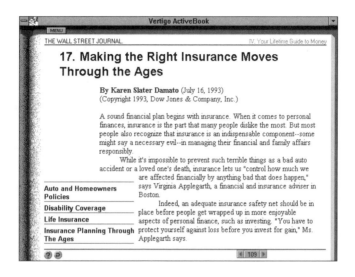

Figure 8.7 The Wall Street Journal Personal Finance Library offers general information on several types of insurance.

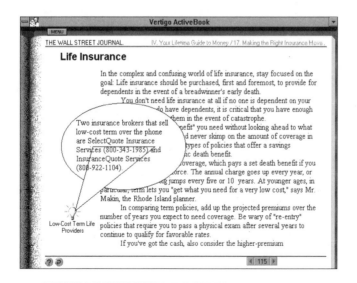

Figure 8.8 The Personal Finance Library is an ActiveBook with built-in calculators and tips, such as these on insurance.

Managing Your Money

Managing Your Money may not be as big a seller as Quicken, but it is a more complete program, with features such as life insurance planing and calculation built right in. It can help you estimate your life insurance needs in three steps: life expectancy, replacement dollars necessary, and the probable cost of those insurance dollars (see Figures 8.9 to 8.11).

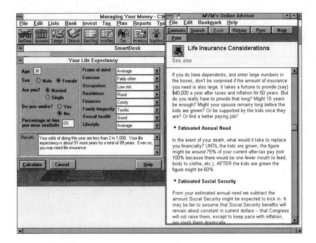

Figure 8.9 Managing Your Money flavors its insurance calculations with relevant and humorous advice.

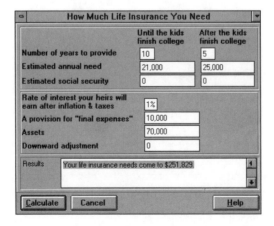

Figure 8.10 Managing Your Money calculates how much insurance you need.

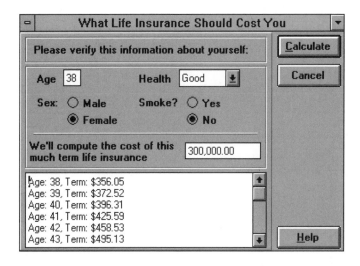

Figure 8.11 Managing Your Money estimates how much your insurance should cost.

For now you'll have to turn to human advisors and books to learn what insurance you should get. But in the meantime you can encourage software makers to follow and extend Managing Your Money's scheme of questioning, calculating, and advising you on insurance amounts and types.

Avoid Scams and Rip-Offs

There's another form of insurance you need. A necessary element of any financial plan, it's called *Caveat Emptor*: Buyer Beware. No matter how hard you work to make money, how much you sacrifice to save it, and how thoroughly you analyze investment opportunities to grow it, you can still lose a little—or a lot—to all the people out there working hard to steal it.

You need to be smart when buying a house, a car, or, for that matter, any large item, even stocks, bonds, and real estate. You can't get smart automatically or instantly, but you can head in that direction. There are two rules of thumb to carry you in the right direction:

1.   Always ask "what's in it for you (the seller)" when someone tries to sell you something.

2. Always say "I'd like to think it over and discuss it with my spouse or parents or best friend" before buying anything.

The first is key because it will make sense of all sorts of "special" offers you get. "This is sure to double in value in a year," someone will say. If so, why are they selling it to you? Why don't they keep it and have twice their own money in a year? "This would be a deal at twice the price," someone else will say. If so, why don't they sell it at twice the price?

The second is important because many scams are "one-time things" or "you must act now" deals. Quick action means less thinking time, and less thinking time means less likelihood you'll see through the scam.

And while you're keeping those rules in mind, you can turn to some programs on your computer for words of wisdom on buying and selling intelligently.

Your Best Money Moves

The ActiveBooks again come in handy, with words and tips on finance. In this case, turn to the Your Best Money Moves disc for its insights on consuming (see Figures 8.12 and 8.13).

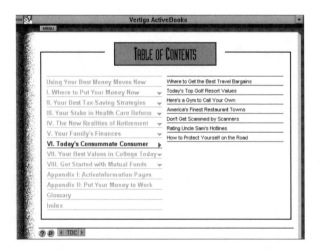

Figure 8.12 The Your Best Money Moves ActiveBook includes several chapters on avoiding bad deals.

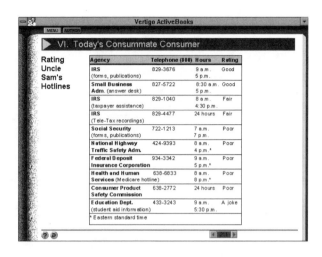

Figure 8.13 Within the text of Your Best Money Moves are explanations and resources, such as this table of government information numbers.

Clark Howard's Consumer Survival Kit

Clark Howard's Consumer Survival Kit focuses on smart buying. Mr. Howard's public relations folks bill him as "one of America's premier consumer advocates." Now his syndicated radio show advice has been packaged as a CD-ROM from The Mescon Group. On it you'll read, see, and hear (with 50 minutes of video) Clark's ideas on car leasing, disability insurance, divorce, and telemarketing scams (see Figures 8.14 and 8.15). There's an index and a variety of search commands for finding what you want to know. With the sections on budgeting for vacation, selling a house, and investing a 401(k) payout, this disc could aid your planning.

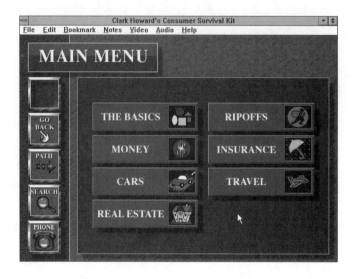

Figure 8.14 Clark Howard's Consumer Survival Kit contains advice on planning in many areas.

Figure 8.15 Clark Howard suggests what to look out for and offers specific letters and other tools for avoiding trouble.

Wills

Only 30% of Americans have a will, and that's usually because of procrastination, not expense. There are computer programs that will help you start putting a will together. The wills they generate are completely legal documents. I wouldn't just pop them up on screen, print them out, and send them off. But if I can take a basic document to my attorney and say "please give this the once-over to make sure I haven't missed anything big," I expect to pay for fewer of his or her hours. With this legal software costing only $10 to $200, I only need to save a few minutes of bill-able time to be ahead of the game.

Another return on your legal software investment is understanding. These programs, including Jonathan Pond's ActiveBook on financial planning, can include clear explanations of the legal whys and whens of the various documents and terms (see Figure 8.16). That'll save you attorney time too, plus make you a smarter legal consumer.

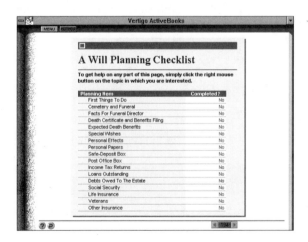

Figure 8.16 Jonathan Pond's ActiveBook on financial planning includes information on wills, such as this checklist.

What should you look for in legal software? First, it should have the documents you need, whether personal or business or some specific category of either. Second, it should customize the document as much as possible, molding it for your own family, estate, business, or locale. Laws differ some from state to state, but all except Louisiana and the possessions (such as Puerto Rico) are similar on many basic documents. Next, the program should be easy to use—find the right document, fill in the blanks, check for omissions. Finally it should be flexible in producing the document—it should allow you to preview it before printing, then print or export it to a word processor for polishing, even advise you where and how to send or save it.

Remember, *run it by an attorney*. You'll have saved money anyway. The attorney won't need as much time because you'll have carved out most of the major issues.

It's Legal

This inexpensive program from Parsons Technology for DOS or Windows helps you draw up a will and many other legal documents. It includes 41 personal, business, and consumer legal documents, all reviewed by attorneys, that are legal in 49 states and the District of Columbia (see Figure 8.17). (Louisiana has a different law, with a very different structure from all other states. Some of these documents won't be official there.) It guides you through filling in the blanks of the forms with a glossary and plain English descriptions. When you finish, there's a page preview feature so that you can see the document on screen as it will print. It's Legal also tells you which signatures will be necessary and advises you on safekeeping of the document, and it stores your notes on where you put the document. There's also a Canadian version. A CD-ROM version includes more legal information guides. As a freebie, along with It's Legal you get a copy of the InterestVision calculator program. You type in loan, annuity, savings, and investment amounts, and InterestVision calculates the missing values—how large the payments are, for how long, at what interest rate, and so on. It is surprisingly powerful for a quick and cheap program. It even offers a choice of different compounding periods and deposits in either advance or arrears (beginning or end of a period).

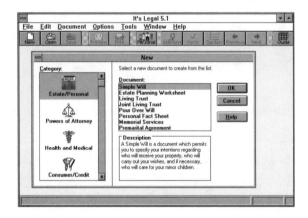

Figure 8.17 It's Legal helps you create, sign, and store 50 different legal forms, including wills.

Home Lawyer

The same company that sells the Managing Your Money personal finance program also makes a PC legal program called Home Lawyer. It has 16 legal documents including wills, powers of attorney, employment forms, credit and collection documents, a consumer complaint letter, leases, and bills of sale. The program interviews you to see what you need, and from your typed answers suggests which topics you should read and follow. When you're done, the program creates a document you can print or move to a word processor.

LegalPoint for Windows

LegalPoint for Windows also starts by asking for personal information. Then you see its list of documents by category or name. You can ask LegalPoint to search through all of its documents for any that contain particular words. The categories are Financial, Sales and Marketing, Personnel and Employment, Sales and Purchase of Goods, Corporate, Technology, Real Estate, and Personal Asset Protection. That last category includes wills, living wills, and powers of attorney. The other categories have half-a-dozen to a dozen specific documents each, 82 in all, mostly for business (see Figure 8.18). Point to any of these and you'll see a short description of the uses of the document. Click on a **Help** button and you can read page-long descriptions of what the document is for and why you would use it. Once you choose a document, it will appear with important technical phrases in green—you can double-click on them to see background information and explanation. The phrases in red—surrounded by brackets—are also "double-clickable." But these are the blanks you must fill, so the explanations that appear guide you in customizing the document. As you work through the document, filling these phrases, there are buttons to automatically leap forward or backward to any unfilled blank. There's both clear and organized help information on using the program and context-sensitive business law information available at all times. You'll also discover that LegalPoint has rulers, font choices, and alignment and tabbing options, as well as cut, copy, and paste commands. LegalPoint can then print documents or save them in the RTF (rich text format) disk file that most word processors can pull in for more polishing.

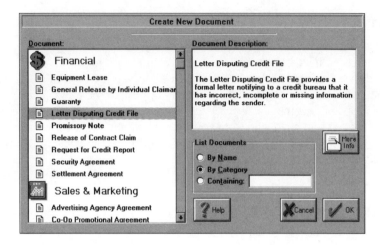

Figure 8.18 LegalPoint for Windows can help make wills, although it focuses more on business documents.

PC Attorney

PC Attorney (Cosmi Software, 310-886-3510, for Windows at $14.95 list or for DOS at $10.95 list) packs 60 personal legal documents and is as simple as it is cheap. You choose a document—from prenuptials to wills—and the program asks for the details it needs to fill in the blanks. There's help available, but it isn't as thorough as in the competition. When you're done, the document is saved in Windows Write format. The documents aren't tailored to any particular state; they seem to be the least-common-denominators acceptable in most jurisdictions. Cosmi also makes a business version called PC Attorney Office Edition for DOS with business forms and the PC Law Library for DOS or Windows, which combines the personal and business, with more than 200 forms, for $34.95 list. They're all the lowest commercial software prices you'll find anywhere and are sold through such stores as Wal-Mart and Target.

WillMaker

Nolo Press, famous for its books that demystify legalese and for its collections of lawyer jokes, makes a variety of legal software targeted at specific documents. This software tends to lack the latest, shiniest appearance on the computer screen—the interface is even a little ugly—but it has the most extensive explanations and advice of any legal software I've seen. Each also comes with a book that further expands on the law and what you can do about it.

WillMaker 5.0 does only wills, but does them well. It comes in Windows, DOS, and Macintosh versions. WillMaker interviews you about your life—dependents, belongings, responsibilities—and uses your answers to create a legal will (Figure 8.19). It highlights the important issues and asks you for decisions on what goes to whom, offering clear explanations of the legal meanings of trusts, beneficiaries, and other such terms. There are even examples, often the clearest kind of explanation, something the other programs should try. You can then print the will. Unlike the brochure-size "how to find the commands" manuals that come with most legal programs, here you'll find a hefty book all about the program and the relevant law.

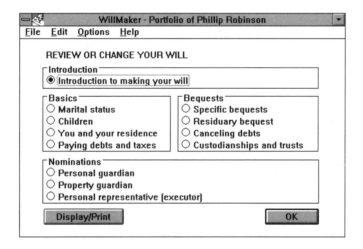

Figure 8.19 WillMaker walks you through all the details of creating a will and produces a legal document you can store or pass by an attorney for a professional opinion and polishing.

WillMaker handles:

💲 State and inheritance taxes;

💲 Estate planning;

💲 Choosing an executor;

- 💰 Handling debts;
- 💰 Naming a trust guardian for children;
- 💰 Choosing the best way to leave property to minor children;
- 💰 Providing management for property left to minors;
- 💰 How marriage affects property ownership;
- 💰 Keeping the will current.

The result should be a document that will legally establish what you want to give to each person including, through the Uniform Transfer to Minors Act trust, which guardian will take charge of your minor children. You can use it legally or have a lawyer review it.

For living wills or health care directions—the sort of thing you might want in case of a coma or terminal illness—WillMaker guides you through the following:

- 💰 Types of final medical care to consider;
- 💰 Directing health care if you have a terminal condition;
- 💰 Directing health care if you are in a permanent coma;
- 💰 Choosing a person to see that your wishes are followed;
- 💰 How pregnancy may affect your situation.

The result will tell others whether you want your life prolonged artificially and what procedures you approve in advance.

For final arrangements, WillMaker walks you through the following:

- 💰 Body and organ donations
- 💰 Burial and cremation details
- 💰 Choosing a mortuary
- 💰 Ceremonies
- 💰 Funerals
- 💰 Markers, epitaphs, and obituaries

WillMaker has legal and program help from a company that has been publishing self-help legal books for two decades. You use its interviews to make your choices. That is, you don't have to know what to look for, you just answer questions about your circumstances and your wishes.

Living Trust Maker

Living Trust Maker 2.0 for Windows or Macintosh follows a similar procedure. Instead of a will, though, this program makes a revocable living trust for a single person or a couple. Done right, this can avoid some of the trouble of probate—the process of settling your estate after you die (Figure 8.20). Thought a will was enough? Often it's not. Items left through a will must work through the probate process. Living trusts aren't probated this way. It all works more smoothly if you've given much of your estate away before you die, with rules allowing you its use as long as you survive. This also helps to handle your estate if you're incapacitated. The interview makes it easy. The explanations are again the star of the program, such as the advice on choosing between a child's subtrust or a custodianship. The manual is thick and complete.

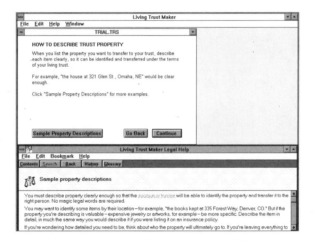

Figure 8.20 Living Trust Maker walks you through the steps of making a living trust that will help you pass on your possessions while losing the least to probate and the state.

Tutorial Example Using WillMaker

When you start using WillMaker, you answer a series of questions about the locations and names of those to whom you want to leave your estate. As you answer, WillMaker will show you the phrases it is building for the will (see Figure 8.21).

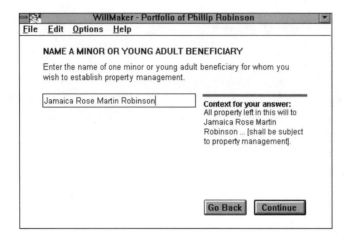

Figure 8.21 WillMaker asks for names and details and shows how it is using those in the will.

Many of WillMaker's questions offer simple choices—click in the box next to the answer you want. If you need to know more about the choice, you can press the **F1** key for help related to the current question (see Figure 8.22).

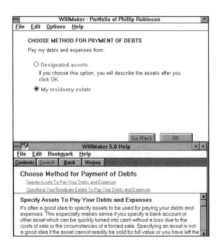

Figure 8.22 WillMaker offers help directly concerning the question on screen.

When you're done with the questions, you can display, print, or export the will (Figure 8.23). You may also go back and change answers, now or after inspecting your will.

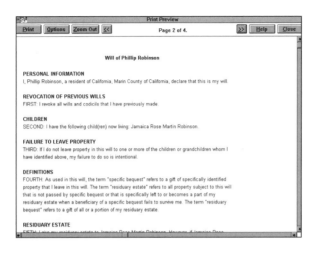

Figure 8.23 WillMaker displays your finished will on screen.

WillMaker then offers similar interviews for creating documents that will direct your health care—if you can't tell the doctors what you want—and your final arrangements when dying or dead. You can create portfolios of these documents for more than one person, and WillMaker will track which are complete and which in process (Figure 8.24).

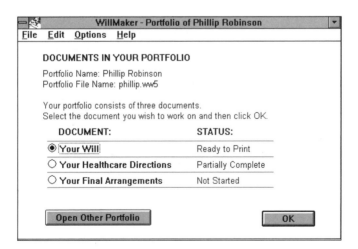

Figure 8.24 WillMaker can make several kinds of documents for more than one person.

Take your finished works, pass them by your favorite attorney, and have them witnessed legally and stored safely.

Summary

Protecting money can be as hard as making it. Record what you have, keep it insured adequately, avoid blowing it on bad buys, and pass it on to your heirs or favorite charities instead of just letting it fall to the state. Software can help you every step of the way, though you'll find great programs for recording (such as the inventory features inside Quicken or Managing Your Money or the entire Personal Recordkeeper program) and for willing to your heirs (WillMaker particularly); decent programs for warning you about scams (the ActiveBooks or Clark Howard's CD-ROM); and only the barest help for insurance (calculators here and there, a little written advice, and the life insurance calculator inside Managing Your Money).

Your next step, the step that doesn't ever have to end, is to learn more. Chapter 9 tells you how to use your computer to find more information on personal finances, especially by going "on-line" through a modem.

CHAPTER 9

Learn

You can always improve your personal financial plans by learning more. More about your money choices, more about your computer's abilities to help, and even more about yourself.

Don't take this too far, though. Don't think that you must learn more and more just to have a fighting chance in the financial world. You'll get most of the benefit of personal financial attention from the basics. Pretty soon you'll move into rarefied spheres where extra effort and time will yield only a fraction of a percent better return. Too much attention may even lose you money if you churn your securities and so pay a lot in commissions, or if you invest in obscurities which end up having a tendency to collapse.

Certainly too much time spent on finance can lose you time, time you could have spent with friends or family, or just being outside on a nice day.

If you do want to know more about your finances and your computer, here are some suggestions. You can look into books and magazines, and you can use a modem to go on-line.

Magazines

There are two kinds of magazines to look at: those about computing and those about personal finance. Each focuses on its own area but will also have a few articles about the intersection of these topics. There are also a few magazines which actively cover both subjects. Remember to look at both the articles and the ads. Although you don't have to believe all the claims made in the ads, you can learn what is considered important and often encounter special deals and trial offers. (I've included addresses only for those magazines difficult to find on newsstands.)

Computer Magazines

These magazines approach finance from the computer side. They assume you know terms such as *Windows* OLE *support* and *database file export*.

PC Magazine

The most popular magazine on using PC-compatible computers, this biweekly has brief stories on new programs of all kinds and regularly compares the latest versions of financial managers and investment advisors.

PC World

The direct competitor of PC *Magazine*, this monthly magazine also has news on the latest programs and comparison reviews of financial software.

PC/Computing

Aimed less at managerial types than PC *Magazine* or PC *World*, this is more for individual computer enthusiasts.

Windows Magazine

Now that most PCs run Windows, this magazine is becoming a thick and important source of news and reviews for all kinds of PC programs.

MacWorld and MacUser

These magazines are to Mac owners what PC *Magazine* and PC *World* are to PC owners: the place for news and reviews. *MacWorld* is more sober; *MacUser* more playful.

Home Office Computing

Just as its name says, this magazine is aimed at the person with a home office. It offers reviews and news, and includes tips and information on phone systems, insurance, and other noncomputer topics.

Mac Home Journal

As the name indicates, this is aimed at home use of the Macintosh. It leaves out heavy business topics such as expensive printers and complex networking and instead talks more about education, games, and personal finance.

Home PC

Similar to *Mac Home Journal*, but for PC owners.

Family PC

Again a home magazine, this is heavily oriented to child and parent computer users. It sometimes includes personal finance for the parents.

Computer Life

This is a key example of a new spate of home and family-oriented computer magazines appearing during 1994. Aimed at an older and more enthusiastic audience than *Family* PC, it includes a regular finance column by Timothy Middleton.

General Business Magazines

These magazines contain information you might use in one of the analysis programs about where prices and values are going. They include *Business Week, The Economist, Fortune,* and *Forbes.* The best-known newspapers in this same area are *The Wall Street Journal* and *Barron's.*

Personal Finance Magazines

These magazines approach finance from the money side. They'll often assume you know terms such as *price-to-earnings ratio* and *beta.*

Kiplinger's

The magazine used to be called *Changing Times.* It includes general-purpose personal finance articles and is the oldest of the financial magazines. It's from the same Kiplinger group that puts its name on software and produces a newsletter.

Worth

An expensive-looking new magazine that spends a lot of time on the idea of living with money, lots of money. It does run some good computer investment advice articles.

Money

Full of news on mutual funds, government policies, and the like that will affect your finances. This magazine is aimed more at middle-class audiences than *Worth.*

Smart Money

Subtitled *The Wall Street Journal Magazine of Personal Business,* this magazine pays attention to real investments, even showing you how its own choices are performing.

Individual Investor

If you get up to check your investments before work, automatically track them during the day, and can't wait for some after-work time playing with charts, this is your magazine.

> PO Box 2070
> Marion, OH 43305
> 212-689-2777
> 800-669-1002

Investor's Software Review

A quarterly newsletter that costs $54 a year or $90 for two years. It has reviews, comparisons, and tips.

> Investor's Research Institute
> PO Box 44875
> Rio Rancho, NM 87174
> 505-891-2241 fax
> 800-845-8997

Technical Analysis of Stocks & Commodities

Devoted to figuring out just what's going up and down and when.

> 4757 California Ave. S.W.
> Seattle, WA 98116-4499

Artificial Intelligence in Finance

For those who believe computers can outguess people in the market. It contains lots of ads for obscure programs.

> Miller Freeman
> 600 Harrison St.
> San Francisco, CA 94107
> 415-905-2200

NeuroVe$t Journal

Specializing in neural networks, genetic algorithms, fuzzy logic, expert systems, chaos theory, fractals, data visualization, and other new math models to outguess the market. $49 for 6 issues.

> PO Box 764
> Haymarket, VA 22069

On-Line Resources

With a computer and a modem and a phone line you can connect to information stored on other computers all over the world. Chapter 1 explained how this on-line world can be a wonderful source of news, stock prices, and conversation about personal finance. For technical analysis you'll need the on-line statistics. For fundamental analysis you'll want the reports and studies. And for fun and thinking you'll want the people—where you'll find communities of others with your same interests.

I don't want to repeat that information from Chapter 1 here. Nor do I want to get into too much detail, because what you can find on-line is changing very quickly, growing larger every day.

Here are some suggestions for learning more through on-line services.

Prodigy

Prodigy has a surprising amount of personal finance information for a service that focuses on home and family. As you've seen in previous chapters, it even offers on-line bill paying and stock trading. You can get there by clicking on the **Business/Finance** button or by using the Jump command to a specific "jumpword" (see Figure 9.1).

Investment Digest (**jump investment digest**) and *Kiplinger's Personal Finance Magazine* (**jump kiplinger's magazine**) are here. The Home Business section is by the editors of *Home Office Computing* (**jump home business**). And there's a discussion area for investment theories (**jump money talk bb**). Brendan Boyd's, financial analyst for UPI, writes a column.

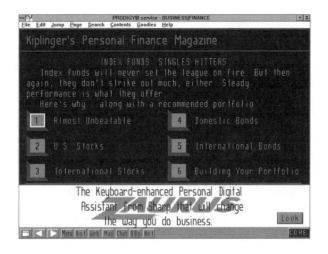

Figure 9.1 Prodigy lets you read several finance magazines on-line.

The Wall St. Edge compiles more than two hundred newsletters and advisory services (**jump wall st edge**). A sample issue costs $2 (see Figure 9.2).

Figure 9.2 The Wall St. Edge collects newsletters in Prodigy.

The Mutual Fund Analyst in Prodigy (see Figure 9.3) helps you search through 3600 mutual funds to compare their performance records. It costs $6 per day to view as many reports as you like or download up to 100 per day (**jump mutual fund analyst**).

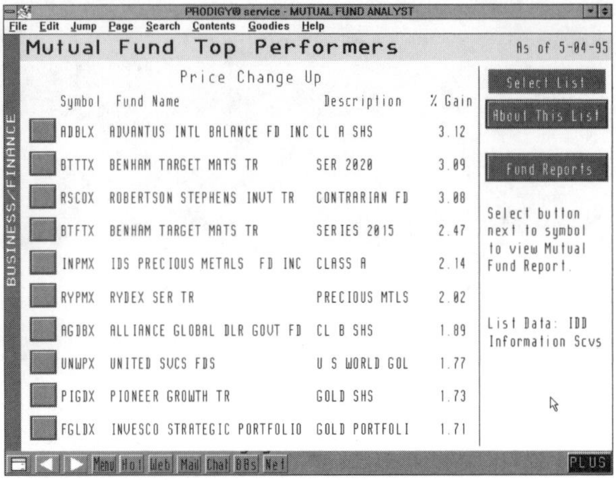

Figure 9.3 Mutual Fund Analyst on Prodigy.

America Online

America Online has lots of data and chat areas. You get at them either by clicking on the buttons and menus on screen or by using a keyword to go directly to the area.

The News and Finance area of America Online is a key place to go for personal finance. You'll find the Hoover's Business Resources (keyword: **hoovers**) and company profiles (keyword: **company**). You'll find transcripts of the Nightly Business Report from TV (keyword: **nbr**). The Cowles/SIMBA Media Information Network (keyword: **cowles**) has articles on the communications business. The Top Business window (keyword: **business**) has the latest news on all of business (see Figure 9.4). And *Worth* magazine (keyword: **worth**) and the *New York Times* (keyword: **nyt**) have their news on-line, as do papers I contribute to (see Figure 9.5)—the *San Jose Mercury News* (keyword: **mc news**) and the *Chicago Tribune* (keyword: **chicago**).

The Motley Fool service brings you the Gardner brothers, moderating and joking their way through the windows of personal finance theories and news. Look to this and the America Online Personal Finance Software Center (see Figure 9.6).

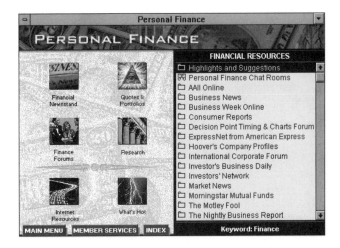

Figure 9.4 America Online's Top Business window with current news.

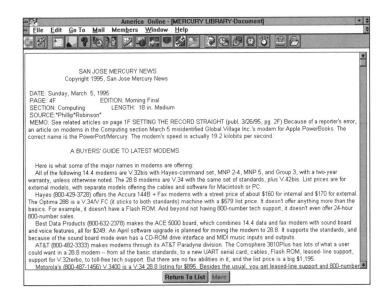

Figure 9.5 One of my own articles in America Online's San Jose Mercury News area.

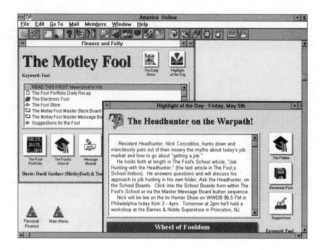

Figure 9.6 The Motley Fool personal finance talk show on America Online.

CompuServe

CompuServe has more business information than any other on-line service. You can get to it with the text-only menus (CompuServe works with older, less graphic PCs, which Prodigy and America Online cannot help) or with the new CompuServe graphic interface software. You can also use the **go** command to leap directly to an area.

Go Money is your key leap. You can also visit related areas such as the business menu (**go business**) for getting to the Working From Home Forum (**go work**) (see Figure 9.7), Legal Forum (**go lawsig**), and International Trade Forum (**go trade**). The Associated Press wire news is here (**go aponline**) and the Business Wire press releases too (**go tbw-1**). Older news stories are in the archives (**go newsarchive**) and the News Source (**go newsusa**). Magazines are in the Magazine Database Plus (**go magdb**). TRW credit reports (**go trwreport**) and demographic information (**go demographics**) and even the Commerce Business Daily (**go combus**) (see Figure 9.8) are here. Watch out though: many CompuServe databases will cost you extra, beyond the basic monthly fee. Stick to Basic Services if you want to pay the least.

CompuServe charges a monthly fee—only extended services are charged hourly. This is their basic plan. America Online charges by the hour.

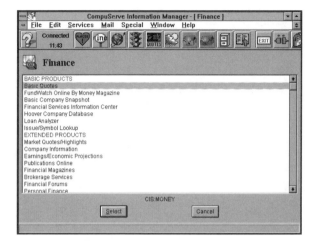

Figure 9.7 CompuServe's Working From Home forum.

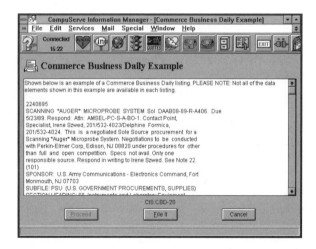

Figure 9.8 CompuServe's Commerce Business Daily database.

The FundWatch Online by *Money Magazine* is part of Basic Services. It has information on 1900 mutual funds, rating and ranking them (see Figure 9.9).

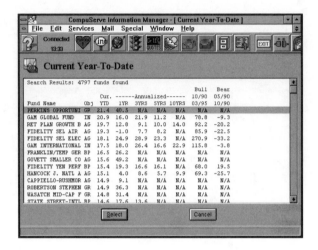

Figure 9.9 FundWatch mutual fund analysis on CompuServe.

And for discussions of investment theories (see Figure 9.10), try the Investors Forum.

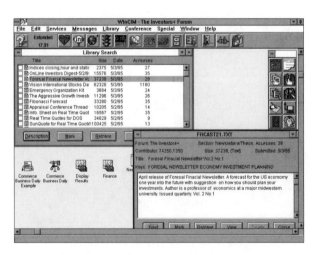

Figure 9.10 The Investor's Forum on CompuServe.

Naturally you can get quotes on your securities, and in lots of different ways. Choose **go basicquote** for the free stock quotes (Figure 9.11).

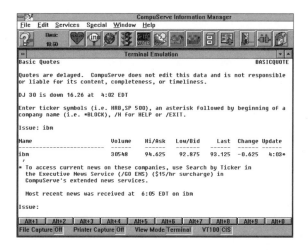

Figure 9.11 Free quotes within CompuServe.

eWorld

For Macintosh owners, eWorld is a small but comfortable on-line service. You click on the places within the graphic world or you use the shortcut terms to move directly to specific information.

The Business and Finance Plaza (see Figure 9.12) has plenty of finance information. The Working Solo (shortcut: **solo**) forum is for entrepreneurs and home-business operators. There is advice and software, such as templates for common Macintosh programs. *Inc. Magazine* has a forum (shortcut: **inc online**) with excerpts from the magazine. Nolo Press has its Self-Help Law Center (shortcut: **nolo**) for information on contracts, patents, and so on (see Figure 9.13). The Business Sector Profiles forum (shortcut: **bsp**) has reports and forecasts from the US government on more than 200 industries. More statistics are in the Real-Time Marketing forum (shortcut: **rtm**) and Hoover's Company Profiles (shortcut: **hoovers**). You'll find investment discussions in Money Matters (shortcut: **money matters**) as well as news from Dow Jones.

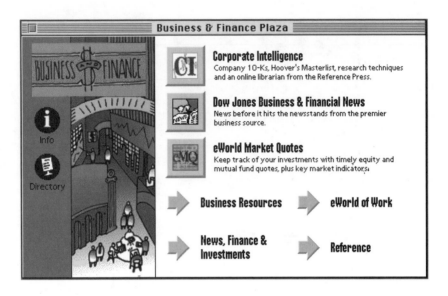

Figure 9.12 eWorld's Business and Finance Plaza.

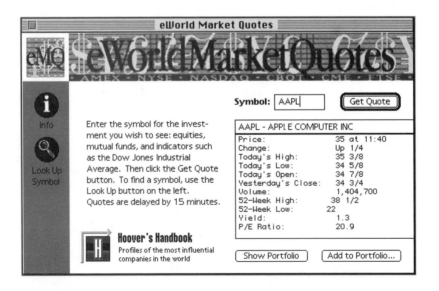

Figure 9.13 eWorld has statistics on industry prospects.

The Internet

On the vast Internet of information, you'll find lots of personal finance help.

For example, Networth (see Figure 9.14) is a free Internet service with advice or more than 5000 mutual funds. It is a research tool for digging into the prospectus and performance of these funds. It includes the complete Morningstar database and pricing quotes from Standard & Poor's. There is also discussion for swapping ideas with other investors.

To get at Networth, from Galt Technologies, use a World Wide Web browser to access **http://networth.galt.com**

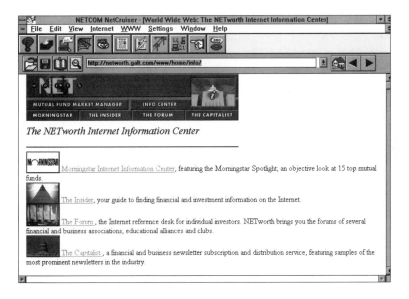

Figure 9.14 Networth, a free mutual fund information site on the Internet.

The Global Network Navigator is an Internet Web site with directions to lots of other places on the net. One part of it is the Personal Finance Center (see Figure 9.15) and in this you'll find information such CPA Joe Markunas advice on taxes (author of *Tax Guide for the Intimidated* by Career Press). Go with a Web browser to **http://gnn.com/meta/finance**.

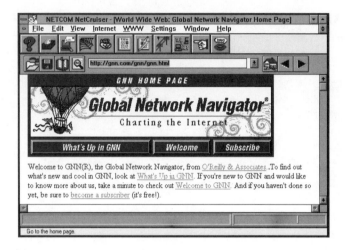

Figure 9.15 The Personal Finance Center of the Global Network Navigator.

Some other Web sites for personal finance are:

🐷   http://www.ai.mit.edu/stocks/

🐷   http://www.secapl.com/secapl/

🐷   http://riskweb.bus.utexas.edu/finweb.html

Many companies are now creating their own web sites, which often include their annual reports.

Internet Periodicals

You can find a number of investment periodicals on-line. In most cases you can get either the periodical itself or excerpts and a subscription offer by sending E-mail to a particular address, with the word *subscribe* in either the subject or the body of the message.

eINVEST is the Electronic Journal of Investing on the Internet. You can get information on this by sending E-mail to **listserv@vm.temple.edu**, and put in the message body

```
subscribe e_invest<your full name>
```

The Electronic Journal of Finance has similar information. Send to the same address but in your message put

```
subscribe finance<your full name>
```

The Internet Personal Finance Letter, edited by Michael P. Griffin, tries to keep simple and smart. Send E-mail to **pfl-request@umassd.edu,** and put in your body

```
subscribe pfl<your full name>
```

Finally, Tom Petruno's Market Beat column in *The Los Angeles Times* can be found on-line if you send E-mail to **petruno@netcom.com**, and in your subject line put

```
subscribe
```

Individual Investor magazine is a monthly about personal investments. You can read free excerpts on-line at the Electronic Newsstand (see Figure 9.16). Use a Gopher utility to access **gopher.enews.com**.

Figure 9.16 Example of reading investor information at the electronic newsstand.

Newsgroups

The Usenet part of the Internet is *newsgroups*. These are essentially bulletin boards to which anyone can contribute. The one of most interest here is called *misc.invest* and all its subgroups (see Figure 9.17). Most Internet programs should have a newsgroup reader. Browse though the messages others have left and then leave your own—commenting, asking, suggesting.

Figure 9.17 Reading the misc.invest newsgroups for rumors and ideas.

A Word of Warning

Remember that anyone can contribute to most on-line services and the Internet. In fact, in many cases, you can even contribute anonymously or with a false name, so there's no accountability. That means you can't believe everything you read, especially on the Internet. If someone or even a bunch of someones say a particular stock is headed up or down, they may be right, they may be uninformed, or they may be trying to cheat everyone with a completely unfounded rumor. "They" may even be just a single person, using various false names. Watch out for such scams.

CHAPTER 10

Shop

You've set up a computer, dreamed your future and guessed the reality, planned your house, college and retirement savings, automated your checkbook, tracked and recorded your expenses and income, budgeted your weeks or months, paid your bills electronically, prepared your tax returns, analyzed and chosen investments, organized your portfolio, estimated and bought insurance, drafted a will, and gone on-line to learn more (or you've at least read about those things, which can be almost as tiring). Now it's...shopping time!

Not that you should blow all that money you've saved and invested, but perhaps you can afford to reward yourself. You don't even have to leave the keyboard to do so.

And if you choose intelligently from the new floppy, CD-ROM and on-line shopping centers, you might even save more money or time over buying from print catalogs or walk-in stores.

Shopping is now a 24-hour, from-your-living room (or office!) activity. And I'm not talking some home shopping cable TV show. I'm talking about putting your computer, disk drives, and modem to work. They'll help you find, inspect, order, and pay for anything from a book to a car, a vacation trip to a coffee grinder, groceries to mortgages, and jewelry to a new hard disk (yes, there's plenty of hardware and software to buy).

These are some of the advantages:

💰 24-hour access—do it when you want.

💰 Weather won't stop you—who cares if it's raining or snowing?

💰 No parking troubles—no parking at all.

💰 No crowds to fight—unless you share your computer.

💰 Quick location of specific items—tireless computer assistance.

💰 Direct comparison of different colors and styles—like a catalog where you put the clothes you want on the model you prefer.

💰 More ecological—no gas to drive to a mall, no paper to mail out catalogs.

These can be some of the disadvantages:

💰 No hands-on touch before you buy—it's just pictures or even just words on a screen.

💰 Smaller selection—far fewer than in any store or mall.

💰 Less personal contact—none in many cases, compared to stores with clerks or other shoppers.

💰 Overly-easy spending—when you can call a credit card number in any time, 24-hours a day, thrift is harder to retain.

All sorts of companies, from tiny software firms to major retailers, are entering this age of teleselling, or cybermalls, to try to find another way to your heart and your wallet.

There are two basic types of computer shopping: on-line and on-disc. This chapter lists a few of each. More will follow, probably in about the same profusion as local strip malls.

On-Line Shopping

On-line, as you read in Chapters 1 and 9, means communicating with other computers through the telephone network (and someday through your cable TV network too). For this you need a modem, telecommunications software, and a subscription to some on-line service or bulletin board.

Many of the well-known on-line services now have on-line shopping as one of their features. Most of these are available anywhere in the country where you can tap into the phone network. They offer descriptions of goods, search commands to help find what you want, and a chance to order either directly through the computer connection or by calling a toll-free number. The most recent versions of these on-line malls add pictures of the goods. But there are also local services, available only in small areas, that depend on a computer and a modem.

Peapod

Peapod (see Figure 10.1) started in 1990 with the Jewel Food Stores, a major grocery chain, in Chicago. You pay for the software (for PC or Mac) an annual membership fee, a monthly fee, plus the cost of your groceries and a service charge for each delivery.

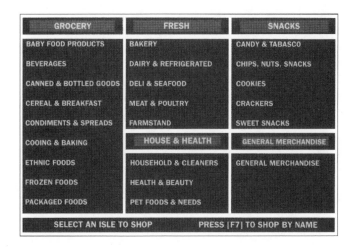

Figure 10.1 Peapod on-line grocery shopping aisle.

You run the program and see a store catalog on screen, such as the Safeway catalog for Peapod in the San Francisco area. From the lists on screen you choose the groceries you want, as well as other items including bus passes, film, and prescription medicines. You can shop by wandering through the on-screen aisles or by naming specific items. You can indicate special requests such as grinding coffee extra fine. And you'll see on-screen notices of special deals.

Then you specify a 90-minute delivery window, chosen from those available. The San Francisco service has these in late afternoon through the evening on Wednesday through Sunday. You pay by check, credit card, or Peapod Electronic Payment. The delivery person will accept any standard coupons and give you their value off your next order. "You order, we shop, we deliver," is their promise and they guarantee to correct any problems.

This may be an expensive store for those on a tight money budget, but it could be deliverance for those on a big money but tight time budget. Besides freeing you from having to visit the store in person and letting you shop at any time, the Peapod service takes advantage of the computer to let you build your own personal lists for easily and automatically ordering your favorite items. The software helps you create and track a grocery budget. It also makes sure you don't miss any specials that you may not have seen in the crowded aisles of a physical store.

CompuServe's Electronic Mall

CompuServe, one of the largest on-line services, has long had an electronic mall. A recent upgrade added more graphics to that mall and more search features. The result: CompuServe's New Electronic Mall (see Figure 10.2). To begin shopping there you sign on to CompuServe and use the command.

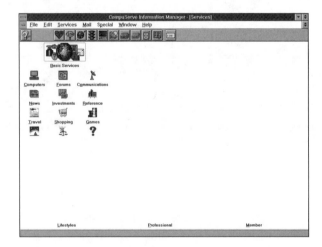

Figure 10.2 CompuServe's New Electronic Mall.

Besides computer software and hardware, you can browse through appliances, contact lenses, publications, even cars—though on that last you really only get information from an Electronic Showroom. These goods come from companies such as 800-FLOWERS, Absolut Vodka, Air France, Express America Mortgage, Macmillan Publishing, University of Phoenix, and Sears.

Prodigy and America Online

The Prodigy Service has its own on-line shopping service that lets you search through a long list of goods. Prodigy shopping might also be said to appear in another form: this is the only on-line service with ads directly on your screen (see Figure 10.3).

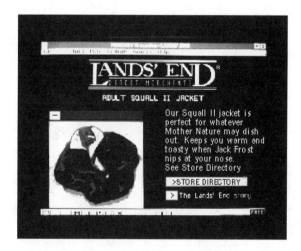

Figure 10.3 Prodigy shopping screen.

America Online has been quickly growing and recently either tied or surpassed—depending on who you talk to—both CompuServe and Prodigy in number of subscribers. Here too you'll find shopping (see Figure 10.4), which you can get at directly from the main menu. Just click on the Shopping button and then make your particular choices (see Figure 10.5).

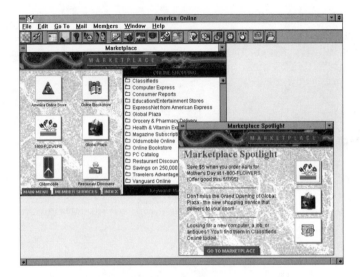

Figure 10.4 America Online has shopping along with its other main choices.

Figure 10.5 America Online shopping offers a variety of goods.

Travel Shopping

If you want to learn about places to go and things to see, look to on-line services such as CompuServe and America Online. Then you can go farther and actually shop for airline flights and hotel rooms, booking reservations and buying tickets through Eaasy Sabre and OAG (see Figure 10.6).

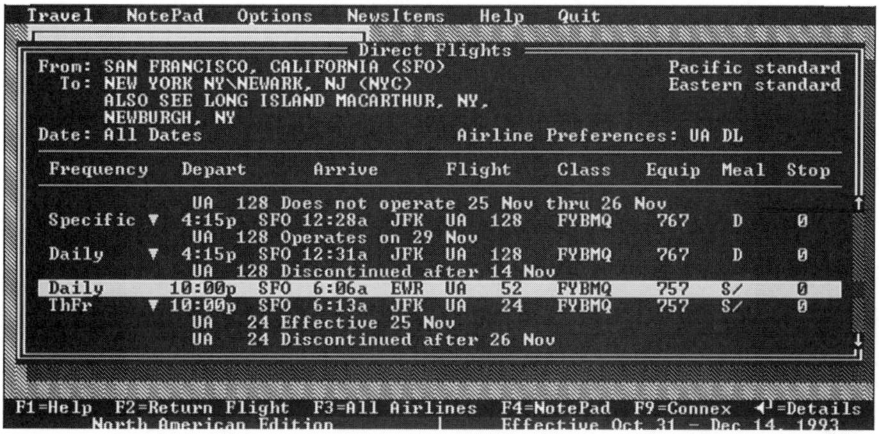

Figure 10.6 OAG screen for buying airline tickets on-line.

Example of Shopping for Travel Tickets On-Line: Eaasy Sabre on Compuserve

Getting to the Eaasy Sabre service on CompuServe is easy. It's right there in the initial menu, where you just select Travel and then the Eaasy Sabre option. After signing up for the service, you choose what sort of information you're looking for (see Figure 10.7).

```
To select one of the options above, enter the number:

** Quick Tip:  These system navigation commands are always available:
     /Help or  ? for assistance
     /Res  or /R to go to the Reservations Menu
     /Top  or /T to return to the Main Menu
     /Exit or /E to return to your System Operator
[24;1H[0m> 2
[2J[1;1H[0m                          RESERVATIONS MENU

   1  Flight Reservations and Availability   5  Airline Fares
   2  Flight Arrival/Departure Information    6  Itinerary Review and Change
   3  Hotels                                  7  Sign On for Reservations
   4  Rental Cars                             8  Flight Schedules
                                             9  Specific Flight Details

To select one of the options above, enter the number:

Quick Tip:  The following system navigation commands are always available:
     /Help or  ? for assistance, or
     /Res  or /R to return to this menu or
     /Top  or /T to return to the MAIN MENU or
     /Exit or /E to return to the System Operator
[24;1H[0m> _
```

Figure 10.7 Eaasy Sabre lets you investigate and book airlines, hotels, and rental cars.

If you choose 1 for Flight Reservations and Availability, you are then asked which city you're flying from, where to, and when. You type this information as codes—such as SFO for San Francisco and AUG30 for August 30th—though there is plenty of intelligence in the program to guess what you're trying to say. There is also help in figuring out the codes. Enter the information and you'll get a list of flights meeting those requirements (see Figure 10.8).

```
1  View more participating airlines
[24;1H[0m> ua
[2J[1;1H[0m                          FLIGHT AVAILABILITY

From:  (SFO) SAN FRANCISCO, CA
  To:  (NYC) NEW YORK CITY, NY                    FRIDAY     AUG-19-94
------------------------------------------------------------------------
   Flight  Leave     Arrive    Meal  ST FC Equip  OnTime  Classes of Service**
1 UA 900  SFO  730A  JFK  400P  BS   0  Y  767     8    P  C  Y  B  M  Q  H  U
2 UA  12  SFO  800A  EWR  417P  BS   0  Y  757     8    F  Y  B  M  Q  H  U
3 UA  22  SFO  900A  EWR  517P  BS   0  Y  757     4    F  Y  B  M  Q  H  U
4 UA 862  SFO  900A  JFK  533P  BS   0  Y  767     5    P  C  Y  B  M  H
5 UA 278  SFO 1130A  EWR  744P  L    0  Y  757     7    F  Y  B  M  Q  H  U
6 UA 828  SFO 1145A  JFK  809P  L    0  Y  767     8    P  C  Y  B  M  Q  H  U
------------------------------------------------------------------------
To SELECT a flight, enter the line number, or            FC = Fast Confirm

  8  View MORE flights           11  View all FARES
  9  CHANGE flight request        12  Translate CODES
 10  View FIRST flight display    13  View LOWest one-way fares

** Quick Tip:  Select your flight, then choose Bargain Finder when prompted and
   EAASY SABRE will select the class of service for the lowest available fare.
[24;1H[0m>
```

Figure 10.8 Eaasy Sabre flight list example.

You may also view the fares for these flights, sorted in a variety of ways (see Figure 10.9).

```
[24;1H[0m> 11
[2J[1;1H[0mFrom: <EWR> NEWARK, NJ                                    TUESDAY    AU4
   To: <SFO> SAN FRANCISCO, CA
   On:       UNITED AIRLINES                            Fares in: USD
----------------------------------------------------------------------------
       One          Round      Book    Advance    Min    Max    Fare
       Way          Trip       In      Purchase   Stay   Stay   Code
       ----         -----      ----    --------   ----   ----   ----------
   1                373.00     U       Yes        Yes    30     U1E7NTV8
   2                468.00     Q       Yes        Yes    No     QE14ONQ
   3                508.00     Q       Yes        Yes    No     QE14PNQ
   4                508.00     H       Yes        Yes    No     HE7ONQ
   5                548.00     H       Yes        Yes    No     HE7PNQ
   6                659.00     H       Yes        Yes    30     HE14NQ
   7                719.00     M       Yes        Yes    No     ME7NQ
----------------------------------------------------------------------------
To view fare RULES, enter the line number of the fare desired, α

 8  View MORE fares                    11  View available FLIGHTS
 9  CHANGE fare request                12  View fares for ALL airlines
10  View the FIRST fare display        13  View fares from HIGHEST to LOWEST
[24;1H[0m>
```

Figure 10.9 Eaasy Sabre fare display example.

Finally, before booking, you ought to read the rules and restrictions on those fares (see Figure 10.10).

```
[2J[1;1H[0m

Booking Code −

Penalty − A USD 35 SERVICE CHARGE INCLUDING TAX WILL BE ASSESSED ON ANY
ITINERARY CHANGE WITH/ WITHOUT TICKET REISSUE. 100 PERCENT PENALTY APPLIES FOR
REFUNDS/CANCELLATIONS.

Res/Ticketing − RES MUST BE MADE NO LATER THAN 7 DAYS BEFORE DPTR FROM ORIGIN.
TKT MUST BE PURCHASED NO LATER THAN 7 DAYS BEFORE DPTR FROM ORIGIN OR 1 DAY
AFTER RES IS

MADE, WHICHEVER COMES FIRST. SGMTS USING THIS RULE MUST BE CONFIRMED.

Minimum Stay − IF TRAVEL FROM THE POINT OF ORIGIN COMMENCES ON/BEFORE 19NOV94,
THEN RETURN TRVL IS VALID ON THE 1ST SUN AFTER 12:01 A.M.. MEASURED FROM DPTR
FROM ORIGIN TO DPTR FROM THE FARTHEST GEOGRAPHICAL POINT. IF TRAVEL FROM THE
POINT OF ORIGIN COMMENCES BETWEEN 20NOV AND 23NOV94, THEN RETURN TRVL IS VALID
ON THE 1ST THU AFTER 12:01 A.M.. MEASURED FROM DPTR FROM ORIGIN TO DPTR FROM
Tress <ENTER> to continue, or
 1  Return to fare RULES menu
 2  Return to FARES display
 3  View available FLIGHTS
>
```

Figure 10.10 Eaasy Sabre rules and restrictions example.

Internet and the World Wide Web

As you remember from Chapter 1, the Internet is the interconnected network of computers in academic, government, corporate, and now individual sites all around the world. Some estimates say 20 to 30 million people now get on to the Internet, either through Internet service providers or through the new Internet features in services such as CompuServe, Prodigy, and America Online.

Because it is not owned by a single central company, and because it has so many subscribers, the Internet is becoming a popular place for future on-line shopping plans. More and more companies are opening up *Web sites*—a particular kind of graphic Internet home—for displaying their wares (see Figure 10.11). A few are actually selling on-line, though this is generally through you viewing and then calling in with a credit card number.Companies are testing the technological improvements that will let you give your credit-card number or bank account access directly through the computer, with no need for a separate call.

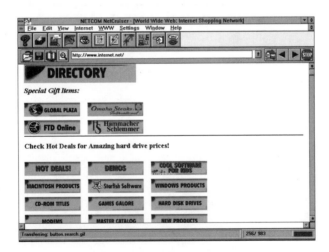

Figure 10.11 Example Internet shopping Web site.

Even the Home Shopping Network people are getting into "the action" with their Internet Shopping Network.

Web sites are organized into a World Wide Web that even beginning Internet users can navigate simply by clicking buttons on screen (see Figure 10.12). Because the web can hold a variety of media, sending it to your computer on request, you'll find not just computer wares and consumer goods: you'll find musical samples, movie clips, and more.

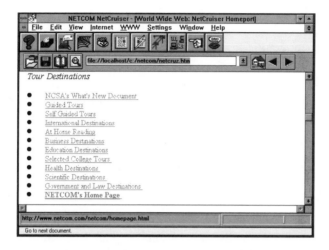

Figure 10.12 Clicking on the highlighted and underlined text of an Internet Web site will jump you immediately to another site or page.

CD-ROM Shopping

On-line shopping has its drawbacks:

- 🐷 You need a modem.
- 🐷 You pay telephone charges.
- 🐷 Often you get low-quality graphics that can't compete with in-person shopping or even catalogs, making it harder to see what you're considering buying.

You can avoid these problems by shopping from a CD-ROM catalog, so let's talk about them now. CD-ROM discs, as explained in Chapter 1, can hold wonderful graphics as well as video clips and sound. All of these can make CD-ROM catalog shopping more realistic than an on-line shopping service.

In fact, because CD-ROMs can hold so much of so many kinds of information, the catalog can even have articles, games, stories, movies and running software programs—more than you'd find in person at a store.

CD-ROMs for Software

Here's a natural: shopping from a disc catalog for software. There are a number of such software catalogs available now. Typically they bundle dozens or even hundreds of programs onto a single CD-ROM, along with the documentation (instruction manuals) for those programs, and even demo versions of the programs. (A little like the disc that comes with this book!) The CD-ROMs themselves are typically free.

You run the demo versions of the programs, which range from bare screen images of what the programs do to nearly complete versions of the programs, limited only in the amount of information they can handle or whether or not they can print the results.

When you decide you like a program, you call a toll-free number and give them a credit card number, and in return you'll be given a password that will unlock the complete version of the program. That means also that if you have the CD-ROM on hand, you can get any of its programs at any time, 24-hours a day. That may come in handy if you needed a new kind of program at some odd hour. If you want the regular printed documents to go with it, most shopping services will send them to you for free.

The TestDrive CD-ROM has 60 Windows programs for business, home and even games. They come in pairs: a demo and the complete program. To use the complete program you must pay to get the password.

The Club KidSoft CD-ROM is full of educational and game software. There's also a KidSoft quarterly magazine. The programs—from companies such as Davidson, EA Kids, and Broderbund—are accompanied by articles, activities, video clips, and more. Half the programs on the CD-ROM are demos. You can try and then buy these. There's a Power Shopping function to help you find programs that fit certain educational subjects, age groups, letter headings, and so on.

If you want Macintosh software you can try Software Dispatch from Apple Computer. With a new set of programs every few months, this CD-ROM has 75 programs and 12,000 pages of documentation. The software ranges from MacWrite Pro to games such as Spectre. Again, the deal is that you try the demos, call with your credit card number when there's a program you like, use the password to unlock the program, and then run the program and read the documentation from disc. Each program is covered by a 30-day warranty from Software Dispatch and is covered by the same technical support you get when you buy it from a software store.

Another collection of Macintosh software is on The Mac Zone CD-ROM. The Mac Zone is a mail-order company. The 150 wares on the disc are sold at 5% less than even their regular discount mail-order prices. Any documentation you need will be mailed to you after you call and pay for items you want.

Example of Buying Software from a CD-ROM: Mac Zone Instant Access

Here's an example in pictures of finding and then ordering Quicken from the Mac Zone CD-ROM.

1.   First you insert the CD-ROM into the drive. Its icon should appear on screen.

Figure 10.13 Mac Zone Instant Access icon.

2.   Double-click on that icon. You'll soon see the main menu, with categories of software (see Figure 10.14).

3.   Click on the category you want. In this example, we're looking for financial software—no surprise—so let's try **General Business**.

4.   Within the General Business category you'll see subcategories. Let's try **Accounts** here (see Figure 10.15).

Quicken! We got here the hard way, but we're here (see Figure 10.16). We could also have tried to search for it with the Find command at the main menu. Anyway, now you can choose to see product details, watch a tour, or try the demo. When you're done with those choices, you can click on the **Purchase** button. The price is already there on screen.

Naturally you can always retreat or move on, by using the **Find Application** command or the **Main Menu** command.

Figure 10.14 Mac Zone Instant Access main menu.

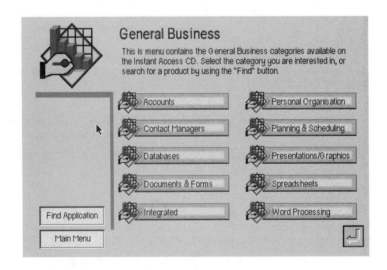

Figure 10.15 Mac Zone Instant Access business programs menu.

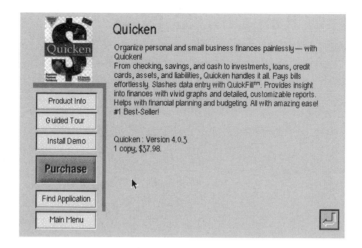

Figure 10.16 Mac Zone Instant Access offer for Quicken—
with demos, information and order specifications.

Here's the order form you can use for buying Quicken (see Figure 10.17). You must call in your order using the old-fashioned phone. Some day this will probably be done on-line.

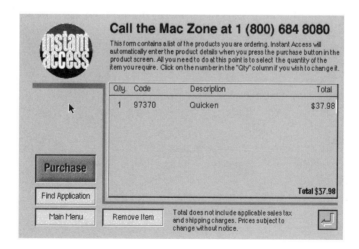

Figure 10.17 Mac Zone Instant Access order form for Quicken.

Consumer Items on CD-ROM

It's not all software in the CD-ROM catalogs. There are also plenty of goods totally unrelated to computers. These goods can't actually be on the CD-ROMs, as the software can. (Well, music and movies can be as clips, as selections, but today's CD-ROMs can't hold more than one movie or one album, yet.) The CD-ROM can hold words and pictures and even voice descriptions of goods. And using a built-in program, the CD-ROM can give you easy easy to search for, take notes on, and remember just what the perfect gift might be for others or even for yourself.

For example, Magellan Systems has a CD-ROM catalog called *The Merchant*. With products fro more than two-dozen companies—from Spiegel to Buick—The Merchant offers interactive shopping, music (such as world beat and children's songs), and film samples (such as clips from *Casablanca*). The **Find** function can search through all of the catalogs on the disc, and take you directly to a particular catalog and page to find what you want. The **Browse** function will flip the pages as you watch. Ordering means calling a separate 800 number for each catalog, but the disc itself is free, and even offers you chances to win prizes such as Caribbean cruises.

The En Passant shopping software for Mac computers—developed by Apple Computer, EDS and Redgate Communications—comes on a CD-ROM. You simply slip the disc into the drive and double-click to start shopping. You can go through this mall in two ways: by catalog or by department.

The catalog shopping reproduces what you'd find in the catalogs of famous companies such as Tiffany & Co., Pottery Barn, Land's End, Patagonia, The Nature Company, Biodi (art imports), Williams-Sonoma, Self Care, bio bottoms, L.L. Bean, WinterSilks, The Wall Street Journal, 800*Flowers, The Right Start Catalog, and even Apple itself. You can click on the catalog you want, then see its wares pictured on screen, along with text descriptions and price. Click on any item you like and an order form appears. There you can specify a quantity and other such details and see the final price summary.

You could instead decide to shop by department. In that case the similar goods of the various merchants are brought together, such as jewelry, clothing, and so on. These are the departments:

- 💰 Fashion Avenue
- 💰 For The Home
- 💰 Electronic Gallery
- 💰 For Kids
- 💰 Discoveries

- 💰 Healthy Living
- 💰 At the Office
- 💰 For Someone Special
- 💰 Going Places
- 💰 Personal Finance

Again you see the pictures, descriptions, and prices, and can click on any you want to order. Or you can just list those you're considering. Putting the computer's abilities to work, En Passant even lets you see the same outfits in different colors on a single model. And you can hear audio product descriptions or see video clips along with the still pictures and text.

When you do order, you need only call a single 800 number. That's easier than some discs—such as The Merchant—which have a separate number for each catalog or retailer, making for lots of calls for those with lots of shopping.

Example of Buying Consumer Items from a CD-ROM: En Passant

Let's look at En Passant as an example of CD-ROM shopping.

1. You start by putting the disc into your Mac and then double-clicking on the icon (see Figure 10.18).

En Passant v1.0

Figure **10.18** En Passant icon.

2. Soon you see the initial En Passant display (see Figure 10.19). On the left are four buttons: **Begin!**, **Introduction**, **About En Passant**, and **Adjust Monitor**. You move the mouse cursor to any of them and press the mouse button. Here's what they do:

💰 **Adjust Monitor**—brings up a display for you to adjust the color on screen.

💰 **About En Passant**—brings up a screen listing the people who made En Passant.

💰 **Introduction**—plays a video clip of a woman explaining what En Passant has and how to use it.

💰 **Begin!**—starts the actual shopping.

Figure 10.19 En Passant's first display.

3. Click on **Begin!** and you'll see the entrance to this mall (see Figure 10.20). There are five buttons on the left: **Valet**, **Gift Register**, **Order List**, **Messages**, and **EP Magazine**. On the right are simply the buttons **Catalogs** and **Departments**.

💰 The **EP Magazine** button will take you to the collection of articles and information on disc (see Figure 10.21). There's a table of contents for leaping to the particular articles such as Tom Peters on career survival, Leah Feldon on wardrobe design, Dr. Dean Edell on health, and others on art, stories, travel, and more.

💰 You'll find articles on personal finance, along with lots of other less-serious subjects (Figure 10.22).

Figure 10.20 En Passant lets you shop by merchant (Catalogs) or by merchandise type (Departments).

Figure 10.21 EP Magazine table of contents.

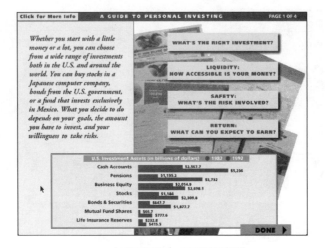

Figure 10.22 EP Magazine article.

There are also suggestions on gifts, alerts to specials, and even a program called Gift Register for matching your budget to your personal interests and for tracking birthdays and important dates (see Figure 10.23). You enter suggestions for the person's birthday gift and the date, and when that time rolls around the program will alert you that it is time to shop.

Figure 10.23 Gift Register in En Passant.

4. Let's get down to business, though. The **Catalogs** button in that main screen lets you see a list of catalogs on this disc (see Figure 10.24). Click on the one you want to try first. For this example I clicked on WinterSilks and soon saw the contents listing for that catalog (see Figure 10.25).

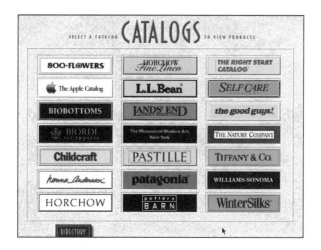

Figure 10.24 Catalogs in En Passant.

5. I could choose areas of the WinterSilks catalog from the contents list. But I paged through by clicking in the lower right corner.

Figure 10.25 WinterSilks Catalog.

6. When I found something of interest I clicked on it and saw the specific ordering information (see Figure 10.26).

Figure 10.26 Ordering information in En Passant.

7. You can also return to the Directory—click the button at the bottom of most any screen—and use the Departments route to buying (see Figure 10.27). There the items from different companies are all mixed together and then divided by type instead of by source.

Figure 10.27 En Passant departments.

8. After your run through departments and catalogs, any items you enter an order for will turn up on the main order list (see Figure 10.28). En Passant then lets you fax or call these orders in, and will make sure the goods are delivered to you, and the charges made to you.

That's all there is to it. Eventually the service should include a modem connection so you don't have to manually call or fax, and can just have your computer call their computer with the order.

Figure 10.28 En Passant order list.

Virtual Reality

How will your computer help you spend in the future? Surely the on-line services will offer more and more goods, until nearly anything will be available through a modem. Better service, such as immediate home delivery, will probably escalate as well. And the graphics, sounds, and other familiar aspects of shopping will certainly be improved in each generation of on-line and CD-ROM shopping.

But for those who don't want to go to a mall, technology may, oddly enough, take them there anyway. Virtually. Using 3-D immersion graphics and the technology called virtual reality, you may someday get dressed for shopping in a special suit, slip on high-tech goggles, and then experience walking, talking, and touching your way through a mall that's built entirely of computer graphics. Synthetic assistants will cater to your needs and show you just how that dress, car, or house will look, in the color, size, and style you want, and may even let you simulate wearing, driving, or living in it.

Visionary Shopping from MarketWare in Norcross, Georgia may be a first step in that direction. It lets you shop on a display screen, using a trackball (similar to a mouse) to point to your purchases. AT&T and a small software company called eShop are working on a PersonaLink network that will offer consumer products and services from national retail merchants. This will appear as a series of graphical storefronts that you'll move into to find items. It will depend on the Magic Cap software built into some of the latest Personal Digital Assistants.

Let's hope you've saved a little before then. Or that you know where the power-off button is on your PC so you can bail out before going broke.

Summary—Where the Deals Are

Unfortunately, on-line and CD-ROM shopping are not home to fantastic discounts. They are interesting ways to spend some time and money, and definitely more convenient than driving all over town, but you won't save much on your final bill. In the next few years they'll probably be more important to large institutions buying from one another. Still, if you have a modem or a CD-ROM drive, perhaps you should look back at that budget you created in Chapter 4 and the planning way back in Chapter 2 to see if you can afford a reward. Watch out, though, for on-line cons. Be very sure before you give your credit-card number to anyone on-line, as sure as you would be for giving it out over the telephone.

APPENDIX A

Addresses

AccuTrade
800-972-3400

American Association of Individual Investors (AAII)
312-280-0170

AIQ Inc.
800-332-2999

America Online
8619 Westwood Center Dr.
Vienna, VA 22182-2285
800-827-6364
703-448-8700

American River Software
916-483-1600

AM Software Inc.
1500B NW Vivion Rd.
P.O. Box 25010
Kansas City, MO 64118
816-741-6848 voice
816-741-1517 fax
800-859-8537

Axcelis, Inc.
4668 Eastern Ave. N.
Seattle, Wa 98103-6932
206-632-0885

BT&T Consumer Technology
714-363-7185

California Scientific Software
10024 Newtown Rd.
Nevada City, CA 95959
916-478-9040 voice
916-478-9041 fax
800-284-8112

Cauldwell Data
800-216-9829

Charles Schwab & Co.
800-334-4455

Citibank
212-657-3597
800-842-8405

Club KidSoft
408-354-6100
800-354-6150

CompuServe
5000 Arlington Centre Blvd.
P.O. Box 20212
Columbus, OH 43220
614-457-8650
800-848-8199

Computer Associates International
One Computer Associates Plaza
Islandia, NY 11788-7000
516-342-5224 voice
516-342-5734 fax
800-225-5224

Comtrad Industries
2820 Waterford Lake Dr., Suite 106
Midlothian, VA 23223
800-992-2966

Data Broadcasting Corp.
415-571-1800

DataTech Software
800-556-7526

Data Transmission Network Corporation
9110 W. Dodge Rd., Suite 200
Omaha, NB 68114
800-475-4755

Delphi
1030 Massachusetts Ave.
Cambridge, MA 02138
800-695-4005
800-365-4636

Disclosure
800-945-3647, x300

Dow Jones & Co.
P.O. Box 300
Princeton, NJ 08543-0300
609-452-1511
609-520-4775 fax

Dow Jones Market Monitor
P.O. Box 300
Princeton, NY 08543
800-522-3567

Dow Jones News Retrieval
609-452-1511
800-522-3567

Dow Jones Telerate Software
1017 Pleasant St.
New Orleans, LA 70115
504-895-1474
800-535-7990

Duvall International
615-385-5331 fax
800-533-5345

EDMS
5859 New Peachtree Rd., Suite 119
Atlanta, GA 30340
404-998-4088
800-395-7670

Engineering Management
Consultants
904-668-0635

En Passant
P.O. Box 764
Camp Hill, PA 17001
800-437-4121

Equis International Inc.
801-265-8886
800-882-3040

Essex Trading Company
800-726-2140

Fidelity Brokerage Services
161 Devonshire St.
Boston, MA 02110
800-544-7272
800-457-1769

Financial Services Marketing Corp.
500 N. Dallas Bank Tower
12900 Preston Rd.
Dallas, TX 75230
800-525-5611
214-386-6320
214-386-6323 fax

Friendly Software
419-868-6090
800-968-4654

Frontier Analytics
310-301-3988

Future Wave Software
1330 S. Gertruda Ave.
Redondo Beach, CA 90277
310-540-5373

Genie
401 N. Washington St.
Rockville, MD 20850
800-638-9636
301-251-6415

Howardsoft
1224 Prospect St., Ste 150
La Jolla, CA 92037
800-822-4829
619-454-0121

**Huntington Associates
Financial Inc.**
800-883-3863

International Pacific Trading Co.
1050 Calle Cordillera, Suite 105
San Clemente, CA 92673
800-444-9993
714-498-4009

Intex Solutions
35 Highland Circle
Needham, MA 02194
617-449-6222

Intuit (for Quicken)
P.O. Box 3014
Menlo Park, CA 94026
415-322-0573
800-624-8742

Intuit South (for TurboTax)
6256 Greenwich Dr., Suite 100
San Diego, CA 92122
619-453-4445
800-964-1040
800-756-1040 fax

Kiplinger
1729 H St. NW
Washington, DC 20006
800-235-0229
800-365-1546

Knight-Ridder Financial Publishing
30 S. Wacker Dr., Suite 1820
Chicago, IL 60606
312-454-1801
800-526-DATA

Laser Resources Inc.
310-324-9999 fax
800-535-2737

Macro*World Research Corp.
800-841-5398

Magellan Systems
800-561-3114

Man Machine Interfaces
555 Broad Hollow Rd.
Melville, NY 11747
516-249-4700

MarketArts Inc.
1420 Presidential Dr.
Richardson, TX 75081
800-998-8439
214-783-6792
214-235-9594

MCI Global Messaging Service (MCI Mail)
1133 19th St. NW
Washington, DC 20036
202-833-8484
800-444-6245

MECA Software
55 Walls Dr.
Fairfield, CT 06430-0912
800-288-6322
800-370-9016
203-255-1441
203-256-5000
203-255-6300 fax

Media Logic Inc.
6216 Indian Canyon Dr.
Austin, TX 78746-6352
800-305-7575
512-328-4166
512-328-4167 fax

Microsoft Corp.
800-426-9400

Morningstar, Inc.
800-876-5005

Mortgage Matchmaker
206-644-2546

NeuralWare Inc.
412-787-8222

NIBS, Inc.
62 Fowlie Rd.
Republic of Singapore, 1542
+65 344 2357
+65 344 2130 fax

Nirvana Systems Inc.
800-880-0338

Nolo Press
950 Parker St.
Berkeley, CA 94710
510-549-1976
800-992-6656

North Systems
(*was* N-*Squared Systems*)
4443 Nalani Ct., SE
Salem, OR 97302
503-364-3829

Novell
800-451-5151

Omega Research
9200 Sunset Dr.
Miami, FL 33173
305-270-1095
800-556-2022

Option Research Inc.
800-334-0854

Parsons Technology
One Parsons Dr.
P.O. Box 100
Hiawatha, IA 52233-0100
800-223-6925
319-395-9626
319-395-7449 fax

Patrick Consult Inc.
810 Matson Place
Cincinnati, OH 45204
513-244-6666

Peapod
1426 Fillmore, Suite 201
San Francisco, CA 94115
415-929-1600

Price Waterhouse
800-752-6234

Prodigy Services Co.
445 Hamilton Ave.
White Plains, NY 10601
800-284-5933
800-776-3449
914-993-8000
914-684-0278 fax

Programmed Press
516-599-6527

Quant IX Software Inc.
800-247-6354

Reality Technologies, Inc.
2200 Renaissance Blvd.
King of Prussia, PA 19406
800-346-2024
215-277-7600
215-278-6115 fax

Scientific Consultant Services
20 Stagecoach Rd.
Selden, NY 11784
516-696-3333

Software Dispatch
800-937-2828 x600

Steele Systems
800-237-8400

Stock Data Corp.
905 Bywater Rd.
Annapolis, MD 21401
410-280-5533
410-280-6664 fax

StockTracker
800-662-8256

Talon Development
P.O. Box 11069
Milwaukee, WI 53211-0069
414-962-7246

Telescan, Inc.
10550 Richmond, Suite 250
Houston, TX 77042
800-324-8246

Teranet IA Inc.
1615 Bowen Rd.
Nanaimo, B.C.
V9S 1G5 Canada
604-754-4223
800-663-8611

TestDrive Corporation
Fulfillment Center
2933 Bunker Hill Lane, Suite 101
Santa Clara, CA 95054-9639

Tetra Solutions Inc.
415-802-9896

The Mac Zone Instant Access CD
800-684-8080
206-881-1148

The Mescon Group Multimedia Division
800-656-1932

Tick Data Inc.
720 Kipling St., Suite 115
Lakewood, CO 80215
800-822-8425
303-232-3701
303-232-0329 fax

Track Data Corporation
95 Rockwell Place
Brooklyn, NY 11217
800-935-7788

Trendsetter Software
2020 N. Broadway, Suite 102
Santa Ana, CA 92706
714-457-5005

T. Rowe Price
800-541-3036

Ultra Financial Systems, Inc.
1633 Arrowhead Dr.
Flower Mound, TX 75028
800-364-4883
214-539-3803 fax

Value Line Software
220 E. 42 St.
New York, NY 10017-5891

Vertigo Development Group, Inc.
58 Charles St.
Cambridge, MA 02141
617-225-2065
800-688-4750

Visual Solutions
487 Groton Rd.
Westford, MA 01886
508-392-0100
508-692-3102 fax

Worden Brothers
4905 Pine Cone Dr., Suite 12
Durham, NC 27707
800-776-4940

Index

A

N

O

S

How to use the CD-ROM that accompanies Personal Finance on Your Computer: Starter Kit

This CD-ROM contains both PC and Macintosh files. The Windows and DOS files are readable on a PC only, while the Mac files are readable on a Mac only. For additional help at any time, turn to the Readme files within each program's directory. For specific help, see below, or contact the technical support numbers for each product.

Quicken

Quicken for DOS and Windows

At the C: prompt, type in **install.exe.** This is a self-extracting file that will prompt you for further information. In DOS, Quicken will be installed in a directory called /QUICKEN on your hard drive. To start Quicken, type **Q** and press **Enter**. You will see Quicken's main menu. From here you can choose commands that will take you anywhere you'd like to go in Quicken.

For Windows users, once you have properly installed Quicken (by typing in **install.exe** in the Run dialog box) you can click on the appropriate icons and use the standard Windows menus and dialog boxes to get around. The start-up window and help function will provide further information.

Quicken for the Mac

Double-click the Quicken 5 Trial Edition Installer icon. Follow the instructions on screen. Information is provided on making backups, moving data files, converting from past versions of Quicken, and working with compression software.

Quicken Technical Support

For further information about any of the Quicken products call 1-(800) 624-8742 or 1-(415) 858-6095 outside the United States.

TurboTax

TurboTax for DOS and Windows

At the C: prompt, type in **install.exe**. This is a self-extracting file that will prompt you for further information. Refer to the Readme file for additional material on importing to specific tax forms and graphic formats, and new options available with this version of TurboTax.

Windows users will install TurboTax by typing in **setup.exe** in the run dialog box. Click on the appropriate icons and use the standard Windows menus and dialog boxes to get around. The start up window and help function will provide further information.

MacInTax

You will need 15MB of memory for a complete installation. Double-click the MacInTax Installer icon. Then follow the installation instructions on screen.

TurboTax Technical Support

Before calling technical support, try using the various options in the Help menu, then call the automated technical support number at 800-685-7012. If you still require support from technical assistance, please have your Intuit customer number and documentation at hand, and have the application open when you call. You can reach technical support at (520) 295-3080, or by overseas fax at (520) 295-3095.